Westfield Memorial Library
Westfield, New Jersey

W9-ABE-781

PRESERVING
ITALY

Westfield Memorial Library
Westfield, New Jersey

PRESERVING ITALY

Canning, Curing, Infusing, and Bottling
Italian Flavors and Traditions

DOMENICA MARCHETTI

PHOTOGRAPHY BY LAUREN VOLO

Houghton Mifflin Harcourt

BOSTON   NEW YORK   2016

Copyright © 2016 by Domenica Marchetti

Interior photography © 2016 by Lauren Volo

All rights reserved.

Food styling by Molly Shuster

Prop styling by Richard Vassilatos

For information about permission to reproduce selections from this book, write to trade.permissions@hmhco.com or to Permissions, Houghton Mifflin Harcourt Publishing Company, 3 Park Avenue, 19th Floor, New York, New York 10016.

Design by Jan Derevjanik

www.hmhco.com

Library of Congress Cataloging-in-Publication Data

Names: Marchetti, Domenica, author. | Volo, Lauren, photographer.

Title: Preserving Italy : canning, curing, infusing, and bottling Italian flavors and traditions / Domenica Marchetti ; photography by Lauren Volo.

Description: Boston : Houghton Mifflin Harcourt, [2016] | Includes bibliographical references and index.

Identifiers: LCCN 2015037882| ISBN 9780544611627 (trade paper) | ISBN 9780544612358 (ebook)

Subjects: LCSH: Cooking, Italian. | Canning and preserving—Italy. | LCGFT: Cookbooks.

Classification: LCC TX723 .M32655 2016 | DDC 641.5945—dc23

LC record available at http://lccn.loc.gov/2015037882

Printed in China

TOP 10 9 8 7 6 5 4 3 2

4500612472

CONTENTS

INTRODUCTION

When my grandmother passed away in 1971, she left behind four grieving daughters and a large jar of her liquor-soaked cherries. The amber glass vessel was filled with tiny sour Amarena cherries that had been dried in the sun and then submerged in a sweet and potent syrup of sugar, alcohol, and spices. The jar was kept in a dark, cool pantry in the family apartment in Rome and the cherries doled out *very* parsimoniously by my mom and aunts. Even though we were pretty young, my sister and I loved those tiny flavor bombs and their boozy syrup. I can't tell you how many times we feigned *mal di pancia* (stomach cramps) to get a spoonful. We savored each one until the last was finally consumed four or five years later (yes, they lasted that long).

But when they were gone, they were gone; my grandmother never wrote down the recipe. For years I dreamed of the intense, winey flavor of those tiny cherries and their heavy, spiked syrup. Finally, with help from my mom—who recalled her mother making them but had never done it herself—I began working on re-creating the recipe. That quest was the beginning of this book.

I have always enjoyed home preserving. My mother, born and raised in the central-south region of Abruzzo, made a variety of Italian pickles and preserves when I was growing up, from classic giardiniera (mixed vegetable pickle) to sweet, sticky quince jam from fruit that grew on the tree in our New Jersey backyard. I myself was hooked on canning as a hobby from my first attempt at making blueberry jam in my tiny apartment in Michigan, where I worked as a newspaper reporter. Technically the jam was a failure—it never set—but the jars "pinged," signaling a successful seal, and I ended up with several half-pints of delicious blueberry syrup. For years my specialty was bread-and-butter pickles, which I still put up every August (my brothers-in-law would never forgive me if they didn't get their annual allotment). But over time, my interest naturally gravitated toward the sorts of preserves I had enjoyed growing up—my mother's colorful giardiniera, marinated eggplant packed in oil, vinegary peppers.

The art and craft of preserving is an ancient one, born of necessity and essential to all the world's cuisines. As with so many culinary endeavors, Italians are masters at it. This is not surprising, given the variety of fruits and vegetables that thrive in the country's Mediterranean climate and within its many microclimates, and also given the Italian tendency—or compulsion—toward resourcefulness.

Italian cooks put up everything from artichokes to zucchini, in vinegar and in oil; they turn summer's berries into jams, and fall's apples and quince into russet-hued pastes; they make marmalade from citrus and liqueur out of roots and nuts. In August and September, out come the heavy-duty tomato-milling machines as families get together to can tomatoes every which way. In October, during the *vendemmia* (grape harvest), the Abruzzesi turn their beloved Montepulciano d'Abruzzo grapes not only into wine, but also into *mosto cotto*, cooked grape must, a cara-melly syrup used in cakes and cookies. Then there are the more specialized forms of preser-vation—the curing of meat; the transformation of milk into cheese; and the metamorphosis of olives from bitter, inedible fruit to tasty antipasto, not to mention that indispensible ingredient, oil.

These days, we tend to think of pre-serves as extras—a dollop of fig jam on toast, a mound of silky roasted peppers in oil to accompany roast chicken. But in fact, these foods kept families nourished all year long in the days before refrigeration and super-markets. What's more, they have played an essential part in defining the regional character of Italian cuisine. In Umbria, cured sausages and salami might be flavored with local truffles; in Calabria they are tinged red from hot chile pepper. Only in Emilia-Romagna and parts of neighboring Lombardy and the Veneto will you find that alluring, ultra-spicy condiment known as mostarda, made from whole pieces of fruit suspended in a nose-tingling hot mustard syrup. In Abruzzo there is *scrucchjata*, a thick, coarse grape jam made from Montepulciano grapes that is used as a filling for traditional Christmas cookies.

Preserving Italy is a tribute to the many wonderful ways Italians put up food. What began with a search for my grandmother's recipe quickly turned into a full-blown obsession. The more I researched, the more I wanted to know. I wondered about other recipes that were in danger of being lost. After all, life in Italy has changed in the decades since I was a child. Fast-food joints abound and supermarkets are filled with prepared and convenience foods. Fewer people have the time or the inclination to occupy themselves with lengthy, laborious, and sometimes out-dated techniques when commercially prepared jars of giardiniera or *carciofi sott'olio* are right at their fingertips on store shelves. But that, I'm happy to report, is only part of the story.

Traveling throughout Italy I've found that, far from disappearing, the art of pre-serving is thriving, in homes, in restaurants, and in the *agriturismi* that have opened in the countryside in recent decades. There are also a growing number of artisan producers throughout Italy whose high-quality goods are helping to fuel the movement. In many cases, young people are leading the way. It reminds me of the canning revival that has taken place this side of the Atlantic, with com-munities of cooks, new and seasoned, coming together to can, preserve, ferment, and brew.

Much of the revival has to do with the Slow Food movement, which began in Italy in 1986 in response to the opening of a McDonald's in Rome's Piazza di Spagna. The movement, which became an official organiza-tion in 1989, now exists in 150 countries and remains especially active in Italy. Among its various programs is the Slow Food Presidia, which supports producers who work to preserve traditional food-processing methods and foods that are at risk of extinction. One of those producers is Sabato Abagnale, who is dedicated to reviving endangered toma-toes and other vegetables grown around Mt.

Vesuvius. You'll meet him within the pages of this book. You'll also meet Paolo Anselmino and Noemi Lora, who switched careers mid-life to start a small business preserving the foods of their native Alta Langa region in Piedmont. I'll introduce you to my friend Francesca Di Nisio, who produces organic olive oil and wine in Abruzzo, and other artisans who are doing wonderful things with food.

In my life and in my travels, I've interviewed professionals and home cooks who have generously shared knowledge, recipes, and stories. As I refined these recipes at home, my kitchen became a laboratory of sorts, with jars of green walnuts submerged in alcohol steeping on the windowsill and crocks of green tomatoes fermenting on the stoop outside. My refrigerators—both the one in the kitchen and the one in the garage—filled up with jars; the garage became a curing room for olives and pork.

When you open the pages of this book, I want you to feel like you are opening the door to a beautifully stocked Italian pantry. In organizing the book, I've chosen to interpret the word *preserving* broadly, so I've included everything from jams and marmalades to techniques for making cheese, brining olives, and curing pancetta. There are chapters on food preserved in vinegar and food preserved in oil. I've assembled a rather lengthy condiments chapter that includes everything from classic pesto Genovese to seasoned salts and vinegars. Tomatoes and sauce, so central to Italian cooking, merit their own chapter, where you will also find techniques for making and storing pasta. On the sweet side, there is a chapter on syrups and liqueurs, and one on classic confections, including fig and almond salami, almond paste, and *panforte di Siena* (hooray for the preservative qualities of sugar!).

Within each chapter you will also find recipes and suggestions for how to use what you preserve. The Sweet-and-Sour Roasted Peppers with Capers on page 38 make a great topping for crostini (page 48) or Pickled Vegetable Pizza (page 78). In winter, I love having a jar of Bottled Beans in Tomato Sauce (page 124) at the ready to turn into a pot of Zuppa di Pasta e Fagioli (page 129). If there is a batch of Sweet Almond Paste (page 279) stored in my freezer, I know I can easily turn it into Almond Gelato (page 289)—which, of course, will be topped with a generous spoonful of Sour Cherries in Boozy Syrup, my grandmother's tart cherries.

Those cherries. You may be wondering whether I was successful in re-creating my grandmother's recipe. You'll find the answer on page 267. But before you head there, please do yourself a favor and read the next section, all about basic techniques and safety. It's important, for while preserving is an art, it is also a science that requires care and precision.

For me, and probably for you, preserving is not so much a matter of necessity as it is of choice, a desire to spend time preparing food now that you can rely on later. I honestly get a thrill when I see a row of jars filled with deep red *passata*, made from ripe farmers' market tomatoes, lined up on the kitchen counter; or when I pull a piece of my own cured pancetta from the freezer to flavor that *passata* and turn it into sauce. Growing my repertoire of preserved food has deepened my understanding of Italian cuisine and made me a better cook, and I promise it will do the same for you.

SAFETY

In preserving, ingredients and techniques work together to yield food that is at once delicious and safe to eat. Ingredients like salt, sugar, vinegar, oil, and alcohol not only provide flavor; they kill or inhibit micro-organisms that would otherwise spoil food or make it dangerous for consumption. Techniques including canning, drying, curing, and freezing also work to make a hostile environment for spoilers. Spoilers in food include:

Enzymes. These molecules are in all living things. Enzymes control biochemical reactions, including the breakdown of food. While this is great for digestion, it's not for preserving. Blanching, cooking, or processing food, or even refrigerating it, slows down or stops enzyme activity.

Molds and yeasts. These two types of fungi are not always undesirable. Think of blue cheese (mold) or beer (yeast). Some molds are bad, however, and can cause allergic reactions or sickness. Yeast causes fermentation, which makes food sour. Freezing food inhibits the growth of mold and yeast, but it doesn't kill them. Both, however, are easily destroyed by heating food to 140 to 212°F.

Bacteria. If this word makes you nervous, it should. Bacteria can be deadly, and they are not as easily destroyed as molds or yeasts.

We have all read news stories about people sickened or even killed by bacteria-contaminated food. Among the most common culprits are *Escherichia coli* (*E. coli*), listeria, salmonella, *Staphylococcus aureus*, and *Clostridium botulinum*, which causes botulism. Some bacteria, such as salmonella, are destroyed when heated to 140°F for a specific amount of time. Processing jars of food in a water bath is more than enough to kill these bacteria. Others, including staphylococcus and *Clostridium botulinum*, are more tenacious and must be heated to 240°F for a prolonged period in order to be destroyed. The only piece of equipment that can generate this heat in a home kitchen is a pressure canner. ***Clostridium botulinum*** is of special concern in preserving. The bacterium's spores do not need air to survive; in fact, they love a warm, moist, low-oxygen, low-acid environment. When all of these conditions are present, the bacterium can produce the botulism toxin, which can cause paralysis and even death if ingested. Certain time-tested preserving techniques, if done properly, will render *C. botulinum* harmless: pickling (acidifying food), drying and curing (removing moisture), and freezing (subjecting food to cold) all serve to inhibit *C. botulinum* and make food safe. But the only way to kill it outright is through pressure canning (see page 18).

PRESERVING SAFELY

Please don't let this information about bacteria and spoilers put you off preserving. Instead, use it to guide you, to remind you to be responsible and cautious, never casual. Here's what you can do to ensure you safely enjoy the fruits (and vegetables) of your labor.

Read the next two sections to become familiar with water-bath and pressure canning, and read the chapter introductions for information on other techniques. Always carefully read each recipe, in full, before proceeding with it.

Work in a clean environment. Make sure all equipment, utensils, and work surfaces have been washed and dried before use and that everything is in working order.

Use good-quality ingredients. Preserving is not meant to salvage food that is halfway to becoming compost; it is for capturing seasonal ingredients at their peak of ripeness and flavor.

Follow the recipes as they are written. Don't alter recipes in a way that could render food unsafe, such as decreasing the amount of vinegar called for. Do not change processing times or techniques.

Only keep food for as long as stated in a recipe. Once you have opened a jar, store any leftovers, covered, in the refrigerator. Pickles and jams will keep for at least a month, usually longer; food that has been pressure canned should be eaten within a week of opening.

When in doubt, throw it out. This old adage will serve you well. If something looks suspect—if there is mold growing on the surface of your jam; if the lid to a jar in the pantry is bulging; if something smells rancid or sour or unpleasant or just off—toss it. If you find a jar of asparagus in olive oil in the fridge and you can't remember how long it's been in there, toss it. Label jars carefully so you know how old the contents are.

A word about garlic: Garlic is a common ingredient in many Italian pickles and vegetable preserves, including vegetables preserved in oil. I still see recipes, both in print and online, that call for sticking a raw clove of garlic into a jar of eggplant or green tomatoes that have been salted or pickled and then submerged in oil. Over the years I am sure I have eaten such preserves myself. But garlic is a low-acid vegetable, and submerging it raw in olive oil is not considered safe by the USDA, even when refrigerated. So I don't do it, and neither should you. (Read more about safely preserving vegetables in oil on page 24.)

Read and learn. Although I have been canning and preserving for decades, I still consider myself to be an amateur. Why? Because I'm not a scientist. I've read a lot on the subject over the years, and I continue to read, both online and in print, and learn. The National Center for Home Food Preservation (www.nchfp.uga.edu) is a great place to start. You'll find a complete list of sources I've relied on in the Bibliography on page 294.

WATER-BATH CANNING

Many of the recipes in this book call for processing jars of pickles or preserves in a large pot of boiling water, called a water bath. This accomplishes two important things: It sterilizes the jar and its contents, killing bacteria, enzymes, molds, and other elements that could cause the food to spoil; and it forces oxygen out of the jars, creating a seal that prevents microorganisms from getting in. In short, it makes the food in the jar shelf stable for long-term storage.

Water-bath canning is safe for preserving high-acid foods, including most fruits, as well as fruits and vegetables to which vinegar or another form of acid has been added—think pickles. High-acid foods contain a pH level of 4.5 or less (the lower the number, the higher the acid level). Heating these foods to the boiling point (212°F) for a prescribed amount of time is enough to destroy or block the growth of deadly microorganisms, including *C. botulinum*, the bacterium that causes botulism. Low-acid foods such as meat, fish, and vegetables with no added acid need to be processed at a higher temperature—240°F— and must be pressure canned to be made shelf stable (see page 18).

We think of tomatoes as acidic, but in fact their pH levels vary, especially with golden or low-acid varieties. For this reason, you must add acid to tomatoes—either lemon juice or citric acid—in order to safely can them in a water bath. If you have a pressure canner, you can process tomatoes without adding acid.

Water-bath canning is not difficult, but it is important—extremely important—that you follow the specific directions in each recipe, especially as they pertain to processing times. Different foods require different processing times depending on how dense they are, how much acid they contain, and the size of the jar you are using. Be diligent about timing and about following every step.

This method of canning does require some special equipment, but it's not expensive and is a worthy investment; I bought my canner more than two decades ago and it is still in tip-top shape. You can find basic canning kits at hardware stores, kitchen supply stores, and many supermarkets, where they tend to be stocked seasonally. Here's what you need:

Canning kettle or large, deep pot with a lid. I bought a speckled black graniteware canning kettle back in the early 1990s and it has held up beautifully. A 12- to 16-quart aluminum or stainless stockpot or other pot of similar size will also work.

Rack. Most canning sets come with a metal one with folding handles. The rack is placed in the bottom of the pot as a platform on which to set the jars. Its job is to hold the jars in place and prevent them from rattling around and chipping. Two excellent alternatives: My friend (and canning maven) Cathy Barrow uses a round stainless steel baking rack, which she says is sturdier; another friend, Marisa McClellan (author of *Food in Jars*) uses a flexible silicone trivet.

Jars. I use standard Ball glass jars in a variety of sizes for most of my preserves and pickles that require water-bath canning. The jars range in size from 4 ounces (120 ml) to 1 quart (950 ml). I also like to use Bormioli glass jars, which are made in Italy and have an appealing rounded shape. Their sizes don't quite correspond to American measurements, so they are not quite as practical. Jars can be reused many times, as long as they are not cracked or chipped. Be sure to inspect your jars for nicks or cracks before using.

Lids and rings. Standard Ball jars are capped with a flat metal lid and screw-on band. The lids have a ring of rubber on the underside that sits flush with the rim of the glass jar. The rubber softens while in the boiling-water bath, allowing air to escape, then becomes firm as the processed jar cools, helping to create the seal. Although the screw-on ring (also called a band) that fits over the lid can be reused, the lids themselves can only be used once for canning. After that, the seal is no longer reliable.

Other useful canning tools. **Silicone spatulas** are great for stirring down bubbling jams and other preserves. I use a **ladle** to fill jars and a plastic or metal **wide-mouth funnel** to guide food into the jars without making a mess. A **jar lifter**, a clamp of sorts, makes easy work of lifting hot jars out of boiling water. The small magnetic wand known as a **lid lifter** easily fishes lids and rings out of hot water. A **bubble remover** is a long, flat plastic tool

used to dislodge any air bubbles that form in a filled jar. A clean **plastic chopstick** also does the trick.

Basic instructions for canning with a water-bath canner

1 · Start with clean equipment. Make sure your canner and canning tools have been washed in hot soapy water and thoroughly dried. Spread a clean kitchen towel out on the work surface near the canner; this is where you will set the jars after they have been processed. Fill the canner about halfway with water and bring to a boil. The level of water will rise once you add your filled jars.

2 · Sterilize your jars and rings. Sterilizing is only necessary if your processing time is less than 10 minutes. Jars processed for 10 minutes or longer will become sterilized while boiling. All the recipes in this book call for processing times of at least 10 minutes. However, I have a long-standing habit of sterilizing all my jars before water-bath canning, so I continue to do it. First, wash jars in hot soapy water. Sterilize by immersing them in a covered pot of boiling water for 10 minutes. I use the water in the canning kettle, and then I use the same water (replenished if necessary) to process the jars once filled. (Alternatively, you can place the jars in a 285°F oven for 30 minutes.) Place the rings in a small covered pot of boiling water and boil for 10 minutes, then turn off the heat and leave them in the water. Do not boil the lids, as it could compromise the seal; just add them to the pot of hot water right before filling the jars.

3 · Fill the jars with the hot preserves or pickles. Remove the hot jars from the canner right before filling, dumping any excess water back into the pot. Fit the jars with the funnel and ladle the hot food into them, taking care to leave the amount of headspace—the space between the top of the food and the top of the jar—specified in the recipe. Leaving too much space could prevent the lid from sealing properly; too little might cause food to seep out and also prevent a seal. Gently run the bubble remover or a plastic chopstick around the inside of the jar, moving it up and down, to dislodge any air bubbles.

4 · Carefully wipe the rims of the filled jars with a damp paper towel to remove any drips or spills. Set the lids on top of the jars and screw on the rings, tightening them with your fingers but without too much force— remember that air needs to escape during processing.

5 · Using the jar lifter, set the jars on the rack in the pot of boiling water, making sure they are submerged by 1 to 2 inches. Return the water to a boil and boil the jars for the amount of time specified in the recipe, allowing adjustments for altitude (see step 8).

6 · When time is up, turn off the heat under the canner and let the jars sit until the bubbling stops. Remove the jars with the jar lifter and set them on a clean kitchen towel to cool. Within a few minutes, you should start to hear that satisfying "ping" indicating that the seal has taken, though not all jars will make noise. Let the jars cool for 12 to 24 hours; do not retighten the lids.

7 · When the jars are cool, remove the rings around the lids and test the seal: Press your finger into the center of the lid; it should remain concave and not flex back up. Lift the jar by the edge of the lid. If the lid stays on, you have a good seal. If, however, your jar has not sealed, transfer the contents to a clean or sterilized jar with a new lid and reprocess within 24 hours. Or, if it is a matter of a single unsealed jar, store it in the refrigerator and consume the food within a week.

8 · Inspect your canning equipment regularly for chips, cracks, rust, and general wear. Replace tools as necessary. The National Center for Home Food Preservation (www.nchfp.uga.edu) and Ball Corporation (www.freshpreserving.com) have more information on water-bath canning, including recommended processing times, altitude adjustments, and troubleshooting information.

PRESSURE CANNING

I wish I hadn't waited so long to start pressure canning. This method uses steam pressure to create high heat and is used to preserve low-acid foods such as beans, broth, fish, meat, and most vegetables that have not been pickled. Having a pressure canner has allowed me to greatly expand my canning repertoire.

For years I was intimidated by the idea of boiling-hot steam pressure building up inside a locked-down pot, and by the insistent rattling of the weighted gauge. My mother never used a pressure canner but she did have a pressure cooker, which she used occasionally to cook potatoes quickly. The gauge would hiss and rattle maniacally, and my mother would hiss and rattle back in Italian. I steered clear.

It was my friend Cathy Barrow who convinced me to take the pressure-canning plunge. In her book, *Mrs. Wheelbarrow's Practical Pantry*, she gives a convincing argument for pressure canning: reducing dependency on commercially processed foods. Two of the foods she pressure-cans are beans and broth. Since I use both of these regularly in my Italian kitchen, I decided it was time to dive in.

Pressure canning works by heating jars of food to 240°F for a prescribed amount of time through the buildup of steam pressure. It is the only safe method for preserving low-acid foods (foods with a pH level of 4.6 or higher) for long-term storage, including vegetables that have not been acidified with vinegar, lemon juice, or citric acid.

Clostridium botulinum, the bacteria that causes botulism, resides on most foods. In the open air, the bacteria are harmless; they only thrive in moist, low-acid, oxygen-free environments—in other words, places like a sealed jar. Processing low-acid foods in a boiling-water bath is not enough to kill the deadly toxin. But bringing them to 240°F in a pressure canner destroys any botulism spores that may be lurking, making food completely safe to eat.

A pressure canner is an expensive and bulky piece of equipment; buy one only if you are committed to using it. In this book, a pressure canner is employed to can Bottled Beans in Tomato Sauce (page 124) and Homemade Meat Broth (page 126). But beyond those recipes, you can use a pressure canner to safely can most vegetables and fruits, as well as meat, poultry, and fish.

You can also use it to can tomatoes. Although we think of tomatoes as acidic, their acidity is variable, hovering right around 4.5 pH. Tomatoes can be safely canned in a water bath *as long as* acid (usually in the form of lemon juice or citric acid) is added. If you use a pressure canner, there is no need to add the extra acid.

While it is safe to can some meat sauces in a pressure canner, I don't do it. I prefer thick meat sauces, and I just can't be sure that the heat from the pressure-canning process penetrates through to the center of the jar. For that reason, I freeze meat sauces.

Certain foods cannot be safely canned, even in a pressure canner. These include dairy and egg products; dense foods, such as mashed potatoes or pumpkin; and pasta, grains, and products made with flour. Then there are the foods that literally turn to mush under the extreme heat: broccoli, cauliflower, and zucchini and other summer squashes. As always when it comes to canning, be sure to follow the recipe closely and refer to the manufacturer's instructions and guidelines before proceeding.

Pressure canners. All American and Presto are two leading manufacturers of pressure canners in the United States. Canners range in price from about $70 to $350 and in size from 10 quarts to 40 quarts, the latter of which can hold up to 32 pint jars or 19 quarts (!) at one time. I use an All American 21-quart pressure canner that can hold up to 19 pint jars or 7 quart jars. It is plenty big for my needs.

Pressure canners come with lids that lock on tightly. Some models have lids with rubber gaskets and handles that clamp down; others are beveled along the rim to fit the top of the pot and are secured with bolts and wing nuts that screw the lid down. A pressure canner lid is outfitted with several pieces, depending on the make and model: a weighted gauge or a dial gauge to regulate and monitor pressure; a steam vent or pipe; and a safety lock or plug to ensure that the canner is sufficiently depressurized before you can open it.

Most pressure canners also come with a **perforated rack**; some have two so you can stack the jars. You will also need **clean jars, lids** and **rings,** and the other tools listed in the section on water-bath canning (page 15).

Basic instructions for canning with a pressure canner

Before you start, read the instruction booklet that comes with your pressure canner and follow the directions to the letter to properly set up and use the canner.

1 · Start with clean equipment. Make sure your canner and canning tools have been washed in hot soapy water and thoroughly dried. Spread a clean kitchen towel out on the work surface near the canner; this is where you will set the jars after they have been processed.

2 · Set up your canner. Set the rack in the bottom of the pot and add 2 to 3 inches of water. There is no need to fill the pot; you just need enough to create the steam pressure that will raise the temperature inside to 240°F. Add a splash of distilled white vinegar to the water to help keep the jars shiny.

3 · Thoroughly wash and dry your jars, rings, and lids. There is no need to sterilize jars destined for pressure canning. The extreme heat will sterilize them during processing.

4 · Fill the jars with the food you are canning. Fit the jars with the wide-mouth funnel and ladle or pack in the food, taking care to leave the amount of headspace—the space between the top of the food and the top of the jar—specified in the recipe. Leaving too much space could prevent the lid from sealing properly; too little might cause food to seep out and also prevent a seal. Gently run a bubble remover or a plastic chopstick around the inside of the jar, moving it up and down, to dislodge any air bubbles.

5 · Carefully wipe the rims of the filled jars clean with a damp paper towel. If there is oily residue on the rim, dip the paper towel in distilled white vinegar; an oily surface may prevent jars from sealing properly.

6 · Set the jars in the canner on top of the rack. Do not set them directly on the floor of the canner. Secure the lid on the canner, following the manufacturer's instructions, so that it is properly locked. My model, for example, requires a light oiling of the beveled surface of the rim of the pot. The lid is then placed on the pot, lined up, and locked into place, and the bolts and wing nuts tightened.

7 · Place the canner over high heat and let it heat up until steam begins to escape from the steam vent or pipe; the steam will be intermittent at first, then rise in a steady column. Once the column of steam is escaping at a steady stream (you should be able to see and hear it), set a timer and let the steam vent for 10 minutes. Then place the gauge onto the vent, making sure you choose the pressure setting called for in the recipe. For example, the recipe for Bottled Beans in Tomato Sauce (page 124) calls for processing the jars at 10 pounds of pressure. Choose the hole in the gauge marked "10" and slide it over the vent pipe. (If you are processing at an altitude higher than sea level, you will need to adjust the pressure and the processing time; see the paragraph at the end of these instructions.)

8 · If you are using a dial gauge, monitor the dial and begin timing the canning process when it reaches the correct pressure (bottled beans, for example, need to process for 75 minutes from the time the gauge indicates the canner has reached 10 pounds of pressure). Adjust the heat as necessary to keep the pressure at the correct level. If you are using a weighted gauge, listen for the first rattle indicating the pot has reached the correct pressure. Once that happens, start timing the canning process and keep listening. You want the gauge to jiggle one to four times per minute. If it is rattling constantly, you need to lower the heat; if it is barely rattling at all, you need to raise it. Over time, you will get a feel for how high or low you need to maintain the heat on your burner to maintain the proper pressure.

9 · Once the food is done processing, turn off the heat and let the canner cool gradually until the pressure dial gauge has dropped to zero (this can take 30 minutes or longer). Once the dial is at zero, use a pot holder to remove the weighted gauge. Wait 2 minutes before loosening the wing nuts or unlocking the lid. Remove the cover by lifting the edge away from you to protect your face from steam. Remove the jars with a jar lifter and set them on a clean kitchen towel. Their contents will be bubbling. Let the jars rest and cool completely before testing the seal on the lid. To test, press your finger into the center of the lid; it should remain concave and not spring back up. Lift the jar by the edge of the lid. If the lid stays on, you have a good seal. If a jar has not sealed properly, remove the lid and carefully wipe the rim of the jar. Replace the lid with a new one and screw on the ring. Reprocess any improperly sealed jars within 24 hours, or store them in the refrigerator and use within a week.

10 · Inspect your pressure-canning equipment regularly for chips, cracks, rust, and general wear. The dial gauge, which displays the amount of pressure in the canner, needs to be tested for accuracy every year. A hardware store or your local county Cooperative Extension office should be able to offer this service. To determine the proper pressure and processing time for higher altitudes, refer to the manual that comes with your canner.

For more information, including how to adjust these instructions for high altitude, visit the National Center for Home Food Preservation (www.nchfp.uga.edu), All American Canner (www.allamericancanner.com), and Ball Corporation (www.freshpreserving.com).

Oil-Preserved Asparagus, page 29

FOODS
PRESERVED
IN OIL

Of all the preserving techniques in this book, this is the one I most associate with Italian food. Duck into an *alimentari* (deli) or peruse the shelves of any supermarket in Italy, and you will find jars of vegetables—literally from artichokes to zucchini—artfully arranged in colorful layers and submerged in oil. They share space with oil-packed anchovies, sardines, and tuna, as well as some oil-preserved cured meats and cheeses.

Like pickling in vinegar, preserving in oil was a way to extend food's edible lifespan in the days before refrigeration. Submerging food in oil prevents its exposure to air, inhibiting mold and delaying oxidation and deterioration. Many families, especially in central and southern regions such as Abruzzo, Calabria, Campania, Puglia, and Sicily, continue to put up eggplant, mushrooms, peppers, squash, and so on even though fresh produce is available year-round in stores. They do it not only because it's a practical and economical way of dealing with the generous output of the garden, but also because oil-preserved foods are delicious, brightly flavored with vinegar, salt, and spice. I love to pile oil-preserved rapini on a porchetta sandwich, and I rely almost daily on roasted peppers, asparagus spears, mushrooms, and other oil-preserved vegetables to accompany roast chicken or grilled sausages, to embellish frittatas or rice or grain salads, and as pizza toppings, among other things.

Vegetables preserved in oil are not just packed raw in a jar and topped off. Because most vegetables are low in acid, they must first be cooked or salted or partially dried and pickled—usually it's a combination of these methods—to make them safe for preserving.

These steps kill or inhibit microorganisms, draw out moisture from the food, and make it acidic; the vegetables are, in essence, being pickled and then preserved.

It is essential to follow all the necessary steps when preserving food in oil. While oil acts as a barrier against molds, yeasts, and oxidation, it **does not** inhibit all microorganisms commonly found in the environment. One of those microorganisms is *Clostridium botulinum*, the bacterium that causes botulism, a potentially deadly toxin. If present, *C. botulinum* can multiply in a moist, low-acid, low-oxygen environment, such as a jar of vegetables in oil—unless those vegetables have been properly cooked, pickled, or acidified first. The USDA does not currently provide guidelines for preserving vegetables in oil.

I am not telling you this to keep you from making and enjoying all the wonderful oil-preserved food in this chapter; after all, Italians—and home cooks across the globe—have been preserving in oil for centuries. I grew up eating artichokes and eggplant and peppers *sott'olio*, and I'm still here to write about it. I'm telling you so that you will be armed with the information and knowledge necessary to preserve confidently and safely.

Safety Tips

- First, read the Safety section on page 13.

- Start with high-quality produce that is free of blemishes.

- Work in a clean environment. Make sure equipment is clean and dry; wash and dry your hands before proceeding.

- Wash and dry vegetables thoroughly before proceeding with a recipe.

- Wash and sterilize jars and lids according to the directions on page 16.

- Follow the directions in each recipe carefully. Don't alter quantities of ingredients and don't lessen blanching, cooking, or marinating times.

- Use good-quality, fresh oil. I use extra-virgin olive oil or sunflower oil. Avoid old or cheap oil, as the off flavor will permeate the food.

- Do not submerge raw garlic in oil. I still encounter plenty of recipes that call for adding raw garlic to vegetables preserved in oil. Because raw garlic may carry the spores of *Clostridium botulinum*, this is a potentially serious hazard. On the few occasions in which I do call for garlic in this chapter, it is always sliced paper-thin and thoroughly pickled before being added to vegetables in oil. If you prefer, you can omit it altogether. You can always season your preserved vegetables with garlic when you serve them.

- Always refrigerate food preserved in oil. Many traditional Italian recipes call for storing jars in a pantry or cool, dark spot. Those environments may not be cold enough to inhibit bacteria growth. Refrigerating your preserves will make them keep longer, but it may also make the oil congeal. To serve, use a clean fork or spoon to scoop out only as much as you plan to eat and then return the jar to the fridge. Don't let the jar sit out on the countertop to allow the oil to liquefy, as this could encourage bacterial growth.

- Think of your oil preserves as short-term preserves. Consume them within the time period indicated in the recipe.

- Use common sense. Use your eyes and your nose to look for anything that might be amiss. Because foods preserved in oil are usually not water-bath canned or pressure canned, you won't be able to tell if a seal is broken. If a jar's lid is bulging, toss it. If the food looks suspect—moldy, slimy—or smells off, throw it away. If you are not sure how long a jar has been in the refrigerator, throw it away. Be sure to clearly label jars at the time of preserving so you know how old the food is.

- I don't recommend water-bath canning or pressure canning for vegetables in oil for a very simple reason: It makes them mushy. Food preserved in oil is generally denser than food preserved in brine. It takes longer for heat to penetrate to the center of the jar. If you are water-bath canning, it is difficult to determine how long the jars of vegetables should boil because the National Center for Home Food Preservation does not give any recommended times for food preserved in oil. Without those guidelines, you would have to boil food for a good long while to be sure all the contents were brought up to the boiling point. As for pressure canning, the heat is simply too intense. Believe me; I tried to pressure-can Caponata (page 173), and it turned into baby food. (Now when I make a big batch of caponata, I freeze it.)

BABY ARTICHOKES IN OIL

In spring and fall, farmers' markets all over Italy bloom with green and purple artichokes, otherworldly and slightly inhospitable in their appearance, with their spiny leaves and long stems still attached. They are not quite so easy to come by in the United States, and they are expensive. But they are worth the occasional splurge if you can find them, especially tender baby ones. Enjoy these home-preserved artichokes in salad, as a topping for pizza, or stuffed into a panino with salami and sharp cheese.

3 lemons

3 cups (710 g) cold water

2 pounds (907 g) baby artichokes

2 cups (473 g) white wine vinegar

2 cups (473 g) dry white wine, such as Orvieto, Pecorino, or Soave

1 teaspoon fine sea salt

1 teaspoon dried parsley

¼ teaspoon crushed red chile pepper

¼ teaspoon dried oregano

¼ teaspoon dried rosemary

Extra-virgin olive oil

EQUIPMENT

1 sterilized 1-pint jar and its lid

1 · Using a vegetable peeler, peel the zest off one of the lemons in strips and set aside. Squeeze the juice from all 3 lemons into a bowl and add the water.

2 · Cut off the artichoke stem and peel off the tough outer layer. Toss the stem into the bowl of lemon water. Pull off the tough outer leaves of the artichoke until you're left with the smooth, tender lemon-colored leaves. Trim around the bottom to remove any tough bits, and then trim off the top third. Cut the cleaned artichoke in half and toss into the bowl. Clean the remaining artichokes in the same way and immerse them in the water.

3 · Combine the vinegar, wine, and salt in a high-sided saucepan. Set aside two strips of lemon zest and add the rest to the brine. Bring to a boil over medium-high heat. Drain the artichokes and carefully add them to the pot. Return the brine to a boil and boil the artichokes until they are just tender, 4 to 5 minutes. Drain in a colander and let cool briefly.

(recipe continues)

4 · Spread a clean kitchen towel on a baking sheet or directly on your work surface. Arrange the artichoke halves on the towel so that they are not touching. Let them air-dry for several hours and up to overnight.

5 · In a small bowl, combine the parsley, crushed red pepper, oregano, and rosemary.

6 · Pour a small quantity of olive oil into the sterilized jar. Arrange a layer of artichokes in the bottom of the jar and sprinkle with a little of the herb mixture. Tuck in one of the reserved strips of lemon zest. Continue to layer the artichokes and herbs until you have packed them all in tightly. Tuck in the last piece of lemon zest.

7 · Slowly pour enough olive oil into the jar to completely cover the artichokes. Clasp on the lid and let stand at cool room temperature for 24 to 48 hours. Check to make sure the artichokes remain completely covered; if not, add additional oil.

8 · Let the artichokes cure in the refrigerator for 1 week before eating, then store in the refrigerator for up to 3 months. To serve, remove from the jar only as much as you plan to serve and let it come to room temperature. Top off the jar with more oil as necessary to keep the remaining artichokes submerged.

OIL-PRESERVED ASPARAGUS

Ever since I started making these mildly pickled asparagus spears a few years ago, I try to have at least one jar stashed in my fridge at all times. They go with almost everything—grilled salmon, roast chicken, frittatas. One of my favorite work-at-home lunches in summer is a hard-boiled egg, some olives, a slice of good mozzarella, and a few of these tangy spears, straight from the fridge.

2 pounds (1 kg) asparagus spears

1 cup (237 g) white wine vinegar

1 cup (237 g) water

1 teaspoon fine sea salt

½ teaspoon whole black peppercorns

1 bay leaf

2 cups (220 g) extra-virgin olive oil

¼ teaspoon crushed red chile pepper

EQUIPMENT

3 sterilized 12-ounce jars and their lids

1 • Trim the asparagus spears from the bottom so they will fit upright in the jars with 1 inch headspace—enough to cover them with oil. Depending on the length of the spears, reserve the bottom halves for another use, or, if you like, preserve them along with the tops.

2 • Combine the vinegar, water, salt, peppercorns, and bay leaf in a pot large enough to hold the trimmed asparagus. Bring to a boil over medium-high heat and then add the asparagus. Almost immediately they will turn from green to yellow-green and some of the tips will turn reddish. Cook until barely tender, about 2 minutes.

3 • Place a clean kitchen towel near the stove. Using tongs, remove the asparagus from the pot and line them up on the towel to dry. Once dry, pack the spears, tip side up, in the jars, taking care to pack them in tightly. You should be able to fill two or three jars, depending on whether you use some of the bottom halves of the spears along with the tips.

4 • In a large skillet, heat the olive oil with the crushed red pepper until warmed through. Carefully fill the jars with the oil, taking care to cover the asparagus completely. Screw the lids on tightly and let the jars sit at room temperature for 24 to 48 hours. Check to make sure the asparagus remain completely covered; if not, add additional oil.

5 • Let the asparagus cure in the refrigerator for at least 1 week before eating, then store in the refrigerator for up to 3 months. To serve, remove from the jar only as much as you plan to use and let it come to room temperature. Top off the jar with more oil as necessary to keep the remaining asparagus submerged.

PICKLED GARLIC SCAPES IN OIL

The city of Sulmona, in Abruzzo, is famous for its red garlic. The bulbs, with their gorgeous, fat, purple-red-clad cloves, grow in the surrounding Peligna Valley. The garlic is prized for its intense fragrance and for its keeping ability. It is a staple at the farmers' market, where you will often find it hanging or stacked in braided lengths. The scapes from the plant—the long, swirly green stalks— are harvested in spring. This allows the plant to focus its energy on growing the bulb. The scapes, called zolle *in the local dialect, are enjoyed fresh or turned into these delicious pickles. The garlic flavor in the scapes is mild and appetizing. Serve pickled scapes with cheese and* salumi *as part of an antipasto platter.*

1 pound (454 g) garlic scapes
2 cups (473 g) white wine vinegar
1 teaspoon fine sea salt
Extra-virgin olive oil

EQUIPMENT
4 sterilized ½-pint jars and their lids

1 · Cut the scapes into 1½- to 2-inch lengths, removing any tough parts at the bottom and the thinnest part at the top above the small bulbous tip.

2 · In a saucepan large enough to hold all the scapes, bring the vinegar to a boil over medium-high heat. Stir in the salt and let it dissolve. Add the scapes to the pot and cover. Return the vinegar to a boil, cover, and boil, stirring once or twice, until the scapes have lost their bright green color and are just tender, 4 to 5 minutes.

3 · Drain the scapes in a colander set in the sink. Spread on a clean kitchen towel and let dry for about 1 hour. Shuffle them around once or twice during this time to make sure they dry on all sides.

4 · Pack the scapes into the jars, leaving 1 inch headspace. Pour enough olive oil into the jars to cover the scapes completely. Use a bubble remover or a clean chopstick to dislodge any bubbles and press down on the scapes to submerge them.

5 · Screw the lids on tightly and let sit at room temperature for 24 hours. Let the scapes cure in the refrigerator for at least 1 week before using, then store in the refrigerator for up to 1 month. To serve, remove from the jar only as much as you plan to use and let it come to room temperature. Top off the jar with more oil as necessary to keep the remaining scapes submerged.

GRILLED MIXED MUSHROOMS IN OIL

· · · MAKES 1 PINT · · ·

Drive along the mountain roads in Umbria in the fall and you're likely to come across precariously parked cars, temporarily abandoned by drivers out searching for fresh porcini mushrooms. The meaty mushrooms are perfect for grilling and preserving in oil. If only they weren't such a rarity—and so prohibitively expensive—here in the United States. The good news is that many supermarkets now stock a good variety of other mushrooms with their own attributes. Look for fat king trumpets and clumps of clamshell mushrooms. Use a mix to give this savory preserve extra visual and textural appeal.

2 pounds (907 g) mixed mushrooms of various sizes, such as white and brown beech (clamshell), king trumpet, and portobello

2 tablespoons coarse sea salt or kosher salt

2 cups (473 g) white wine vinegar

½ cup (110 g) extra-virgin olive oil, plus more as needed

3 strips lemon zest (no white pith)

1 small dried chile pepper, crushed, or a generous pinch of crushed red chile pepper

1 bay leaf

6 whole black peppercorns

EQUIPMENT
1 sterilized 1-pint jar and its lid

1 • Wash and dry the mushrooms. Separate the beech mushrooms into small clumps. Cut the trumpet mushrooms in half lengthwise. Scrape the gills from the portobellos and cut the portobellos into thick slices.

2 • Place the mushrooms in a bowl and toss gently with the salt. Place a plate on top of the mushrooms and weight it down with a heavy object. Let the mushrooms sit for 1 hour. Drain the mushrooms, spread them on a clean kitchen towel, and pat them dry.

3 • Bring the vinegar to a boil in a medium saucepan over medium-high heat. Add the mushrooms, return to a boil, and boil until they have softened slightly but still have a nice meaty texture, 3 to 5 minutes. Drain and spread the mushrooms out on a clean kitchen towel and pat them dry. Let them dry until they are no longer damp, about 2 hours.

4 • Prepare a medium-hot charcoal grill or preheat a gas grill to medium-high. To grill inside, preheat a stovetop grill to medium-high. Working carefully and in batches, quickly char the mushrooms on both sides so that they become blackened in spots. Using tongs, transfer them to a bowl and let cool.

(recipe continues)

5 · Combine the ½ cup oil, the lemon zest, chile pepper, bay leaf, and peppercorns in a small saucepan over medium heat. Heat, stirring from time to time, to just below a simmer (look for small bubbles to appear). Remove from the heat and let cool slightly.

6 · Pour the infused oil and spices over the mushrooms. Toss gently and let marinate at room temperature for 24 hours. Then pack the mushrooms and the seasoned oil, including the spices, into the jar, pressing them down. Pour enough additional oil over the mushrooms to cover them completely and then secure the lid tightly. Let the mushrooms rest at room temperature for 24 hours. Check the oil and add more if necessary so that the mushrooms are completely submerged.

7 · Let the mushrooms cure in the refrigerator for 1 week before eating, then store in the refrigerator for up to 3 months. To serve, remove from the jar only as much as you plan to use and let it come to room temperature. Top off the jar with more oil as necessary to keep the remaining mushrooms submerged.

ROSETTA'S TUNA-STUFFED CHERRY PEPPERS

Cookbook author Rosetta Costantino was born in Calabria, in southern Italy, and lived there until her family moved to California when she was a teenager. Now, like me, she splits her time between her two homelands. Her book My Calabria *is one of my favorites on southern Italian cuisine. When Rosetta heard I was working on this book she offered to share her recipe for this classic antipasto,* peperoncini ripieni di tonno sott'olio—*hot cherry peppers filled with a savory stuffing of tuna, capers, and anchovies. Warning: these little cherry bombs are seriously hot and seriously addictive.*

2 pounds (907 g) hot cherry peppers

2 cups (473 g) white wine vinegar

2 cups (473 g) water

2 (7-ounce) cans best-quality solid tuna in olive oil, drained

2 tablespoons capers, rinsed and drained

6 to 8 best-quality anchovy fillets in oil, patted dry

Extra-virgin olive oil

EQUIPMENT

Disposable kitchen gloves (such as Playtex)

3 sterilized 1-pint jars and their lids

1 · Wearing gloves, cut out the stems from the peppers with a paring knife and carefully remove all the seeds and pith inside. Put the peppers in a high-sided saucepan and pour in the vinegar and water. Bring to a boil over medium-high heat and boil for 5 minutes.

2 · Drain the peppers in a colander and let them sit until cool enough to handle. Set them, cut-side-down, on a clean kitchen towel to dry for 2 hours. Turn them over and let dry for at least another 2 hours, and up to overnight (if drying overnight, turn them back over so they are cut side down).

3 · Prepare the filling by finely chopping the tuna with the capers and anchovies. Stuff the peppers with the tuna mixture and pack them snugly into the jars, leaving about 1 inch headspace. Slowly pour in enough oil to completely cover the peppers. Screw the lids on tightly and let sit at room temperature for 24 hours. Check to make sure the peppers remain completely covered; if not, add more oil.

4 · Let the peppers cure in the refrigerator for 1 week before using, then store in the refrigerator for up to 3 months. To serve, remove from the jar only what you plan to use and let it come to room temperature. Top off the jar with more oil as necessary to keep the remaining peppers submerged.

EGGPLANT IN OIL

Pressing the eggplant, as I do in this recipe, gives it a satisfyingly chewy texture and prevents it from becoming saturated with oil during the preserving process. Choose long, slim eggplants or young bulbous ones, either of which will have fewer seeds than other types. Enjoy these pickles as part of an antipasto platter, in a sandwich, or as an ingredient in Insalata di Riso (page 71).

4 large ripe but firm eggplants
  (2½ to 3 pounds/1.1 to 1.4 kg)

¼ cup (128 g) fine sea salt

1 or 2 small fresh chile peppers, minced

2 cups (473 g) white wine vinegar

1 cup (237 g) water

½ small red bell pepper, trimmed, seeded,
  and cut into ⅜-inch-thick strips

2 cloves garlic, cut into thin slices

1 bay leaf

1 tablespoon minced fresh oregano, or
  1 teaspoon dried oregano

2 cups (439 g) extra-virgin olive oil,
  plus more as needed

EQUIPMENT

4 sterilized ½-pint jars and their lids

1 • Peel the eggplants and cut them into slices about ⅜ inch thick, then again into ⅜-inch-thick strips. Place the strips in a bowl, sprinkle with the salt, and toss thoroughly. Set a plate on top and weight it down with a heavy object. Let the eggplant sit overnight. Drain, pressing down to extract as much liquid as possible. Transfer the eggplant to a heatproof bowl and scatter the chile peppers on top.

2 • Combine the vinegar and water in a saucepan. Add the bell pepper, garlic, and bay leaf. Bring to a boil over medium-high heat and boil for 1 minute. Remove from the heat and remove and discard the bay leaf. Pour the boiling brine over the eggplant and let cool to room temperature. Drain, again pressing out as much liquid as possible. Spread the eggplant out on clean kitchen towels and let air dry for a couple of hours.

3 • Transfer the eggplant to a bowl and sprinkle the oregano on top. Stir in the 2 cups olive oil and let marinate for 1 hour. Pack the eggplant into the jars, leaving 1 inch headspace. Make sure to get a couple of garlic slivers and strips of pepper in each jar. Pour the oil from the bowl over the eggplant. If necessary, top off with more oil until the eggplant is completely submerged. Screw the lids on tightly and let sit at room temperature for 24 hours.

4 • Let the eggplant cure in the refrigerator for at least 1 week before eating, then store in the refrigerator for up to 3 months. To serve, remove from the jar only as much as you plan to use, and let it come to room temperature. Top off the jar with more oil as necessary to keep the remaining eggplant submerged.

Olive Oil: Cultivating a Sacred Substance

To Francesca Di Nisio, olive oil is not just a vehicle for frying and sautéing, or a finishing touch to be tossed with lettuce or drizzled over a bowl of soup. When she speaks about it, it is with reverence.

"For us Italians, olive oil is a sacred substance," she says. "We are anointed with it at our birth and our death. It is present at the opening and closing of our lives and it nourishes us throughout."

Di Nisio, a small producer of organic olive oil in Abruzzo, has brought me to a hillside outside of the medieval town of Navelli to see some of her trees. We scramble up terrain that is all stones, dry as a bone. Eventually we reach our destination, an enormous, ancient tree with a split-open trunk that is so wide you could furnish a room inside it. How the tree has survived so long on this arid slope is beyond me. And yet the tree, and all the others around it, is full of small, hard fruit that will ripen over the next few months.

"Olive trees are immortal," Di Nisio says. Her fascination dates back to her childhood, much of it spent at her grandparents' home in the countryside. "My maternal grandmother, Maria, had a simple and genuine life," she says. "Her family produced wine, oil, and grains. I always had a strong desire to follow in her footsteps."

So that's what she did. After studying winemaking and earning a master's degree in marketing in Florence, Di Nisio opened her business, CantinArte, in 2007. She and her husband, Diego Gasbarri, produce and sell organic oil, wine, grains, and saffron from the Navelli plain (where the microclimate produces some of the world's best).

But it's the olive oil that holds Di Nisio's heart. *"Puo mancare anche il vino, ma non puo mai mancare l'olio,"* she says—you can do without wine, but you can't do without oil.

CantinArte produces just 4,000 to 5,000 (500 ml) bottles of oil per year, depending on the harvest. The oil comes from a blend of three olives—Leccino, Dritta, and Frantoio—each of which imparts a different quality. "I like to harvest olives when they're not super mature, while you can still taste the herbaceous quality," Di Nisio says. "When I taste our oil I taste so many flavors: artichokes, bitter almonds, freshly cut grass, tomatoes."

The olives are harvested in mid-October, picked by hand and with small hand rakes. The fruit collects on tarps spread out under the trees and then is transferred to ventilated crates. The work begins at 6 a.m. and by 5 p.m. the olives are already at the *frantoio*, the press.

It's hard work, and a long day, but one filled with ritual and symbolism and celebration. "All of the families get involved," she says. "People who moved away come back for it." Some stay up all night awaiting the first taste of the newly pressed oil.

"We bring it back to our homes and we have an early breakfast of bread and fresh olive oil. Can you imagine anything better?"

SWEET-AND-SOUR ROASTED PEPPERS
with Capers

Peppers were a New World import to Italy. And yet, the aroma of roasting peppers is, to me, the aroma of Italy. Walk down a side street at lunchtime, and you will be hit with their sweet and pungent perfume from a nearby trattoria or house. That beautiful, assertive flavor is captured here in this colorful preserve.

3 pounds (1.4 kg) ripe bell peppers

2 tablespoons tiny capers

2 tablespoons finely chopped fresh flat-leaf parsley

1 cup (237 g) white wine vinegar

1 cup (237 g) water

¼ cup sugar

1½ teaspoons fine sea salt

2 cloves garlic, sliced paper-thin

Extra-virgin olive oil

EQUIPMENT
2 sterilized 1-pint jars and their lids

1 · Arrange an oven rack 4 inches below the broiler and preheat the broiler.

2 · Place the peppers on a baking sheet and broil, turning every couple of minutes with tongs, until they are blistered and somewhat blackened on all sides. (Alternatively, you can char the peppers on a grill.) Transfer to a bowl, cover with plastic wrap, and let steam for about 10 minutes.

3 · Lay a pepper on a cutting board near the sink and slice or gently pull off the stem. Let any juice from the pepper drain into the sink.

Cut the pepper in half and scrape off the charred skins, seeds, and innards. Cut the halves lengthwise into thin strips, about ¼ inch thick. Clean and slice the remaining peppers and transfer them to a heatproof bowl. Stir in the capers and parsley.

4 · Bring the vinegar, water, sugar, salt, and garlic to a boil in a saucepan set over medium-high heat. Boil the brine for 2 minutes to dissolve the sugar and salt, and then pour it over the peppers. Let steep for 1 hour.

5 · Drain the peppers, reserving a little of the brine. Pack the peppers tightly into the sterilized jars. Spoon 1 tablespoon brine over the peppers; then fill each jar with enough oil to cover the peppers completely. Cover tightly and let sit at cool room temperature for 24 hours. Check to make sure the peppers are still submerged; if not, add more oil.

6 · Let the peppers cure for at least 2 days before using, then store in the refrigerator for up to 3 months. To serve, remove from the jar only as much as you plan to use and let it come to room temperature. Top off the jar with more oil as necessary to keep the remaining peppers submerged.

GRILLED ZUCCHINI IN OIL

It never occurred to me to put grilled zucchini under oil until I came across one at an artisan food shop in Abruzzo. What an excellent idea. Be sure to use hardwood coals to get the best smoky taste. Serve these with grilled pork chops or roast chicken, or dice them up and use as a topping for crostini, along with a dollop of ricotta. They are also delicious in the vegetable frittata on page 53.

3 pounds (1.4 kg) medium zucchini
Fine sea salt
2 cups (473 g) white wine vinegar
2 cups (473 g) water
¼ cup (55 g) extra-virgin olive oil
Sunflower oil

EQUIPMENT
2 sterilized 1-pint jars and their lids

1 · Trim the ends off the zucchini and cut the zucchini lengthwise into ¼-inch-thick slices. Layer in a colander, sprinkling lightly with salt as you go. Place a plate on top of the zucchini and weight it down with a heavy object. Let stand for 1 hour, then pat the slices dry with paper towels or clean kitchen towels.

2 · Combine the vinegar, water, and 2 tablespoons salt in a large pot and bring to a boil over medium-high heat. Stir to dissolve the salt. Add the zucchini, using a wooden spoon to submerge it in the brine. Cover and boil until the zucchini slices have lost their bright green color, about 3 minutes. Remove the slices from the brine and lay them on clean kitchen towels to dry for 1 to 2 hours.

3 · Prepare a charcoal grill or heat a gas grill to medium-high. Brush the grate with vegetable oil or spray with high-heat cooking spray.

4 · Brush the zucchini slices on both sides with the olive oil. Grill for about 2 minutes, until there are grill marks on the bottom; carefully turn them and grill for another 2 minutes. Transfer the zucchini to a platter and let cool to room temperature.

5 · Pour a small quantity of sunflower oil into each of the jars. Pack the zucchini into the jars, overlapping them as needed to make the slices fit. If you have especially long slices, you can roll them up cigar-style and tuck them in that way. Slowly pour enough oil into the jars to completely cover the zucchini. Screw the lids on tightly and let sit at cool room temperature for 24 hours. Check to make sure the zucchini remains completely covered; if not, add more oil.

6 · Let the zucchini cure in the refrigerator for 1 week before using, then store in the refrigerator for up to 3 months. To serve, remove from the jar only as much as you plan to use and let it come to room temperature. Top off the jar as necessary to keep the zucchini submerged.

PICKLED RAPINI IN OIL

· · · MAKES 2 PINTS · · ·

*There is no middle ground when it comes to rapini. You either love it, as I do,
or you despise it, as my dad does. It's true, rapini is pungent and assertive; it
can take some getting used to. But if you are on the "despise" side, I urge you
to give this cruciferous vegetable another go, especially lightly pickled. A quick
bath in brine followed by a steeping in good oil mellows the broccoli's flavor.
Pickled rapini makes a great accompaniment to grilled sausages (page 232) and is
delicious smushed into a panino with prosciutto cotto and mozzarella (page 52).*

2 pounds (907 g) broccoli rabe (rapini)

2 cups (473 g) white wine vinegar

2 cups (473 g) water

4 cloves garlic, sliced paper-thin

2 tablespoons sea salt

Extra-virgin olive oil

2 to 4 dried red chile peppers, crushed

EQUIPMENT
2 sterilized 1-pint jars and their lids

1 · Trim the broccoli rabe, keeping the young
leaves and the florets and their tender stems;
discard the tough stems. You should end up
with about 1½ pounds (680 g).

2 · Bring the vinegar, water, garlic, and salt to
a boil in a large saucepan over medium heat.
Stir to dissolve the salt. Add the broccoli rabe,
pushing down with tongs or a wooden spoon
to submerge it in the brine. Once the liquid
returns to a boil, let the broccoli rabe boil
until tender but not soft, about 5 minutes.
Drain the broccoli rabe, discarding the brine,
and let cool for about 10 minutes.

3 · Spread a clean kitchen towel on a baking
sheet or directly on your work surface.
Arrange the broccoli rabe on the towel so that
the pieces are not touching. Let them air-dry
for 1 hour.

4 · Pour a small quantity of olive oil into
each of the jars. Pack the broccoli rabe into
the jars, sprinkling in some of the red chile
peppers as you go (as much or as little as you
like). Slowly pour enough olive oil into the jar
to completely cover the broccoli rabe. Screw
the lids on tightly and let stand at cool room
temperature for 24 hours. Check to make sure
the broccoli rabe remains completely covered;
if not, add additional oil.

5 · Let the broccoli rabe cure in the refrigerator for 1 week before using, then store in
the refrigerator for up to 3 months. To serve,
remove from the jar only as much as you plan
to use and let come to room temperature. Top
off the jar with more oil as necessary to keep
the remaining broccoli rabe submerged.

OIL-PRESERVED BUTTERNUT SQUASH
with Mint

Winter squash tends not to be associated with Italian cooking. But in fall and winter, beautiful big squashes adorn the farmers' markets from north to south. In Emilia-Romagna, squash-filled ravioli are a classic; and in the south, cooks sauté the squash in olive oil, then dress it with vinegar, sugar, and mint. This recipe pays tribute to those southern flavors. I specify butternut here only because it is one of the easiest to peel and cut up. But you can use any variety you like (except spaghetti squash, which would turn to mush). Acorn, buttercup, and kabocha are all good.

1 butternut squash (1½ to 2 pounds/680 to 907 g)

2 cups (473 g) white wine vinegar

1½ cups (300 g) sugar

1 fresh or dried chile pepper, sliced crosswise or crushed

1 teaspoon dried mint

1½ to 2 teaspoons kosher or fine sea salt

Sunflower oil

EQUIPMENT

3 or 4 sterilized ½-pint jars and their lids

1 · Slice the squash in half lengthwise. Scoop out the seeds and any stringy pulp and discard (or reserve the seeds for another use). Peel off the rind with a sharp paring knife and cut the squash halves in half again lengthwise, to yield 4 pieces. Slice each quarter crosswise into wedges about ¼ inch thick and transfer to a large heatproof bowl.

2 · Combine the vinegar, sugar, chile pepper, mint, and salt in a medium saucepan and bring to a boil over medium heat. Stir once or twice to dissolve the sugar. Pour the boiling brine over the squash. Cover with a clean kitchen towel and let steep overnight.

3 · Drain the squash, reserving the brine. Return the brine to the saucepan and bring to a boil over medium-high heat. Boil vigorously for 2 minutes, then carefully add the squash. Return to a boil and boil until the squash is just beginning to soften, about 2 minutes—it should still be a little crunchy. Drain the squash and spread it out on clean kitchen towels to air-dry for a couple of hours.

4 · Pack the pieces tightly into the jars, leaving about 1 inch headspace. Pour enough oil over the squash to cover the pieces completely. Cover tightly with the lids and let stand at room temperature for 24 to 48 hours. Store in the refrigerator for up to 3 months. To serve, remove only as much as you plan to use and let it come to room temperature. Top off the jar with more oil as necessary to keep the remaining squash submerged.

VARIATION · To preserve the squash in the brine rather than in oil, pack the pieces tightly in sterilized jars, leaving about 1 inch headspace. Pour the hot brine over the squash, taking care to cover all the pieces. Cover tightly with the lids and let come to room temperature. Store in the refrigerator for up to 3 months.

LINDA'S SALT-PRESERVED GREEN TOMATOES

My friend Linda Maiello Prospero is a food writer and author of the blog Ciao Chow Linda. *I fell in love with her recipe for these tangy salt-preserved tomatoes, and she kindly gave me permission to share it here. Although this is a classic Calabrian preparation, these tomatoes have less in common with traditional Italian vinegar preserves than they do with dill pickles; that is, they are fermented. You douse them with salt, weight them down, and set them outside on the stoop to do their thing for two weeks. The transformation is remarkable. The hard, mild-flavored green tomatoes turn crunchy and sour. I find them irresistible and often enjoy them for lunch alongside hard-boiled eggs or cheese and salami. If you are a gardener or someone who looks for bargains at the farmers' market, this is a great way to use up those late-season green tomatoes that linger on the vine.*

5 pounds (2.3 kg) hard medium green tomatoes

½ cup (150 g) fine sea salt, plus 1 tablespoon for finishing

3 to 5 cloves garlic, crushed

2 fresh chile peppers, cut crosswise into thin slices

1 tablespoon fennel seeds, plus 1½ teaspoons for finishing

Extra-virgin olive oil

EQUIPMENT

1 (5-quart) plastic bucket or crockery or glass jar (do not use metal vessels), plus a second bucket or jar for weighting

Parchment paper

Heavyweight sturdy plastic grocery bag

7 sterilized ½-pint jars and their lids

1 · Cut out the "eye" from the stem end of the tomatoes and slice them vertically (through the stem end) ⅜ to ½ inch thick. If they are large, slice them in half through the stem and put them cut side down, then slice crosswise. Put them in a bowl as you go.

2 · Sprinkle the ½ cup salt on the tomatoes and use your hands to mix well. Layer the tomatoes in a bucket or crockery jar together with the garlic, chile peppers, and 1 table-spoon fennel seeds. Cut a round of parchment to fit just inside the opening of the bucket or jar and press it down on top of the tomatoes.

3 · Set the bucket or jar in a place where you don't mind some spillage; the tomatoes will give off a lot of water as they cure. I set mine on a back stoop; since I make these in October, the temperature is just right, neither too hot nor too cool.

(recipe continues)

4 • Place another bucket or jar on top of the parchment and weight it down with a very heavy object. My friend Linda fills a crockery jug with water. I fill a second plastic bucket with rocks from Lake Michigan (you get the idea). It's important not to use metal here, as it will react with the tomatoes. Stick to crockery, ceramic, glass, or plastic. Cover the jars with a large plastic bag and let them stew in their own juices, so to speak, until as much liquid as possible has been compressed out of the tomatoes and they are flattened, 10 days to 2 weeks.

5 • Drain the tomatoes in a colander set in the sink. Remove and discard the garlic, but keep the sliced chile pepper in with the tomatoes. In a small bowl, mix together the remaining 1 tablespoon salt and 1½ teaspoons fennel seeds. Pack the tomatoes into the jars, adding a drizzle of olive oil and a sprinkle of the fennel-salt mixture every so often, and leaving about 1 inch headspace. Make sure there are a few pieces of chile pepper in each jar. Press down on the tomatoes and use a bubble remover or a clean chopstick to release any air bubbles. Top off the jars with more oil, making sure the tomatoes are fully submerged. Screw the lids on tightly.

6 • The tomatoes are ready to eat immediately, or store them in the refrigerator, where they will keep for up to 3 months. To serve, remove from the jar only as much you plan to use and let it come to room temperature. Top off the jar with more oil as necessary to keep the remaining tomatoes submerged.

RED CABBAGE PICKLE

· · · MAKES 4 PINTS · · ·

It is always a treat to dine at a friend's house in Italy, because you invariably come away with something new, whether it's a recipe or a cooking or preserving technique. One afternoon, while having lunch with my friend Francesca at her in-laws' home near Navelli, in Abruzzo, she mentioned to her family that I was working on a book about Italian preserves. Out came a jar of this beautiful, scarlet, crunchy cabbage pickle, a sort of quick Italian version of sauerkraut. Francesca's mother-in-law, Anna Gasbarri, kindly shared the recipe, which was given to her by a cousin. This makes an excellent side dish to grilled sausages or pork chops.

1 large head red cabbage, about 2 pounds
   (907 g)

½ cup (150 g) fine sea salt

3 cups (710 g) white wine vinegar

2 cups (473 g) dry white wine

Sunflower oil or other mild-tasting
   vegetable oil

EQUIPMENT

4 sterilized 1-pint or two 1-quart jars and
   their lids

1 · Cut the cabbage lengthwise into quarters and cut out the core. Shred or cut the cabbage into thin slices and place them in a large bowl. Sprinkle the salt over the cabbage and toss thoroughly (I use my hands). Let the cabbage sit overnight; it will release liquid. Drain in a colander set in the sink and squeeze out as much excess liquid as possible.

2 · Place the cabbage in a clean nonreactive bowl and cover with the vinegar and wine. Cover lightly (I use a sheet of waxed paper) and let steep for at least 5 hours and up to overnight. Once again, drain the cabbage in a colander set in the sink and squeeze out as much excess liquid as possible. Spread the cabbage out on clean kitchen towels. Be sure to use clean but old towels that you don't mind staining red. Let the cabbage dry for 1 to 2 hours, until it no longer feels damp.

3 · Pack the cabbage into the jars and cover completely with oil. Use a bubble remover or a clean chopstick to release any air bubbles. Wipe the mouths of the jars clean with a damp paper towel. Screw the lids on tightly and let stand at room temperature overnight, then refrigerate. Store in the refrigerator for up to 3 months. To serve, remove from the jar only what you plan to use and let it come to room temperature. Top off the jar with more oil as necessary to keep the remaining cabbage submerged.

CROSTINI
with Sweet-and-Sour Peppers and Fresh Mozzarella

· · · MAKES ABOUT 32 CROSTINI, ENOUGH FOR 8 TO 10 APPETIZER SERVINGS · · ·

A plate of crostini before dinner rustles up the appetite, especially when the toppings are fresh, oozy mozzarella and bright, assertive sweet-and-sour peppers. The flavors in this easy appetizer shout "Summer!" but one of my favorite times to make it is for winter dinner parties, when I'm looking to banish the cold and conjure warmer days. I sometimes assemble a batch for myself for lunch.

1 thin baguette (ficelle), cut on the bias into ½-inch-thick slices

Extra-virgin olive oil

8 ounces (227 g) fresh mozzarella, cut into thin slices

1 cup (225 g) Sweet-and-Sour Roasted Peppers with Capers (page 38), diced, plus some of the oil from the peppers

Flaky sea salt

1 · Preheat the oven to 400°F. Arrange the baguette slices on a rimmed baking sheet and brush lightly with oil. Bake until they are nicely browned around the edges, 8 to 10 minutes. Let cool to room temperature.

2 · Cut the mozzarella slices to fit (more or less) on the crostini. Lay a piece of mozzarella on top of a crostino and top with about 2 teaspoons of the diced peppers and capers. Assemble all the crostini and arrange them on a serving platter. Drizzle a little of the pepper oil over them and sprinkle lightly with salt before serving.

FARRO SALAD
with Preserved Winter Squash and Dried Cherries

Most people remember their first encounter with love; I remember my first encounter with farro, at a restaurant in the rugged Garfagnana area of Tuscany. This ancient grain with a pleasingly chewy texture and nutty flavor has been around since Roman times but has enjoyed a revival in popularity in recent decades. Traditionally used in hearty vegetable soups, farro now stars in risotto-style dishes and in grain salads. This is but one of many renditions of farro salad that you can make with the preserved foods in this book: Feel free to play around with flavors and ingredients to come up with your own variation.

1 cup pearled farro, rinsed, any small stones or debris removed

1½ teaspoons fine sea salt

1 shallot, thinly sliced

¾ cup (113 g) Oil-Preserved Butternut Squash with Mint (page 42)

¼ cup (28 g) oven-dried cherries or store-bought

2 tablespoons extra-virgin olive oil

1 tablespoon white balsamic vinegar

1 tablespoon honey

Freshly ground black pepper

½ cup (70 g) coarsely chopped toasted hazelnuts

2 ounces (57 g) ricotta salata, diced

1 bunch arugula, for serving

1 · Put the farro in a high-sided saucepan with water to cover by 2 inches. Add 1 teaspoon of the salt and bring to a boil over medium-high heat. Reduce the heat to medium-low and cook, partially covered, until the farro is tender but still a little firm and chewy (al dente), 20 to 25 minutes. Drain the farro in a colander set in the sink and transfer it to a bowl. Fold in the shallot, preserved butternut squash, and dried cherries.

2 · In a small bowl, whisk together the oil, vinegar, and honey. Spoon in a little oil or brine from the squash, if you like. Season with the remaining ½ teaspoon salt and a little pepper and whisk again. Pour the dressing over the farro and fold until thoroughly combined. Fold in the hazelnuts and ricotta salata.

3 · Spread the arugula on a platter and spoon the farro salad on top. Serve warm or at room temperature.

PROSCIUTTO COTTO PANINI
with Pickled Rapini

· · · MAKES 4 SERVINGS · · ·

I don't often crave a sandwich, but when I do it's usually something big and hearty, a meal in itself. These panini fit the bill with a generous helping of prosciutto cotto, creamy mozzarella, and, to tie everything together, assertive pickled rapini. Prosciutto cotto translates to "cooked ham," and that is exactly what it is—not the more well-known cured prosciutto di Parma. It is typically seasoned with rosemary and sage. Look for prosciutto cotto in well-stocked delis and Italian food stores. If you can't find it, substitute a really good-quality deli ham.

4 ciabatta rolls or other fresh, crusty sandwich rolls

About 8 ounces (227 g) Pickled Rapini in Oil (page 41), at room temperature, cut into bite-size pieces, plus about 8 tablespoons of the oil from the rapini jar

8 to 12 ounces (227 to 340 g) sliced prosciutto cotto or best-quality deli ham

8 ounces (227 g) fresh, milky mozzarella, cut into 8 slices

Slice the rolls in half and spoon about 1 tablespoon of the oil on each cut side. Pile the prosciutto cotto onto the bottom half of each roll, folding it to fit. Arrange 2 slices of mozzarella over the prosciutto and top with the rapini. Place the upper halves of the rolls on top and press down gently for a few seconds to compress the sandwiches. Cut the panini in half and enjoy.

PICKLED VEGETABLE FRITTATA

I can't tell you how many times a frittata like this has saved me after a busy workday. I almost never make it the same way twice, so use this recipe as a guideline. Sometimes I use Pickled Rapini (page 41) or Oil-Preserved Butternut Squash with Mint (page 42). Or, instead of pickled asparagus spears, I might arrange some Oven-Roasted Tomatoes in Oil (page 132) on top. With all the vegetables in this frittata, you don't really need another one, but I like to serve a simple green salad on the side, along with some good bread.

½ cup (113 g) Sweet-and-Sour Roasted Peppers with Capers (page 38)

⅓ cup (70 g) Grilled Mixed Mushrooms in Oil (page 32) or Spiced Pickled Mushrooms (page 67)

⅓ cup (57 g) Grilled Zucchini in Oil (page 40)

6 spears Oil-Preserved Asparagus (page 29)

10 large eggs

½ cup (50 g) freshly grated Parmigiano-Reggiano

½ teaspoon fine sea salt

Freshly ground black pepper

2 tablespoons extra-virgin olive oil

2 to 3 ounces (57 to 85g) mozzarella, cut into cubes, or fresh ricotta (page 203)

1 • Pat the vegetables dry with paper towels to remove excess oil or brine. Cut the grilled zucchini slices crosswise into bite-size pieces. Leave the other vegetables as they are; you want a mix of sizes and textures. Set aside the asparagus spears and a few choice, large pieces of mushrooms.

2 • Turn on the broiler of your oven.

3 • In a large bowl, beat the eggs with the Parmigiano, salt, and pepper. Heat the oil in a 10-inch ovenproof skillet (I use a cast-iron skillet) over medium heat. Add the vegetables, except for the reserved asparagus and mushroom pieces. Cook, stirring once or twice, until the vegetables are heated through. Pour in the eggs and either sprinkle the mozzarella on top or dollop the ricotta here and there on top of the eggs. Arrange the reserved asparagus and mushrooms on the surface of the frittata. Reduce the heat to medium-low and cook until the frittata is set and nicely browned on the bottom. Use a spatula to lift an edge to check.

4 • Transfer the skillet to the broiler and broil until puffed and browned on top, about 2 minutes. Let the frittata settle for a couple of minutes before transferring it to a serving platter. Serve warm.

Carrots and Fennel in Agrodolce, page 58

FOODS PRESERVED IN VINEGAR

Google "Italian pickles" and you will get an avalanche of responses—nearly all for the same thing: giardiniera, that classic mix of garden vegetables in vinegar brine. I love giardiniera and on page 61 you will find my recipe, which features colorful carrots, cauliflower, peppers, and green beans and is based on one my mom used to make every year. But Italians pickle plenty of other vegetables as well: squat cipolline onions; crunchy fennel; peppers hot and sweet; beets, mushrooms, zucchini.

Pickling vegetables—preserving them in a vinegar solution—is an easy and tasty way to hold on to the colors and flavors of summer. To me, nothing beats the cold, sour (or sweet-and-sour) crunch of pickled vegetables, especially on a blustery winter day. In fact, a jar of pickled hot-and-sweet peppers (page 70), carrots and fennel (page 58), or giardiniera is often my go-to side dish for a hearty winter roast or stew.

A platter of mixed pickles, accompanied by cheese and *salumi*, makes a great appetizer for a casual get-together, no matter the season. Minced pickled vegetables are delicious mixed into a filling for stuffed peppers and tomatoes, or scattered atop pizza. But the best way to enjoy Italian-style pickles, in my opinion, is folded into Insalata di Riso (page 71), cold rice salad, together with hard-boiled eggs and tuna. This classic summer dish, an appetizing mix of color, flavor, and texture, was a specialty of my Zia Gilda and may just be my favorite recipe in the entire book.

Ingredients

I use a variety of vinegars for pickling. All of the vinegars called for are 5 percent acid. This is essential for preventing the growth of mold, bacteria, and other unwelcome microorganisms. Distilled white vinegar, made from grain (usually corn), has a sharp, clean flavor and no color. Wine vinegar can be either red or white and varies widely in quality. It can be made from a single variety, such as Pinot Grigio, or a mix. Better-quality wine vinegars are aromatic and complex, and less harsh-tasting than cheap ones. Like wine vinegars, balsamic wine vinegars can be dark or light in color and they vary in quality. True red balsamic vinegar is made from the must of Trebbiano grapes and is aged for at least 12 years in a succession of wood barrels that impart flavor and complexity. White balsamic vinegar is a combination of Trebbiano must and white wine vinegar. I use balsamic vinegar sparingly in recipes because it is expensive; also, red balsamic vinegar's intensely dark color changes the color of brine. Apple cider vinegar is not common in Italian pickles, but I like its crisp, fruity flavor and so I call for it in some recipes.

I use non-iodized fine sea salt, which is what I usually have on hand in my cupboard. Pickling salt, which is also pure salt, may be substituted. You can also use kosher salt, but keep in mind that because of kosher salt's larger crystal size, it will take longer to dissolve. You will also need to add up to 50 percent more in volume than the recipe calls for to obtain the same amount in weight as fine salt. Do not use table salt, which contains additives that can turn brine cloudy.

Several recipes call for both salt and sugar to create pickles known as *agrodolce* (sweet and sour). I use plain granulated sugar or, occasionally, vanilla sugar. The latter is made by burying a piece of vanilla bean in your sugar canister.

Black peppercorns, cloves, fennel seeds, and juniper berries are commonly used in Italian pickle preserves. Spices add depth to the flavor of pickles, so be sure yours are fresh (less than a year old). Dull spices make dull pickles.

Essentials of Italian Pickling

- The pickle recipes in this chapter call for water-bath canning to make them stable for long-term storage (up to a year). Before you start, read Water-Bath Canning, beginning on page 15. You will need the equipment and instructions listed in that section. Be sure to also read the section on how to sterilize jars and properly wash lids and rings.

- Follow the instructions for each recipe. Pay careful attention to blanching or cooking times. Overcooking your vegetables will give you mushy pickles.

- Your pickles will be only as good as your vegetables, so for the best pickles, start with the best vegetables: firm zucchini, unblemished mushrooms, freshly picked cauliflower, crunchy green beans, crisp carrots.

- Enjoy your pickles! Allow newly canned pickles to cure in a cool, dark spot for at least a week before opening, preferably a little longer. Once opened, refrigerate any leftovers. And don't forget about them; while water-bath canning makes vinegar pickles shelf-stable for a year, or even longer, they will lose crunch and color over time.

CARROTS AND FENNEL IN AGRODOLCE

· · · MAKES 4 PINTS · · ·

Italians are fond of preserving vegetables—and fruit—in a sweet-and-sour brine known as agrodolce. *Sweet peppers are a classic example, but I like this somewhat more unusual combination of crunchy carrots and sliced fennel bulb. Use a mix of colored carrots—gold, orange, and red—if you can find them. The darker ones turn the brine a pretty shade of sunset pink.*

2 cups (437 g) water

Juice of 2 lemons

2 pounds (907 g) fennel bulbs, plus 4 small fronds

2 pounds (907 g) carrots, peeled

2 cups (437 g) white wine vinegar

2 cups (437 g) apple cider vinegar

2 cups (400 g) sugar or vanilla sugar (see page 57)

2 tablespoons fine sea salt

1 teaspoon whole black peppercorns

1 teaspoon whole fennel seeds

EQUIPMENT

4 sterilized 1-pint jars and their lids

Basic water-bath canning equipment (see page 15)

1 · Combine the water and lemon juice in a bowl.

2 · Cut the tops off the fennel bulbs. Cut each bulb into quarters and each quarter into thin wedges. Drop each wedge in the lemon water as you go to keep it from browning.

3 · Cut the carrots into 2-inch sticks, and cut any large pieces in half or into quarters lengthwise to yield bite-size pieces. Add the carrots to the lemon water.

4 · Combine the vinegars, sugar, salt, peppercorns, and fennel seeds in a large, deep saucepan over medium-high heat. Bring the brine to a boil, stirring occasionally to make sure the sugar dissolves.

5 · Drain the fennel and carrots and add them to the boiling water. Cover the pot, turn off the heat, and let sit for 5 minutes.

6 · Place a fennel frond in the bottom of each jar. Pack the vegetables into the jars, taking care to get a mix of vegetables and some spices in each one. Pour the hot brine over the vegetables, leaving ½ inch headspace. Use a bubble remover or a clean chopstick to get rid of any bubbles. Screw the lids on tightly, and process for 10 minutes in a boiling-water bath (see Water-Bath Canning, page 15).

7 · Store the sealed jars in a cool, dark place and let the vegetables cure for at least 1 week before serving. They will keep for up to 1 year, though they may eventually lose their crisp texture. Refrigerate any jars that fail to seal properly and enjoy those first.

COOK'S NOTE · You may have a fair amount of brine left over. Rather than toss it, use it to make fennel-pickled eggs: Hard-boil and peel 6 eggs. Pack them snugly into a clean jar and pour hot brine over them, making sure the eggs are completely submerged. Cap tightly and refrigerate. Let the eggs cure for a couple of days before using. Enjoy within a week.

CIPOLLINI IN AGRODOLCE

· · · MAKES 2 PINTS · · ·

*Cipollini are those cute little saucer-shaped onions that you find in farmers'
markets and sometimes well-stocked supermarkets. They're sweet and crunchy
and happen to be the perfect size for pickling. Once pickled, I chop them up and
add them to Insalata di Riso (page 71). They are also good for slicing into a salad
or panino. Or chop one finely and add it to your favorite stuffed egg recipe.*

1½ pounds (680 g) cipollini onions

1 cup (237 g) white balsamic vinegar

½ cup (118 g) white wine vinegar

½ cup (118 g) water

⅓ cup (65 g) sugar

1 teaspoon fine sea salt

1 teaspoon whole black peppercorns

½ teaspoon whole coriander seeds

1 bay leaf

2 strips orange zest (no white pith)

EQUIPMENT

2 sterilized 1-pint jars and their lids

Basic water-bath canning equipment
(see page 15)

1 · Peel the onions and submerge them in a
bowl of cold water for 30 minutes.

2 · Combine the vinegars, the water, sugar,
salt, peppercorns, coriander seeds, and bay
leaf in a large, high-sided saucepan and bring
to a boil over medium-high heat. Add the

onions and orange zest. Return to a boil
and boil until you can pierce through the
onions with a fork with a bit of resistance,
about 10 minutes. They should be tender
but not soft.

3 · Using a skimmer or a slotted spoon,
transfer the onions to a bowl. Pack them
into the jars. Pour the brine through a small,
fine-mesh strainer into the jars, leaving
½ inch headspace. Use a bubble remover or
a clean chopstick to dislodge any air bubbles.
Retrieve the two pieces of orange zest and
tuck one into each jar.

4 · Screw the lids on tightly and process for
10 minutes in a boiling-water bath (see
Water-Bath Canning, page 15).

5 · Store the sealed jars in a cool, dark place
and let the onions cure for at least 1 week
before serving. They will keep for up to
1 year, though they may eventually lose their
crisp texture. Refrigerate any jars that fail to
seal properly and enjoy those first.

CLASSIC GIARDINIERA

··· MAKES 3 QUARTS ···

If the bottled supermarket version of giardiniera is your only reference, you are in for a happy surprise. Homemade giardiniera is so much more appealing, crisp and assertive but not abrasive.

1 medium head cauliflower (about 1½ pounds/680 g), separated into florets

1 pound (454 g) young carrots, sliced on the bias if large, left whole if small

8 ounces (227 g) pearl or small cipollini onions, peeled

6 to 7 ounces (170 to 200 g) green beans or mixed green and wax beans, sliced into 2-inch lengths (about 2 cups)

4 large celery stalks, sliced on the bias into 2-inch lengths (about 2 cups)

1 red bell pepper, cored, trimmed, and sliced into thin strips

1 yellow bell pepper, cored, trimmed, and sliced into thin strips

2 cups (473 g) white wine vinegar

2 cups (473 g) distilled white vinegar

2 cups (473 g) water

2 tablespoons fine sea salt

2 tablespoons sugar

1 teaspoon whole black peppercorns

1 teaspoon crushed red chile pepper

½ teaspoon whole cloves (about 10)

½ teaspoon juniper berries (about 9)

2 bay leaves

6 tablespoons extra-virgin olive oil

EQUIPMENT

3 sterilized 1-quart or six 1-pint jars, or a mix, and their lids

Basic water-bath canning equipment (see page 15)

1 • Have the vegetables prepped and ready. Combine the vinegars, water, salt, sugar, peppercorns, crushed red pepper, cloves, juniper berries, and bay leaves in a large pot and bring to a boil. Add all the vegetables and stir. Cover the pot and let the vegetables steep, still on the heat, for 1 minute. Turn off the heat and, with a skimmer or large slotted spoon, transfer the vegetables to a bowl.

2 • Add 2 tablespoons oil to each quart jar or 1 tablespoon to each pint jar. Pack the vegetables into the jars, adding a mix of each vegetable and some of the spices to each jar. Pour the brine over the vegetables, leaving ½ inch headspace. Use a bubble remover to dislodge any bubbles. Screw the lids on tightly and process for 10 minutes in a boiling-water bath (see Water-Bath Canning, page 15).

3 • Store the sealed jars in a cool, dark place and let the giardiniera cure for at least 1 week before serving. It will keep for up to 1 year. Refrigerate any jars that fail to seal properly and enjoy those first.

WINE-SPIKED JULIENNE CARROTS

Carrots are the workhorse of the vegetable world; we all have a bag in the fridge but we rarely think about making them the star of the show. Carrots are essential in Italian cooking, both as a flavoring agent for sauces, soups, and stews and as a center-stage ingredient in their own right. Here they shine in a sweet-and-sour pickle spiked with white wine and lemon zest.

1¼ pounds (567 g) carrots, either orange or rainbow (red, orange, yellow)

2 tablespoons coarse sea salt

1 cup (237 g) white wine vinegar

¾ cup (150 g) sugar

½ cup (118 g) dry white wine, such as Orvieto, Pecorino, or Soave

Pinch of finely grated lemon zest, plus the juice of ½ lemon

18 whole peppercorns

EQUIPMENT

3 sterilized ½-pint jars and their lids

Basic water-bath canning equipment (see page 15)

1 · Cut the carrots crosswise into 2-inch pieces. Cut each piece lengthwise into slices about ⅛ inch thick, then cut each slice into matchstick (julienne) strips about ⅛ inch thick. Place the carrot strips in a bowl as you work.

2 · Sprinkle the salt over the carrots and toss well. Transfer the carrots to a colander and set the colander over the bowl. Set a plate over the carrots and weight it down with a heavy object (a container of grains, a jug of maple

syrup, whatever you have on hand). Let the carrots marinate for 2 hours to release some of their juice.

3 · Rinse and drain the carrots, spread them out on a clean kitchen towel, and pat dry.

4 · Combine the vinegar, sugar, wine, and lemon zest and juice in a medium saucepan and bring to a boil over medium-high heat, stirring to dissolve the sugar. Add the carrots, stir once, and return to a boil. Boil for 2 minutes, then remove from the heat.

5 · Place 6 peppercorns in the bottom of each jar, and then pack the carrots into the jars. Ladle the hot brine over the carrots, leaving ½ inch headspace. Use a bubble remover or a clean chopstick to get rid of any bubbles. Screw the lids on tightly and process for 10 minutes in a boiling-water bath (see Water-Bath Canning, page 15).

6 · Store the sealed jars in a cool, dark place. The carrots will keep for up to 1 year, though they may eventually lose their crisp texture. Store any jars that fail to seal properly in the refrigerator and enjoy those first.

PICKLED CAULIFLOWER with Lemon

· · · MAKES 3 PINTS · · ·

After years of bad press, cauliflower is finally getting the love it deserves, in restaurants, in cookbooks, and on blogs. Italians have always appreciated its sweet, slightly sulfuric flavor, and my mom served it often with dinner, dressed with olive oil and lemon, or sometimes in a rich gratin. Cauliflower is a central ingredient in Classic Giardiniera (page 61), the ubiquitous mixed vinegary pickle that turns up on many an antipasto platter. But I'm so fond of it that I've decided it deserves its own pickle.

3 medium heads cauliflower

2 cups (473 g) white wine vinegar

1 cup (237 g) dry white wine, such as Orvieto, Pecorino, or Soave

1 cup (237 g) water

4 strips lemon peel (no white pith)

1 bay leaf

1½ tablespoons sugar

1 tablespoon fine sea salt

1 teaspoon whole black peppercorns

3 tablespoons extra-virgin olive oil

EQUIPMENT

3 sterilized 1-pint jars and their lids

Basic water-bath canning equipment (see page 15)

1 · Trim the cauliflower and cut the heads into bite-size florets. You should have about 8 cups (2 pounds/907 g) florets after trimming.

2 · Combine the vinegar, wine, water, lemon peel, bay leaf, sugar, salt, and peppercorns in a large saucepan and bring to a boil over medium-high heat. Add the cauliflower to the pot, cover, and cook for 1 minute; the water may not return to a boil. Using a skimmer or slotted spoon, transfer the cauliflower to a bowl. Reserve the brine.

3 · Pack the cauliflower tightly into the jars and add 1 tablespoon of the oil to each. Pour the brine over the cauliflower, leaving ½ inch headspace. Make sure you get a few peppercorns in each jar. Use a bubble remover or a clean chopstick to dislodge any bubbles. Screw the lids on tightly and process for 10 minutes in a boiling-water bath (see Water-Bath Canning, page 15).

4 · Store the sealed jars in a cool, dark place and let the cauliflower cure for 1 week before serving. The cauliflower will keep for up to 1 year, though it may eventually lose its crisp texture. Store any jars that fail to seal properly in the refrigerator and enjoy those first.

VARIATION · Try pickling purple cauliflower for dramatic effect. The florets turn magenta when plunged into the brine and eventually they turn the brine bright pink as well.

PICKLED BEETS AND SPRING ONIONS

· · · MAKES 4 PINTS · · ·

*Beets might not strike you as especially Italian, but they are a staple in the
cooking of the north. The roots are used in salads and the tops are sautéed
in olive oil or tossed into soups. These beautiful magenta pickles, spiced with
juniper, clove, and bay leaf, are delicious alongside simple roast chicken or fish.*

2 pounds (907 g) beets, trimmed

2 tablespoons sunflower oil or vegetable oil

1 pound (454 g) spring bulb onions

2 cups (473 g) white wine vinegar

1 cup (237 g) apple cider vinegar

1 cup (237 g) water

½ cup (100 g) sugar

2 tablespoons fine sea salt

2 teaspoons whole black peppercorns

6 juniper berries, lightly crushed

6 whole cloves

1 bay leaf

1 cinnamon stick

EQUIPMENT

4 sterilized 1-pint jars and their lids

Basic water-bath canning equipment
  (see page 15)

1 · Preheat the oven to 400°F.

2 · Place the beets upright in a roasting pan
and drizzle the oil over them. Rub the oil in
with your fingers. Cover with aluminum foil
and roast until tender, about 45 minutes. Let
cool to room temperature. Peel the beets and
cut them into 1-inch dice. Place them in a
bowl.

3 · Remove the green tops and bottoms from
the onions and slice the bulbs into wedges.

4 · Combine the vinegars, water, sugar, salt,
and spices in a saucepan and bring to a boil
over medium-high heat, stirring to dissolve
the sugar and salt. Add the onion wedges,
cover, turn off the heat, and let the onions
steep for 1 minute. Remove the onions, leaving the brine in the saucepan, and gently toss
the onions with the beets.

5 · Pack the beets and onions into the jars,
leaving ½ inch headspace. Strain the spices out
of the brine and ladle the brine over the vegetables, leaving ½ inch headspace. Screw the
lids on tightly and process for 10 minutes in a
boiling-water bath (see Water-Bath Canning,
page 15).

6 · Store the sealed jars in a cool, dark place
and let the beets cure for 2 weeks before
opening. Sealed jars will keep for up to 1 year.
Store any jars that fail to seal properly in the
refrigerator and use those first.

GIULIA'S PICKLED ZUCCHINI

··· MAKES 3 PINTS ···

If you have an abundance of zucchini in your garden, make these easy, vinegary pickles. I rely on zucchini from the farmers' market, so sometimes I use zucchini, and sometimes a mix of summer squash. Be sure to use firm squash to keep them from becoming too soft during brining and processing. This recipe is adapted from one given to me by my friend Giulia, who serves them at her guesthouse in Abruzzo.

2 pounds (907 g) firm zucchini or a mix of zucchini and summer squash

2 cups (473 g) white wine vinegar or apple cider vinegar, or 1 cup each

1 cup (237 g) water

½ cup (100 g) sugar

2 teaspoons fine sea salt

¾ cup (165 g) extra-virgin olive oil

EQUIPMENT

6 sterilized ½-pint jars and their lids

Basic water-bath canning equipment (see page 15)

1 · Cut off the ends of the zucchini and slice them lengthwise into quarters. Slice the quarters crosswise into ⅛-inch-thick wedges. You should end up with about 8 cups.

2 · In a large saucepan, combine the vinegar, water, sugar, and salt. Bring to a boil over medium-high heat, stirring to dissolve the sugar and salt. Add the zucchini and stir to distribute. Raise the heat to high. Once the brine returns to a boil, cover and boil for 2 minutes.

3 · With a skimmer, transfer the zucchini to a large rimmed baking sheet lined with a clean kitchen towel. Reserve the brine. Spread the wedges out in a single layer and let air-dry for 2 hours, until they no longer feel damp. Place the zucchini in a bowl and toss gently with the olive oil.

4 · Strain the reserved brine through a fine-mesh sieve and return it to the saucepan. Bring to a boil over medium-high heat, and then turn off the heat.

5 · Pack the zucchini into the jars, leaving ½ inch headspace. If there is any oil left in the bowl, divide it among the jars. Ladle the brine over the zucchini, leaving ½ inch headspace. Screw the lids on tightly and process for 10 minutes in a boiling-water bath (see Water-Bath Canning, page 15).

6 · Store the sealed jars in a cool, dark place and let the zucchini cure for 2 weeks before opening. Unopened jars will keep for up to 1 year. Store any jars that fail to seal properly in the refrigerator and use those first.

SPICED PICKLED MUSHROOMS

· · · MAKES 2 PINTS · · ·

There's something appealingly retro about this recipe, just like the starring ingredient. Button mushrooms are far from exotic, but they are readily available and perfect for taking on the flavors of this cinnamon- and clove-laced brine. Enjoy these mushrooms on Pickled Vegetable Pizza (page 78), or folded into Insalata di Riso (page 71).

2 pounds (907 g) firm, unblemished white button mushrooms

2 cups (473 g) distilled white vinegar

1 cup (237 g) white wine vinegar

1½ cups (355 g) water

½ cup (110 g) sunflower oil or vegetable oil

2 tablespoons sea salt

1 teaspoon whole black peppercorns

6 whole cloves

1-inch piece cinnamon stick

1 bay leaf

4 tablespoons extra-virgin olive oil

EQUIPMENT

2 sterilized 1-pint or four ½-pint jars and their lids

Basic water-bath canning equipment (see page 15)

1 · Gently rinse the mushrooms and pat them dry, brushing off any debris with a paper towel. Trim the stems and cut the mushrooms into quarters.

2 · Combine the vinegars, water, oil, salt, and spices in a large saucepan and bring to a boil over medium-high heat, stirring to dissolve the salt. Add the mushrooms, return to a boil, and boil for 5 minutes. Turn off the heat and cover the pot. Let the mushrooms rest for 5 minutes. Remove the mushrooms from the brine with a slotted spoon or skimmer.

3 · Pack the mushrooms into the jars, leaving about 1 inch headspace. Discard the bay leaf from the brine and then ladle the brine into the jars, leaving ¾ inch headspace. Pour 2 tablespoons olive oil into each pint jar or 1 tablespoon into each half-pint jar. Screw the lids on tightly and process for 15 minutes in a boiling-water bath (see Water-Bath Canning, page 15).

4 · Store the sealed jars in a cool, dark place and let the mushrooms cure for 2 weeks before opening. The sealed jars will keep for up to 1 year. Store any jars that fail to seal properly in the refrigerator and use those first.

SWEET, SOUR, AND SPICY PICKLED MELON

· · · MAKES 3 PINTS · · ·

These lightly pickled melon balls are hot, sweet, and tangy but also bursting with the fresh flavor of melon. Use melons that are ripe but not too soft, as they will soften slightly during water-bath processing. Serve this colorful pickle as part of a fruit salad—it is great with watermelon and blueberries. For something savory, put this out as part of an antipasto platter, with a good, rich cheese such as robiola and some slices of prosciutto.

2 large or 3 medium ripe but firm melons, such as cantaloupe, honeydew, or canary, or a mix, (about 6 pounds/2.7 kg total)

2 cups vanilla sugar (see page 57) or sugar

1 cup (237 g) water

¾ cup (177 g) white wine vinegar

¼ cup (4 g) chopped fresh mint

1 teaspoon fine sea salt

1 teaspoon crushed red chile pepper

EQUIPMENT

3 sterilized 1-pint jars (not wide-mouth) and their lids

Basic water-bath canning equipment (see page 15)

1 · Using a melon baller, carve out 6 cups worth of melon balls and place them in a bowl. (Reserve the leftover melon for a fruit salad or smoothie.)

2 · Combine the sugar, water, vinegar, and mint in a nonreactive saucepan. Bring to a boil over medium-high heat, stirring to dissolve the sugar. Turn off the heat, cover, and let steep for 1 hour. Strain the liquid through a fine-mesh strainer and return it to the saucepan.

3 · Stir in the salt and crushed red pepper and bring the brine to a boil again over medium-high heat.

4 · While the brine is heating, pack the melon balls into the jars, arranging them as tightly as you can without smooshing them. (Using jars with standard-size mouths rather than wide mouths will help keep the melon balls below the "shoulders" of the jars and prevent them from floating.) Funnel the hot brine into the jars, leaving ½ inch headspace and making sure the melon balls are completely submerged. Use a bubble remover or a clean chopstick to gently jostle the melon balls to help settle them.

5 · Screw the lids on tightly and process for 25 minutes in a boiling-water bath (see Water-Bath Canning, page 15). Store the sealed jars in a cool, dark place and let cure for at least 1 week before serving. The melon will keep for up to 6 months, though it will eventually lose its crisp texture. Store any jars that fail to seal properly in the refrigerator and enjoy those first.

HOT-AND-SWEET PICKLED PEPPERS

*I never craved ice cream when I was expecting, but I did crave pickles—
specifically pickled peppers. I couldn't find any commercial ones
that I liked well enough, so I had to come up with my own recipe.
These are an adaptation of the pickled peppers that my mom used to
make. I've spiced them up a bit with chile pepper, garlic, and cloves.
Serve them as an accompaniment to a frittata or pork chops.*

2½ pounds (1.1 kg) ripe sweet red
   horn-shaped peppers, red bell peppers,
   or a mix of red and yellow bell peppers

4 cups (946 g) apple cider vinegar

2 cups (473 g) water

1 cup (200 g) sugar

¼ cup (75 g) fine sea salt

3 fresh chile peppers, stemmed and sliced
   crosswise

3 cloves garlic, cut into pieces

1 bay leaf

1 teaspoon whole black peppercorns

3 whole cloves

6 tablespoons (110 g) extra-virgin olive oil

EQUIPMENT

3 sterilized 1-pint jars and their lids

Basic water-bath canning equipment
   (see page 15)

1 · Cut out the stems from the sweet peppers
and slice them in half lengthwise. Remove and
discard the seeds and pith. Slice the peppers
into ½-inch-thick strips.

2 · Combine the vinegar, water, sugar, salt,
chile peppers, garlic, bay leaf, and peppercorns
in a large, high-sided saucepan and bring to a
boil over medium-high heat. Add the peppers,
cover, and cook for 2 minutes; the water does
not need to return to a boil. Using a skimmer
or a slotted spoon, transfer the peppers to a
bowl or a clean kitchen towel.

3 · Pack the peppers into the jars, leaving
about ¾ inch headspace. Make sure to get
some slices of chile pepper and pieces of
garlic into each jar; discard the bay leaf. Use
a bubble remover or a clean chopstick to
dislodge any air bubbles. Add a clove and
2 tablespoons oil to each jar. Pour the brine
over the peppers, leaving ½ inch headspace.
Screw the lids on tightly and process for
10 minutes in a boiling-water bath (see
Water-Bath Canning, page 15).

4 · Store the sealed jars in a cool, dark place
and let the peppers cure for at least 2 weeks
before serving. They will keep for up to 1 year,
though they may eventually lose their crisp
texture. Store any jars that fail to seal properly
in the refrigerator and enjoy those first.

INSALATA DI RISO

··· MAKES 6 TO 8 SERVINGS ···

This salad was a specialty of my mother's oldest sister, Gilda, and it has always been one of my favorites. Is it necessary to use only ingredients you preserved yourself? Absolutely not. You can find just about all the ingredients in a good Italian deli, and of course you may add as many or as few as you like.

Fine sea salt

1½ cups (300 g) Arborio rice

1 (7-ounce) can solid tuna in olive oil, plus a couple tablespoons of oil from the can

1 cup (142 g) chopped Classic Giardiniera (page 61), drained

½ cup (85 g) Brine-Cured Olives (page 179), drained, pitted and cut into 2 or 3 pieces

½ cup (85 g) Sweet-and-Sour Roasted Peppers with Capers (page 38) or Hot-and-Sweet Pickled Peppers (page 70), drained

½ cup (85 g) chopped Baby Artichokes in Oil (page 26), drained

¼ cup (43 g) sliced Oil-Preserved Asparagus (page 29), drained

¼ cup (43 g) Eggplant in Oil (page 36), drained

¼ cup (43 g) Giulia's Pickled Zucchini (page 66), drained

¼ cup (43 g) Spiced Pickled Mushrooms (page 67), drained

2 to 4 tablespoons Wine-Spiked Julienne Carrots (page 63), drained

2 to 4 Cipollini in Agrodolce (page 60), drained and cut into quarters

3 hard-boiled large eggs, cut into pieces

3 best-quality anchovy fillets, finely chopped

2 tablespoons minced fresh flat-leaf parsley

1 tablespoon capers, preferably salt-packed, rinsed, drained, and coarsely chopped

3 tablespoons mayonnaise

Juice of ½ lemon

Freshly ground black pepper

1 · Bring a pot of water to a boil over high heat and salt it generously. Add the rice and let it come to a boil. Cover, reduce the heat to medium-low, and cook at a gentle simmer until the rice is al dente, about 20 minutes. Drain and then transfer to a large bowl.

2 · Add the tuna in large chunks, plus a couple tablespoons of oil from the jar, and toss gently to coat the rice with the oil. Add the remaining vegetables—as many or as few as you like—and toss gently to combine. Add the eggs, anchovies, parsley, capers, mayonnaise, and lemon juice. Fold everything together. Taste and season with salt and pepper.

3 · Cover the salad with plastic wrap and let stand at room temperature for 30 minutes to allow the flavors to mingle. If not serving immediately, store the salad in the refrigerator and remove 20 minutes before serving.

TRAMEZZINI FIVE WAYS

Tramezzini are small, artfully constructed tea sandwiches that are as pretty to look at as they are delicious to eat. Made with soft white bread trimmed of its crust and filled with all sorts of savories and pickled vegetables, they are a staple of Venetian snack food. Here are a few of my favorites. Make any or all, or come up with your own combinations.

EGG SALAD TRAMEZZINI
with Asparagus

8 hard-boiled large eggs

1 tablespoon mayonnaise, plus more
   for the bread

2 tablespoons minced Classic Giardiniera
   (page 61)

Fine sea salt and freshly ground black
   pepper

8 slices good-quality soft white bread
   (I use Vermont Bread Company
   Soft White)

8 spears Oil-Preserved Asparagus (page 29),
   cut crosswise into small pieces

1 · Peel the eggs and set aside 4 of them. Chop the remaining 4 eggs and put them in a bowl. Fold in the mayonnaise and giardiniera. Season lightly with salt and pepper.

2 · Spread a thin layer of mayonnaise on one side of each of the bread slices. Spread the egg salad evenly on four of the slices. Scatter the asparagus pieces on top. Cut the reserved 4 eggs in half lengthwise. Arrange two halves, cut side down, on each *tramezzino* over the asparagus.

3 · Cover each with another slice of bread, mayonnaise side down. Gently press down on the sandwiches to compress them just a little. Using a serrated knife, neatly cut away the crusts. Cut the *tramezzini* in half on the diagonal and serve.

(recipe continues)

TUNA AND OLIVE TRAMEZZINI
with Roasted Peppers

2 (7-ounce) cans good-quality solid tuna in olive oil, drained and coarsely chopped

¼ cup (42 g) coarsely chopped pitted Brine-Cured Olives (page 179) or store-bought purple olives, such as Kalamata

1 tablespoon capers, rinsed, drained, and coarsely chopped (optional)

⅓ cup (85 g) mayonnaise, plus more for the bread

8 slices good-quality soft white bread (I use Vermont Bread Company Soft White)

1 cup (200 g) Sweet-and-Sour Roasted Peppers with Capers (page 38) or bottled roasted red peppers, drained and cut into strips

Several leaves of red leaf lettuce

1 • Combine the tuna, olives, and capers in a bowl and fold in the mayonnaise until well combined.

2 • Spread a thin layer of mayonnaise on one side of each of the bread slices. Spoon the tuna salad onto four of the slices, mounding it slightly in the center and spreading it out to the edges. Scatter the pepper strips over the tuna. Top with lettuce leaves, keeping them within the confines of the bread.

3 • Cover each *tramezzino* with a second slice of bread, mayonnaise side down. Gently press down on the sandwiches to compress them just a little. Using a serrated knife, neatly cut away the crusts. Cut the *tramezzini* in half on the diagonal and serve.

PROSCIUTTO, ROASTED PEPPER, AND MOZZARELLA TRAMEZZINI

Mayonnaise, for spreading on bread

8 slices good-quality soft white bread (I use Vermont Bread Company Soft White)

1 cup (200 g) Sweet-and-Sour Roasted Peppers with Capers (page 38) or bottled roasted red peppers, drained and cut into strips

8 ounces (227 g) thinly sliced prosciutto di Parma

8 ounces (227 g) thinly sliced fresh mozzarella

2 ounces (57 g) arugula, thoroughly dried

Spread a thin layer of mayonnaise on one side of each of the bread slices. Scatter the peppers evenly over four of the slices, then arrange the prosciutto on top, followed by the mozzarella. Place a mound of arugula on top of the cheese. Cover each *tramezzino* with a second slice of bread, mayonnaise side down. Gently press down on the sandwiches to compress them just a little. Using a serrated knife, neatly cut away the crusts. Cut the *tramezzini* in half on the diagonal and serve.

PROSCIUTTO COTTO, PICKLED MUSHROOM, AND ASIAGO FRESCO TRAMEZZINI

Mayonnaise, for spreading on bread

8 slices good-quality soft white bread
(I use Vermont Bread Company
Soft White)

8 ounces (227 g) prosciutto cotto,
or good-quality deli ham

3 to 4 ounces (85 to 113 g) Grilled Mixed
Mushrooms in Oil (page 32), drained
and patted dry

8 ounces (227 g) Asiago fresco, thinly sliced

Several leaves of romaine lettuce

1 · Spread a thin layer of mayonnaise on one side of each of the bread slices. Arrange the prosciutto cotto on four of the slices and scatter the mushrooms on top. Arrange the cheese slices evenly over the mushrooms, then top with the lettuce leaves, keeping them within the confines of the bread.

2 · Cover each *tramezzino* with a second slice of bread, mayonnaise side down. Gently press down on the sandwiches to compress them just a little. Using a serrated knife, neatly cut away the crusts. Cut the *tramezzini* in half on the diagonal and serve.

SPICY SALAMI, ARTICHOKE, ROASTED TOMATO, AND PROVOLONE TRAMEZZINI

Mayonnaise, for spreading on bread

8 slices good-quality soft white bread
(I use Vermont Bread Company
Soft White)

6 ounces (170 g) thinly sliced hot salami
or soppressata

4 Baby Artichokes in Oil (page 26), or
8 bottled marinated artichoke halves,
drained and patted dry

6 ounces (170 g) thinly sliced provolone

1 cup (200 g) Oven-Roasted Tomatoes
in Oil (page 132), or bottled sun-dried
tomatoes in oil, drained, patted dry,
and cut crosswise into strips

1 · Spread a thin layer of mayonnaise on one side of each of the bread slices. Arrange the salami on four of the slices. Cut each artichoke half in half lengthwise and place four pieces on each *tramezzino* on top of the meat. Arrange the cheese over the artichokes and scatter the tomatoes on top.

2 · Cover each *tramezzino* with a second slice of bread, mayonnaise side down. Gently press down on the sandwiches to compress them just a little. Using a serrated knife, neatly cut away the crusts. Cut the *tramezzini* in half on the diagonal and serve.

BAKED PEPPERS AND TOMATOES
with Giardiniera Bread Stuffing

I almost never make this recipe the same way twice, always changing up the type of cheese or herb seasoning. The minced giardiniera is a must, though; it punches up the flavor of the bread crumb stuffing.

2 cups (454 g) Passata di Pomodoro (page 117)

1 clove garlic, lightly crushed

4 tablespoons extra-virgin olive oil

2 large red or yellow bell peppers

4 medium round tomatoes

1 shallot, minced (about 3 tablespoons)

3 cups (170 g) fresh bread crumbs

2 tablespoons minced fresh flat-leaf parsley

2 tablespoons minced fresh basil

¾ cup (180 g) finely chopped Classic Giardiniera (page 61)

½ cup (40 g) shredded Asiago fresco

½ cup (40 g) shredded provolone

2 tablespoons capers, coarsely chopped

½ teaspoon fine sea salt, or to taste

Freshly ground black pepper

Generous pinch of crushed red chile pepper

½ cup (28 g) freshly grated Parmigiano-Reggiano or Pecorino Romano

1 · Preheat the oven to 375°F. Combine the *passata* and garlic in a bowl. Stir in 1 tablespoon of the oil and let steep.

2 · Cut the peppers in half lengthwise through the stems and scoop out the seeds, core, and white pith. Set aside. Slice the tops off the tomatoes and scoop out the seeds and gel. Set them upside down on a paper towel to drain.

3 · Heat the remaining 3 tablespoons oil in a large skillet over medium heat. Add the shallot, reduce the heat to medium-low, and cook until the shallot begins to soften, about 5 minutes. Stir in the bread crumbs, parsley, and basil and cook, stirring often, until the bread crumbs are light golden and crisped, about 8 minutes. Transfer to a bowl and let cool briefly. Fold in the giardiniera, Asiago, provolone, and capers and season with the salt, pepper, and chile pepper. Spoon into the hollowed-out peppers and tomatoes.

4 · Spread about half the tomato *passata* in the bottom of a baking dish just large enough to hold the vegetables snugly. Arrange the peppers and tomatoes in the dish and spoon the remaining *passata* over the top. Sprinkle the Parmigiano on top. Cover with foil and bake for 30 minutes. Uncover and bake until the tops are nicely browned and the peppers and tomatoes are tender, about 30 minutes longer. Turn off the oven but leave the vegetables in for 15 minutes longer, to soften just a bit more. Serve warm or at room temperature.

PICKLED VEGETABLE PIZZA

I concede that pickled vegetable pizza sounds unconventional, and also that you will not find it on most pizzeria menus in Italy. But I can't think of a better way to offset the rich creaminess of fresh mozzarella than some colorful, lightly brined or pickled veggies: artichokes, eggplant, mushrooms, olives, oven-roasted tomatoes, peppers . . . all of them are at home on top of a pizza. Choose from the list of suggestions or add your own touch.

3 cups (380 g) Caputo "00" flour for pizza (see Sources, page 292) or bread flour

2 teaspoons rapid-rise yeast

1½ teaspoons fine sea salt

1 cup (237 g) warm water (100 to 110°F)

2 tablespoons extra-virgin olive oil, or as needed

1½ cups (340 g) Small-Batch Tomato Sauce (page 120) or Bottled Whole Tomatoes (page 115), crushed

8 to 12 ounces (227 to 340 g) fresh mozzarella

Assortment of pickled and preserved vegetables, such as:

Baby Artichokes in Oil (page 26)

Eggplant in Oil (page 36)

Sweet-and-Sour Roasted Peppers with Capers (page 38)

Oven-Roasted Tomatoes in Oil (page 132)

Grilled Mixed Mushrooms in Oil (page 32)

Salt-Cured Olives (page 177) or Brine-Cured Olives (page 179)

EQUIPMENT

13- or 14-inch round pizza pan or 11- by 17-inch rimmed baking sheet

Pizza stone or baking steel (optional; see Cook's Note)

Wooden pizza peel, if using a pizza stone or baking steel

1 · Add the flour, yeast, and salt to the bowl of a food processor fitted with the metal blade and pulse to combine. With the motor running, drizzle in the water and 1 tablespoon of the oil through the feed tube and process until a ball of dough forms.

2 · Turn the dough out onto a lightly floured work surface and knead until it is smooth and elastic, 3 to 5 minutes. Form the dough into a ball. Grease the inside of a large ceramic or glass bowl with the remaining 1 tablespoon oil and place the dough inside, turning it to coat it with oil. Cover with plastic wrap and refrigerate for several hours to allow it to rise slowly—6 to 8 if you have the time. Remove the dough from the refrigerator at least 1 hour

before shaping it. If you are pressed for time, put the bowl in a warm place and let the dough rise until doubled in volume, 1½ to 2 hours.

3 · Preheat the oven to 500°F. If using a pizza stone or a baking steel, place it in the oven while it is preheating.

4 · Lightly coat a 13- or 14-inch round pizza pan or 11- by 17-inch rimmed baking sheet with oil. If you're baking the pizza directly on the stone or steel, place the dough on a lightly floured pizza peel. With oiled fingers, gently stretch and press the dough out toward the rim of the pan or the peel. This will take a little while, since the dough has a tendency to spring back. If this happens, let it rest for a minute, then continue.

5 · Spoon as much (or as little) of the tomato sauce as you like over the dough, leaving a 1-inch border. Arrange the mozzarella slices and your selection of vegetables over the sauce. Don't overdo it or you will weigh the pizza down.

6 · If you are using the stone or steel, gently slide the pizza from the peel onto the stone or steel. Bake until the cheese is melted and just beginning to brown in spots and the crust is crisped and puffed up around the edges, about 5 minutes. If you want to char the crust, turn on the broiler and broil the pizza for about a minute, just until the crust is blackened in a few places.

7 · Let the pizza rest for 5 minutes before cutting into wedges or rectangles and serving.

COOK'S NOTE · Pizza stones for the home cook have been around for a long time, but the baking steel is a recent addition to the world of pizza-making equipment. This slim but hefty sheet of metal is an excellent heat conductor and creates really good chewy-crispy crusts. (See Sources, page 292, for more information.)

Simple Strawberry Jam, page 85

SWEET PRESERVES:
CONSERVES, JAMS, JELLIES, MARMALADES

Fruit grows in shameless abundance all over Italy, along hillsides, by the seaside, and on craggy slopes. I have seen fig trees sprouting up through the cracks of cobbled streets, with more fruit on them, I might add, than on my tree at home in Virginia.

Fresh fruit is part of virtually every meal in Italy; fresh figs or a *spremuta* (freshly squeezed citrus juice) at breakfast, a handful of cherries to close the midday meal, or—my favorite—a ripe peach sliced into a glass of wine at the end of dinner.

But for all that remains? There are fruit spreads—jams, jellies, conserves, marmalades, and the like. This chapter features a handful of my favorite recipes for Italian fruit spreads—fig jam, sour cherry spoon fruit, quince jelly, and more—plus bonus recipes that showcase them. Yes, homemade plum or grape jam is delicious spread on toast, but it's even better as a filling for a lattice-top crostata (page 105).

In Italy it is also common to preserve fruit in syrup and/or alcohol, and to make lovely liqueurs out of fruit. You will find those recipes in another chapter, beginning on page 237.

Essentials of Sweet Preserves

• Most of the recipes in this chapter call for water-bath canning to make them stable for long-term storage. Before you start, read Water-Bath Canning, beginning on page 15. You will need the equipment and instructions listed in that section. Be sure to also read the section on how to sterilize jars and properly wash lids and rings.

• What's the difference? Although jams, jellies, preserves, conserves, and marmalades all contain a mix of fruit, sugar, and pectin (natural or added), there are differences between them. **Jam** is made from mashed or finely chopped fruit that is cooked down to a spoonable, spreadable consistency. **Jelly** is made from the juice strained from cooked fruit. It is a transparent jiggly spread that makes an excellent glaze. **Preserves** are chunks or whole pieces of fruit suspended in a thick syrup, jelly, or jam. These are not to be confused with the umbrella term *preserves*, used to describe any food that is manipulated to improve its keeping capabilities. **Conserves** are jams to which dried fruits and/or nuts have been added. They are extra-thick and delicious with cheese as an appetizer or with roast meats. **Marmalade** is made from the pulp and peel of citrus fruit. Bitterness is typically one of its characteristics, making it good for both sweet and savory uses.

• For best results, use fresh, in-season fruit that is unblemished and ripe—but not overripe. Overripe fruit tends not to jell as well as just-ripe or slightly underripe fruit because **pectin**, the natural thickening agent in fruit, loses strength over time. High-pectin fruits include apples, pears, plums, quince, and citrus fruits; these preserves will set without added pectin. Strawberries and cherries are low in pectin; apricots, peaches, plums, and grapes lie somewhere in between. You can buy commercial pectin to help thicken your preserves, but I prefer not to. Instead, I use lemon juice and peel or a grated apple—both high in pectin—to help my preserves set.

- Most fruits are high in acid; figs are an exception. Lemon juice helps to balance fruit's natural sweetness and raises the acidity level of preserves, making them safe for water-bath canning and long-term storage. Acid also helps to activate fruit's natural pectin, aiding the thickening process.

- Sugar brings everything together, adding sweetness and drawing moisture out of the fruit, thus helping to make the environment inhospitable to microbes. I almost always use vanilla sugar (page 57) when making fruit spreads.

- I have two wide, nonreactive, heavy-bottomed pots that I typically use for making sweet preserves, a 4-quart heavy-bottomed stainless steel deep saucepan, and a 5½-quart enameled Dutch oven. They both cook the fruit evenly, and their materials do not react with the acidity of the preserves, which mean they don't negatively affect color or flavor.

- Follow the cooking instructions in individual recipes. In general, fruit spreads should be cooked at a lively simmer to evaporate the water and thicken the mixture while maintaining the fruit's fresh flavor. Don't boil too hard or you risk evaporating the fruit's natural pectin. Stir continuously with a silicone spatula or wooden spoon to prevent burning.

- Testing for doneness: The preserves are done when they reach 220°F. To test without a thermometer, use the **freezer test**: Chill several small plates in the freezer. Remove the thickened preserves from the heat (to prevent further cooking), spoon a little onto one of the plates, and set it in the freezer for 2 minutes. The spread should be thick enough that it wrinkles slightly when you nudge it with your finger and moves slowly when you tilt the plate. If it's too runny, return the pot to the heat for a few more minutes and test again with another plate. It is important not to overcook fruit spreads, or they can turn unpleasantly rubbery.

- After processing, preserves will continue to set as they cool. Store sealed jars in a cool, dark place to maintain their color and flavor.

APRICOT-ANISE JAM

I grew up eating apricots by the kilo during summers spent in Italy. Finding worthy ones this side of the Atlantic has been a challenge, but in recent years I've had some luck at farmers' markets. If you are new to making preserves, apricots are a great fruit to start with. You don't have to peel them, as their thin skin melts away during cooking. And there is no need to add the jelling agent pectin, since the fruit thickens nicely on its own.

1½ pounds (680 g) ripe apricots
    (12 to 14 medium)

¾ to 1 cup (150 to 200 g) sugar

2 tablespoons orange or lemon juice

3 small strips lemon zest

½ teaspoon anise seeds

EQUIPMENT

2 sterilized ½-pint jars and their lids

3-inch square piece of cheesecloth

Kitchen twine

Basic water-bath canning equipment
    (see page 15)

1 · Cut the apricots in half and remove the pits. Cut each half into 4 pieces and put them in a heavy-bottomed nonreactive pot or preserving pot. Sprinkle ¾ cup (150 g) of the sugar over the apricots and stir in the juice and zest.

2 · Mound the anise seeds on the square of cheesecloth and tie it into a bundle with kitchen twine. Toss the bundle into the pot.

3 · Set the pot over medium-high heat and bring to a boil. Reduce the heat to medium and cook at a lively simmer, stirring often,

until most of the fruit has broken down and the mixture has begun to thicken, about 10 minutes. Taste and add the remaining ¼ cup (50 g) sugar if the mixture is too tart. Cook, stirring, until thickened to a jam-like consistency, about 10 minutes longer. (Reduce the heat to medium-low if the mixture is sputtering too much.)

4 · Turn off the heat and retrieve and discard the cheesecloth bundle. You can fish out the lemon zest as well if you like, but I usually just leave it in (it's hard to locate).

5 · Funnel the hot jam into the sterilized jars, leaving ¼ inch headspace. Wipe the rims clean if necessary with a clean, damp cloth, and screw the lids on the jars.

6 · Process in a boiling-water bath for 10 minutes (see Water-Bath Canning, page 15). Remove the jars and set them upright on a clean kitchen towel. Let the jars cool to room temperature before storing in a cool, dark place for up to 1 year. Refrigerate once opened. Store any jars that fail to seal properly in the refrigerator and enjoy those first.

SIMPLE STRAWBERRY JAM

Strawberries are low in pectin, so most recipes for call for adding commercial powdered pectin and/or lots of sugar to help the mixture set. These preserves tend to be too stiff and too sweet for my taste. For years I added a chopped Granny Smith apple, which is high in pectin, to the pot. This worked nicely but changed the texture of the jam. Recently, while cleaning out my freezer, I came across a batch of frozen strawberries that needed to be used up. I tossed them into a pot and, with no apples on hand, I added some lemon juice and a couple of pieces of orange and lemon peel. The preserves set beautifully, thus confirming my long-held belief that cooking really is an intuitive process. Make sure you use ripe, in-season strawberries and not those giant cottony ones from the supermarket.

1½ pounds (680 g) fresh or frozen
   strawberries, hulled

2 cups (400 g) vanilla sugar (see page 57)

Juice of ½ lemon

1 (3-inch) strip orange zest (no white pith)

1 (3-inch) strip lemon zest (no white pith)

EQUIPMENT

3 sterilized ½-pint jars and their lids

Basic water-bath canning equipment
   (see page 15)

1 • Put the strawberries in a heavy-bottomed saucepan or preserving pot. Add the sugar, lemon juice, and orange and lemon strips. Set the pot on the stovetop over medium-low heat and stir until the sugar is fully dissolved and the strawberries are soft. Use a potato masher to mash up the strawberries, taking care to leave some of them in pieces. Raise the heat to medium-high and bring the mixture to a boil. Cook at a lively simmer, stirring often, until the mixture has darkened and begun to thicken, 20 to 30 minutes. Watch out for spattering.

2 • Continue to boil until the mixture reaches 220°F and you can drag a path along the bottom of the pot with a silicone spatula. Or use the freezer plate method to test for doneness as described on page 83.

3 • Ladle the hot jam into the sterilized jars, leaving ¼ inch headspace. Wipe the rims clean if necessary with a clean, damp cloth, and screw the lids on the jars.

4 • Process the jars in a boiling-water bath for 10 minutes (see Water-Bath Canning, page 15). Remove the jars and set them upright on a clean kitchen towel. Let cool to room temperature before storing in a cool, dark place for up to 1 year. Refrigerate once opened. If any jars have failed to seal properly, store them in the refrigerator and enjoy those first.

STRAWBERRY-APRICOT PRESERVES

··· MAKES 2 PINTS ···

*This is hands-down my favorite jam combination, even though it has little
to do with Italy and much to do with a trio of New York folk-singing sisters
called The Roches. In one of their earlier tunes, called "The Troubles," they
sing fondly about strawberry-apricot pie. For decades (literally) I wondered
about this combination. Finally, I had to make one. It was an outrageously
good pie, with a sunrise-pink filling. I decided it needed to be a jam, too.*

1 full quart ripe, in-season strawberries
(about 1½ pounds/680 g)

1 pound (454 g) ripe apricots

3 cups (600 g) vanilla sugar (see page 57)

¼ cup (59 g) lemon juice, plus 3 strips
lemon zest

EQUIPMENT

4 sterilized ½-pint jars and their lids

Basic water-bath canning equipment
(see page 15)

1 · Hull and quarter the strawberries, placing
them in a wide, heavy-bottomed nonreactive
saucepan or preserving pot as you go. Pit and
quarter the apricots; then cut each quarter in
half crosswise to yield big pieces. Add them to
the saucepan. Stir in the sugar and lemon juice
and zest and let macerate at room temperature
for 1 hour.

2 · Cook the fruit over medium-low heat and
stir until the sugar is fully dissolved. Raise the
heat to medium-high and bring the mixture to
a boil. Cook at a lively simmer, stirring often,
until the mixture has darkened and begun
to thicken, 20 to 30 minutes. Watch out for
spattering.

3 · Continue to boil until the mixture reaches
220°F. Or use the freezer plate method to test
for doneness as described on page 83.

4 · Ladle the hot jam into the sterilized jars,
leaving ¼ inch headspace. Wipe the rims clean
if necessary with a clean, damp cloth, and
screw the lids on the jars.

5 · Process the jars in a boiling-water bath for
10 minutes (see Water-Bath Canning, page
15). Remove the jars and set them upright on a
clean kitchen towel. Let cool to room temperature before storing in a cool, dark place
for up to 1 year. Refrigerate after opening.
If any jars have failed to seal properly, store
them in the refrigerator and enjoy those first.

VARIATION · Substitute Pluots (that lovely
cross between a plum and an apricot) for the
apricots. The resulting jam will be ruby red
in color with a touch of rich, sweet-tart plum
flavor.

SOUR CHERRY SPOON FRUIT

· · · MAKES 1½ PINTS · · ·

*These sticky, sweet-tart preserves are delicious spooned on Greek
yogurt or vanilla ice cream. But my favorite way to enjoy them is this:
Toast a slice or two of good Italian bread. Spread fresh ricotta (page
203) on top and then spoon the fruit on top of that. Heaven.*

1½ pounds (680 g) fresh sour cherries
(about 4 cups), pitted (see Cook's Note)
with pits reserved

1 cup (140 g) dried sour cherries

2 cups (400 g) vanilla sugar (see page 57)

2 tablespoons freshly squeezed lemon juice

½ vanilla bean

EQUIPMENT

3 sterilized ½-pint jars and their lids

Tight-weave cheesecloth

Kitchen twine

Basic water-bath canning equipment
(see page 15)

1 · Combine the fresh and dried cherries,
sugar, and lemon juice in a nonreactive heavy-
bottomed saucepan or preserving pot. Scrape
the seeds from the vanilla bean and add
them to the pan, along with the pod. Let the
cherries macerate for about 1 hour. Tie the
reserved pits in a piece of cheesecloth with the
twine and add the bundle to the pot.

2 · Set the pot over medium-high heat and
bring to a boil. Cook at a lively simmer, stirring often, until the mixture has darkened and
begun to thicken, 20 to 30 minutes.

3 · Continue to boil until the mixture reaches
220°F and you can drag a path along the
bottom of the pot with a silicone spatula.
Or use the freezer plate method to test for
doneness as described on page 83.

4 · Remove and discard the cheesecloth
bundle. Ladle the hot fruit into the jars,
leaving ¼ inch headspace. Wipe the rims
clean if necessary with a clean, damp cloth,
and screw the lids on the jars.

5 · Process the jars in a boiling-water bath for
10 minutes (see Water-Bath Canning, page
15). Remove the jars and set them upright on a
clean kitchen towel. Let the jars cool to room
temperature before storing in a cool, dark
place for up to 1 year. Refrigerate after opening. Store any jars that fail to seal properly in
the refrigerator and use those first.

COOK'S NOTE · To remove the pits from sour
cherries, unbend a clean paper clip into a long
"S"-shaped wire with two curved ends. Gently
push the smaller curved end into the cherry
through the stem end and scoop out the pit.

BITTER CITRUS MARMALADE

··· MAKES ABOUT 3 PINTS ···

Bitter orange marmalade is a classic Sicilian preserve. When I was growing up, I couldn't tolerate the intrusive bits of peel and the sharp taste that my parents seemed to enjoy with such relish. That memory stayed with me for a long time, and I didn't touch it for years. My palate has changed quite a bit and I now find this marmalade irresistible. I think of it as "lazy" bitter marmalade because rather than painstakingly scraping off the white pith after the oranges have cooked, I leave it on. This makes less work for me and gives the preserve that bitter flavor I have come to love.

2½ pounds (1.1 kg) organic, untreated citrus fruit, such as blood oranges, mandarin oranges, lemons, and so on (use more exotic fruit, such as kumquats, mandarinquats, or Buddha's hand, if you like)

Spring or filtered water

Sugar

1 vanilla bean

EQUIPMENT

Cheesecloth

Kitchen twine

Kitchen scale

3 sterilized 1-pint or six ½-pint jars and their lids

Basic water bath canning equipment (see page 15)

1 · If using small citrus, such as kumquats or mandarinquats, cut them crosswise into very thin wheels. Cut the oranges and lemons into quarters and cut the quarters crosswise into very thin wedges. Remove and collect the seeds of the fruit in a bowl as you work. They contain lots of pectin, which will help to set the marmalade.

2 · Place the fruit in a large nonreactive heavy-bottomed saucepan or preserving pot and cover with 3 to 3½ cups water—enough to just cover the fruit. Put the seeds in a piece of cheesecloth and tie it into a bundle with the kitchen twine. Add this to the pot.

3 · Bring the fruit to a boil over medium-high heat and boil for 5 minutes. Remove from the heat and let cool to room temperature; then cover the pot and refrigerate overnight.

(recipe continues)

4 • Bring the fruit to a boil once again over medium-high heat. Reduce the heat to medium and simmer until the peel of the fruit is tender, about 15 minutes. Remove and discard the bundle of seeds.

5 • Weigh the fruit mixture; it should weigh about 2½ pounds (1.1 kg). Add an equal weight of sugar to the pot. Slice open the vanilla bean and scrape the seeds into the pot. Reserve the pod for another use (I use it to make vanilla sugar).

6 • Set the pot on the stovetop over medium-low heat and stir until the sugar is fully dissolved. Raise the heat to medium-high and bring the mixture to a boil. Cook at a lively boil, stirring often, until the mixture has darkened and begun to thicken. This will take about 30 minutes. Watch out for spattering.

7 • Continue to boil until the mixture reaches 220°F and you can drag a path along the bottom of the pot with a silicone spatula. Or use the freezer plate method to test for doneness as described on page 83.

8 • Ladle the hot marmalade into the sterilized jars, leaving ¼ inch headspace. Wipe the rims clean if necessary with a clean, damp cloth, and screw the lids on the jars.

9 • Process the jars in a boiling-water bath for 10 minutes (see Water-Bath Canning, page 15). Remove the jars and set them upright on a clean kitchen towel. Let cool to room temperature before storing in a cool, dark place for up to 1 year. Refrigerate after opening. If any jars have failed to seal properly, refrigerate them and enjoy those first.

PLUM PRESERVES

· · · MAKES 1½ PINTS · · ·

There's a plum tree in our side yard that was planted by a previous owner. One year, out of nowhere, it produced a bumper crop of small but deliciously sweet plums with juicy red flesh, which I then turned into preserves. I'm afraid I'm not much of a fruit tree whisperer and the tree hasn't produced a generous crop since, so I rely on plums from my local farmers' markets. Spread this deliciously tart jam on toast or scones, or use it as a filling for Favorite Jam Crostata (page 105).

2 pounds (907 g) Santa Rosa or other red-fleshed plums

2¼ cups (450 g) sugar

Coarsely chopped zest and freshly squeezed juice of 1 small lemon

EQUIPMENT

3 sterilized ½-pint jars and their lids

Basic water-bath canning equipment (see page 15)

1 · Cut the plums in half and remove the pits. Cut each half into 4 pieces so that you have small chunks. Put the cut-up plums in a large nonreactive heavy-bottomed saucepan or preserving pot. Stir in the sugar, lemon zest, and lemon juice, and let macerate at room temperature for 1 to 2 hours.

2 · Cook the fruit over medium-low heat, stirring, until the sugar is fully dissolved. Raise the heat to medium-high and bring the mixture to a boil. Cook at a lively simmer, stirring often, until the mixture has thickened and turned several shades darker, 15 to 20 minutes. Watch out for spattering.

3 · Continue to boil until the mixture reaches 220°F and you can drag a path through the bottom of the pot with a silicone spatula. Or use the freezer plate method to test for doneness as described on page 83.

4 · Ladle the hot jam into the jars, leaving ¼ inch headspace. Wipe the rims clean if necessary with a clean, damp cloth, and screw the lids on the jars.

5 · Process the jars in a boiling-water bath for 10 minutes (see Water-Bath Canning, page 15). Remove the jars and set them upright on a clean kitchen towel. Let the jars cool to room temperature before storing in a cool, dark place for up to 1 year. Refrigerate after opening. Store any jars that fail to seal properly in the refrigerator and enjoy those first.

PEACH AND ALMOND CONSERVA
with Marsala

*Conserva is a preserve with either nuts or dried fruit—or sometimes both—
mixed in. Here, sliced almonds add a crunchy texture, while a splash of Marsala,
a fortified wine from Sicily, gives the flavor of the peaches a robust boost.*

3 pounds (1.4 kg) ripe peaches

2 cups (400 g) vanilla sugar (see page 57) or
  sugar

Juice of 1 lemon

1 vanilla bean

½ cup (118 g) dry Marsala wine

1 cup (100 g) sliced almonds, lightly toasted
  (see Cook's Note)

EQUIPMENT

4 or 5 sterilized ½-pint jars and their lids

Basic water-bath canning equipment
  (see page 15)

1 · Place a large bowl of ice water near the stove. Bring a large pot of water to a boil over high heat. Carefully drop in the peaches, in batches if necessary, and blanch for 1 minute to loosen the skins. Remove the peaches with a large skimmer or slotted spoon and plunge them into the ice water. Drain in a colander set in the sink.

2 · Peel the peaches, pit them, and cut them into quarters. Place them in a heavy-bottomed saucepan or preserving pot and mash coarsely with a potato masher. Stir in the sugar and lemon juice. Split the vanilla bean lengthwise and scrape the seeds into the pot. (Reserve the pod to make more vanilla sugar.)

3 · Cook over medium-low heat and stir until the sugar is fully dissolved. Raise the heat to medium-high and bring the mixture to a boil. Cook at a lively simmer, stirring often, until the mixture has darkened and begun to thicken, 20 to 30 minutes. Skim any foam that forms on the surface and watch out for spattering.

4 · Stir in the Marsala and continue to boil until the mixture reaches 220°F and you can scrape a path along the bottom of the pot with a silicone spatula, about 30 minutes more. Or use the freezer plate method to test for doneness as described on page 83.

5 · When it's ready, turn off the heat and stir in the almonds. Ladle the hot *conserva* into the sterilized jars, leaving ¼ inch headspace. Wipe the rims clean if necessary with a clean, damp cloth, and screw the lids on the jars.

6 · Process the jars in a boiling-water bath for 10 minutes (see Water-Bath Canning, page 15). Remove the jars and set them upright on a clean kitchen towel. Let the jars cool to room temperature before storing in a cool, dark place. This *conserva* is best enjoyed within 3 months; over time the almonds will lose their crunchy texture and the flavor of the Marsala will become less pronounced. Refrigerate once opened. If any jars have failed to seal properly, store them in the refrigerator and enjoy those first.

COOK'S NOTE · To toast almonds, spread them out on a rimmed baking sheet and bake at 350°F until lightly golden and fragrant, about 7 minutes. Let cool to room temperature before stirring into the *conserva*.

BLACKBERRY-APPLE JAM

· · · MAKES 2½ PINTS · · ·

Together with raspberries and blueberries, blackberries compose a category of fruit known in Italian as frutti di bosco, *or "fruit of the woods." Which is a fancy way of saying mixed berries. You can make this jam with all three, but I prefer just blackberries for their deep color and intense, winey flavor. These berries are low in pectin and need a little help to set. Rather than add commercial pectin, I use a small Granny Smith apple, which gives this jam just the right consistency and an extra hit of tartness. This is an excellent jam to use in Favorite Jam Crostata (page 105).*

6 cups (1 kg) blackberries

1 small Granny Smith apple

5 cups (1 kg) vanilla sugar (see page 57) or
   sugar

3 tablespoons freshly squeezed lemon juice

EQUIPMENT

5 sterilized ½-pint jars and their lids

Food mill

Basic water-bath canning equipment
   (see page 15)

1 · Put the berries in a nonreactive heavy-bottomed saucepan or preserving pot and mash them up a bit with a potato masher or wooden spoon. Cut the apple into chunks and add it, including skin and seeds, to the pot. Cook the fruit over medium heat until the apple pieces are soft, about 30 minutes. Remove from the heat. Puree the mixture through a food mill fitted with the disk with the smallest holes, catching the fruit puree in a bowl. Discard the solids left in the mill.

2 · Measure the puree into a clean pot. You should have about 5 cups. Stir in the sugar and lemon juice. Bring the mixture to a boil over medium-high heat. Cook at a lively simmer, stirring often, until the puree has begun to thicken, 20 to 30 minutes. Watch out for spattering.

3 · Continue to boil until the mixture reaches 220°F. Or use the freezer plate method to test for doneness as described on page 83.

4 · Ladle the hot jam into the jars, leaving ¼ inch headspace. Wipe the rims clean if necessary with a clean, damp cloth, and screw the lids on the jars.

5 · Process the jars in a boiling-water bath for 10 minutes (see Water-Bath Canning, page 15). Remove the jars and set them upright on a clean kitchen towel. Let cool to room temperature before storing in a cool, dark place for up to 1 year. Refrigerate after opening. Store any jars that fail to seal properly in the refrigerator and enjoy those first.

FIG JAM
with Orange Zest

Fig trees grow so well in central and southern Italy that you often see "volunteers" sprouting in the cracks between rocks and sometimes even in cobblestone sidewalks. I have just one small tree in my yard, but most years it gives me a decent crop— enough to make a couple batches of this pretty, seed-speckled jam. Finely chopped orange zest adds a bright note. The recipe is simple, as it requires no pectin and no peeling of the fruit. Stir the preserves into yogurt, use them as a filling for a jam crostata (page 105), or, for a savory twist, brush over pork or chicken for grilling.

2 pounds (907 g) ripe figs

2 cups (400 g) sugar or vanilla sugar
   (see page 57)

Finely minced zest and juice of 2 small
   oranges

EQUIPMENT

3 sterilized ½-pint jars and their lids

Basic water-bath canning equipment
   (see page 15)

1 · Cut the tips off the figs and quarter the figs lengthwise. Place them in a heavy-bottomed nonreactive saucepan or preserving pot. Add the sugar and orange zest and juice. Gently mix everything together and let the figs macerate for 30 minutes or up to several hours.

2 · Set the pot over medium-high heat and bring to a boil. Reduce the heat to medium and cook at a lively simmer until the jam is thick and glossy and has turned a couple of shades darker, 15 to 20 minutes. Be sure to stir often to prevent burning and watch out for spattering.

3 · Continue to boil until the mixture reaches 220°F and you can drag a path through the bottom of the pot with a silicone spatula. Or use the freezer plate method to test for doneness as described on page 83.

4 · Ladle the hot preserves into the sterilized jars, leaving ¼ inch headspace. Wipe the rims clean if necessary with a clean, damp cloth, and screw the lids on the jars.

5 · Process in a boiling-water bath for 10 minutes (see Water-Bath Canning, page 15). Remove the jars and set them upright on a clean kitchen towel. Let the jars cool to room temperature before storing in a cool, dark place for up to 1 year. Refrigerate after opening. Store any jars that fail to seal properly in the refrigerator and enjoy those first.

QUINCE JELLY

It seems impossible that a fruit as inhospitable as quince—tough, bitter, inedible raw—could be transformed into this translucent, jewel-toned jelly. But after chopping, simmering, and straining, the result is a jelly with a sweet, floral flavor. Spread this on your morning toast or set it out as part of a cheese plate.

3 pounds (1.4 kg) ripe quince
Water
Sugar or vanilla sugar (see page 57)

EQUIPMENT

Tight-weave cheesecloth
Kitchen scale
1 sterilized 1-pint jar and its lid
Basic water-bath canning equipment
  (see page 15)

1 · Cut the quince into quarters and remove the seeds and core. Slice the quarters crosswise into ½-inch-thick wedges.

2 · Place the fruit in a large nonreactive heavy-bottomed pot and pour in enough water to cover. Bring to a boil over high heat, reduce the heat to medium or medium-low, and cook at a gentle simmer until the quince is soft and tender, about 1 hour.

3 · Line a colander or large strainer with damp cheesecloth and set it over a bowl. Ladle the fruit into the colander and leave it to drain for several hours, or even overnight. Do not press the mixture or you will end up with cloudy jelly. When fully drained, discard the fruit. Measure and weigh the liquid—you should have 2 cups, weighing about 1 pound (454 g).

4 · Pour the liquid into a heavy-bottomed saucepan or preserving pot. Add three-quarters of the weight in sugar to the liquid. For example, for 1 pound (454 g) liquid, add 12 ounces (340 g or 1½ cups) sugar.

5 · Bring the mixture to a boil over medium heat, stirring to dissolve the sugar and to prevent it from sticking to the bottom of the pot. Use a spoon to skim off and discard any foam from the surface.

6 · The liquid will turn darker and syrupy as it cooks. Continue to boil until it reaches 218 to 220°F. Or use the freezer plate method to test for doneness as described on page 83.

7 · Ladle the hot jelly into the sterilized jar, leaving ¼ inch headspace. Wipe the rim clean if necessary with a clean, damp cloth, and screw the lid on the jar.

8 · Process the jar in a boiling-water bath for 10 minutes (see Water-Bath Canning, page 15). Remove the jar and set it upright on a clean kitchen towel. Let cool to room temperature before storing in a cool, dark place for up to 1 year. Refrigerate after opening. If the jar has failed to seal properly, store it in the refrigerator.

Quince Jelly
1 ⚜ 15

Ball —50

RUSTIC GRAPE JAM

In early October, open-bed trucks appear on the rugged mountain roads of Abruzzo, carrying a precious cargo of Montepulciano d'Abruzzo grapes to be turned into the region's best-known wine. A few of those dusky blue grapes, however, are destined for something else: They are cooked down into a thick, full-bodied jam known as scrucchjata *(skrook-YAH-ta). The dialect name, as far as I've been able to determine, translates more or less to "squished." The jam is almost as prized as Montepulciano wine itself, and the Abruzzese use it in jam tarts and as a filling for delicious half-moon cookies called* calcionetti *(page 109). Montepulciano d'Abruzzo grapes aren't grown in the United States, but with the proliferation of wineries in almost every state, it's gotten easier to find grapes beyond the classic Concord variety (think Welch's grape jelly) and the red and green snacking types found in the supermarket. It's worth seeking out good wine grapes for this recipe; if you can't come up with a nearby source for wine grapes, try ordering them online (see Sources, page 292).*

4 pounds (1.8 kg) wine grapes, such as Syrah, stemmed

About ½ cup (100 g) vanilla sugar (see page 57) or sugar

EQUIPMENT

2 or 3 sterilized ½-pint jars and their lids

Food mill fitted with the disk with the smallest holes

Basic water-bath canning equipment (see page 15)

1 • Place the grapes in a large nonreactive heavy-bottomed saucepan or preserving pot and mash them up a bit with a potato masher. Set the pot over medium heat and bring to a gentle boil. The grapes should start to break down within 10 to 15 minutes. Reduce the heat and cook, stirring often, until the grapes have broken down completely into pulp, 15 to 20 minutes longer.

2 • Let the pulp cool briefly; then pass it through the food mill into a bowl to get rid of the seeds and skins. You should have about 2½ cups pulp. Taste and add just enough sugar without sweetening it too much. For this amount of pulp, I use about ½ cup (100 g) sugar, depending on the grapes' natural sweetness (some traditional *scrucchjata* recipes don't call for any extra sugar).

3 · Transfer the pulp to a clean saucepan or a deep skillet and bring to a boil over medium-high heat.

4 · Continue to boil until the mixture is thick and glossy and the temperature reaches 220°F, about 15 minutes more; you should be able to drag a path along the bottom of the pot with a silicone spatula. Or use the freezer plate method to test for doneness as described on page 83.

5 · Ladle the hot jam into the sterilized jars, leaving ¼ inch headspace. Wipe the rims clean if necessary with a clean, damp cloth, and screw the lids on the jars.

6 · Process the jars in a boiling-water bath for 10 minutes (see Water-Bath Canning, page 15). Remove the jars and set them upright on a clean kitchen towel. Let cool to room temperature before storing in a cool, dark place for up to 1 year. Refrigerate after opening. If any jars have failed to seal properly, store them in the refrigerator and enjoy those first.

BRANDIED CHESTNUT CREAM JAM

There was often a jar of crema di marroni *in the fridge when I was growing up, and to this day one of my favorite breakfasts is a thick slice of toast, generously buttered and topped with this sticky-sweet spread. I've included instructions for cooking and peeling whole chestnuts. But many supermarkets and gourmet food shops now sell vacuum-packed chestnuts that have already been cooked and peeled. They are usually easy to find from Thanksgiving through New Year's. Feel free to take the easy route; I often do.*

1½ pounds (680 g) whole chestnuts in their shell, or 1 pound (454 g) peeled, cooked whole chestnuts (available at some supermarkets and gourmet food shops)

2 cups (473 g) whole milk

1¼ cups (250 g) sugar

½ cup (118 g) water

½ vanilla bean

4 tablespoons Cognac

EQUIPMENT

3 sterilized ½-pint jars and their lids

Kitchen scale

Potato ricer

Immersion blender

Parchment paper

1 · If you're starting with chestnuts in their shells, bring a large pot of water to a boil. With a sharp paring knife, cut a small "X" into the bottom or rounded side of the chestnuts. Plunge them into the boiling water and boil for 30 minutes. Remove from the heat and let the chestnuts sit for a few minutes.

2 · Remove a few at a time and let them cool briefly. Remove the shells and use the paring knife to peel off the inner skins. Weigh the peeled chestnuts; you should have about 1 pound (454 g). If you have more, measure out 1 pound (454 g) and reserve the rest for another use (I usually just eat them while I'm working).

3 • Crumble the peeled chestnuts into a heavy-bottomed saucepan. If using vacuum-packed cooked and peeled chestnuts, crumble them into the saucepan. Pour in the milk and bring to a simmer over medium-low heat. Reduce the heat to low if necessary to keep the milk from boiling. Cook, stirring, until the chestnuts have absorbed the milk and are very soft and crumbly. Press the still-hot chestnut mixture through a potato ricer into a clean heatproof bowl and let cool.

4 • Combine the sugar and water in a heavy-bottomed saucepan. Scrape in the seeds from the vanilla bean. Cook, stirring, over medium heat, until the sugar is completely dissolved. Bring to a boil and boil just until the syrup is slightly thickened but still clear in color, about 2 minutes. Pour the hot syrup over the chestnut mixture and stir it vigorously.

5 • Transfer the mixture to the saucepan and cook over medium heat, stirring all the while, until the chestnut cream is thick enough to mound on a spoon or spread with a knife, about 10 minutes. Stir in 2 tablespoons of the Cognac and cook, stirring, for another minute or two.

6 • Remove the pot from the heat and puree the chestnut cream with an immersion blender until smooth. You can also puree it in a standard blender or in a food processor fitted with the metal blade.

7 • Spoon the jam into the sterilized jars. Cut out 3 rounds of parchment paper to fit inside the jars on top of the jam. Pour the remaining 2 tablespoons Cognac into a small bowl and immerse each of the rounds of parchment paper in the liquor until soaked. Press the parchment rounds right on top of the jam in the jars and screw the lids on tightly. The liquor-soaked parchment will help prevent mold from forming.

8 • Let the jam come to room temperature before refrigerating it. Store the jam in the refrigerator, where it will keep for up to 3 months. If the parchment rounds dry out at any point, replace them with new ones soaked in Cognac. If at any point you see mold forming on the jam, discard it.

GREEN TOMATO PRESERVES

My mother made green tomato preserves almost every year when I was growing up. Back then, I just assumed I wouldn't like them—what kid would choose green tomato preserves over cherry or strawberry or plum? Now I know what I was missing. These preserves are something special: caramelized and sweet, with just the right amount of sour. Spread them on toast for breakfast, or serve with a rich Italian cheese such as Taleggio or robiola.

2 pounds (907 g) firm green tomatoes (about 6 medium)

Finely grated zest and juice of 1 large lemon (about ¼ cup juice)

2½ cups (500 g) sugar

⅓ cup (100 g) mild honey

2 pinches of coarse sea salt

½ vanilla bean

EQUIPMENT

7 sterilized 4-ounce jars and their lids

Basic water-bath canning equipment (see page 15)

1 • Remove the cores from the tomatoes and cut the tomatoes lengthwise into quarters. If the seeds are small, leave them be. If they are mature, scrape them out. Cut each quarter crosswise into thin slices.

2 • Put the tomatoes, lemon zest and juice, sugar, honey, and salt in a large nonreactive heavy-bottomed saucepan or preserving pot. With a small paring knife, slice the vanilla bean open lengthwise. Scrape the seeds into the pot and toss in the pod.

3 • Set the pot over medium-high heat and bring it to a boil, stirring to combine the ingredients. Reduce the heat to medium and cook at a fairly lively simmer until the preserves are glossy and thick enough to spread, 40 to 45 minutes. Be sure to stir often to prevent burning. Remove the vanilla bean pod at the end of cooking.

4 • Ladle the preserves into the sterilized jars, leaving ¼ inch headspace. Wipe the rims clean, if necessary, with a clean, damp cloth and screw the lids on the jars.

5 • Process in a boiling-water bath for 15 minutes (see Water-Bath Canning, page 15). Remove the jars and set them upright on a clean kitchen towel. Let the jars cool to room temperature before storing in a cool, dark place for up to 1 year. Refrigerate after opening. If any jars have failed to seal properly, store them in the refrigerator and enjoy those first.

GRILLED PORK CHOPS
with Apricot-Mustard Sauce

· · · MAKES 4 SERVINGS · · ·

Know what makes a good pork chop? Good pork. By that I don't mean the ultra-lean "other white meat" that is as dry as sawdust and tastes like it, too. For years I've been buying pork from a purveyor at my local farmers' market who raises a small herd of hogs. His pork is beautifully marbled, and juicy and tender—not tough—when cooked. The rich, flavorful meat stands up beautifully to tangy fruit sauce.

4 bone-in pork chops, about ¾ inch thick, about 1½ pounds (680 g) total

Fine sea salt and freshly ground black pepper

½ cup (170 g) Apricot-Anise Jam (page 84)

1 tablespoon smooth Dijon mustard

1 • Prepare a charcoal grill or heat a gas grill to medium-high. Season the pork chops on both sides with salt and pepper. Whisk the apricot-anise jam with the mustard. Dribble in a tablespoon or two of water to loosen the sauce if necessary.

2 • Oil the grill grate. Grill the chops for 2 minutes without moving them. Turn them over and baste with the jam mixture. Grill for 2 minutes more. Turn and baste again. Grill for 2 to 3 minutes more on each side, basting once or twice more, until the chops are cooked through (145 to 150°F).

3 • Transfer the chops to a platter and let rest for 5 minutes before serving.

FAVORITE JAM CROSTATA

··· MAKES ONE 9- OR 10-INCH LATTICE-TOP CROSTATA ···

If you stay at a family-run agriturismo or bed-and-breakfast in Italy, chances are you will be greeted in the morning with a rustic tart such as this—a sweet pastry shell filled with jam and baked just until tender and golden. My crust is a little like shortbread, very buttery, and perfumed with lemon and orange zest. Enjoy crostata with your morning coffee, or serve it as a homespun dessert.

3 cups (380 g) unbleached all-purpose flour, plus more for dusting the work surface

1 cup (200 g) confectioners' sugar, plus more for dusting the crostata

Finely grated zest of 1 orange

Finely grated zest of 1 lemon

¼ teaspoon fine sea salt

8 ounces (2 sticks/227 g) cold unsalted butter, cut into ½-inch pieces

1 large egg

2 large egg yolks

1½ to 2 cups (510 g) Rustic Grape Jam (page 98), Strawberry-Apricot Preserves (page 86), Green Tomato Preserves (page 102), or any favorite jam

1 · Measure the flour, sugar, zests, and salt into the bowl of a food processor fitted with the metal blade. Process briefly to combine. Distribute the butter pieces around the bowl and process until the mixture is crumbly. Add the egg and egg yolks and process just until the dough begins to come together. Turn the dough out onto a lightly floured surface and pat it into a disk. Wrap it tightly in plastic wrap and refrigerate until well chilled, at least 1 hour.

2 · Preheat the oven to 350°F.

3 · Remove the dough from the refrigerator and cut it into two pieces, one slightly larger than the other. Rewrap the smaller piece and set it aside. Roll the larger piece into an 11- or 12-inch circle. Carefully wrap the dough around the rolling pin and drape it over a 9- or 10-inch fluted tart pan with a removable bottom. Gently press the dough into the bottom and up the sides of the pan.

4 · Spoon the jam into the prepared shell and smooth it out with the back of your spoon. Roll out the remaining dough and cut it into ¾-inch-thick strips or use a cookie cutter to cut out shapes such as flowers or stars. Place the strips in a lattice pattern on top of the jam, or arrange the cutouts on top. (Save any excess dough to roll out later; you can cut out shapes and bake cookies.) Fold the edge of the crust over the jam and lattice.

5 · Bake until the crust is lightly browned, about 35 minutes. Let the crostata cool in the pan on a wire rack to room temperature. To serve, remove the rim of the pan, transfer the crostata to a decorative serving platter, and dust lightly with confectioners' sugar.

ALMOND CAKE
with Strawberry-Apricot Preserves

I enjoy a nice slice of layer cake every now and then. But this? This I could eat every day, for breakfast with coffee, as an afternoon snack, or after dinner. It is the definition of a rustic Italian cake; easy to make, easy to eat; crumbly yet tender; and infused with the warm aroma of toasted nuts. There's no need to slather this cake with frosting; just spread a thin layer of jam between the layers and dust with confectioners' sugar.

8 tablespoons (1 stick/113 g) unsalted butter, melted and cooled

2 cups (280 g) lightly toasted skinned almonds, cooled (see Cook's Note, page 108)

½ cup (60 g) unbleached all-purpose flour

2 teaspoons baking powder

4 large eggs, separated

1 cup (200 g) sugar

¼ teaspoon pure almond extract

⅛ teaspoon fine sea salt

1 cup (227 g) Strawberry-Apricot Preserves (page 86) or any favorite jam

Confectioners' sugar, for dusting

1 · Preheat the oven to 350°F. Coat a 9-inch springform pan with about 1 tablespoon of the melted butter. Place a round of parchment paper in the bottom of the pan and lightly coat the parchment with butter. Set the remaining melted butter aside.

2 · Process the almonds in a food processor fitted with the metal blade until finely ground but not pasty. Transfer them to a bowl and stir in the flour and baking powder.

3 · In a large bowl, whisk together the egg yolks and sugar. The mixture will be very thick and will probably clump inside the whisk. Drizzle in about half of the remaining melted butter, whisking all the while, until the mixture has loosened a bit. Add the remaining butter and whisk until fully incorporated. Whisk in the almond extract.

4 · Using a sturdy silicone spatula, stir the almond-flour mixture into the egg yolk–butter mixture. It will be very thick, like nut paste. This is fine.

(recipe continues)

5 · In a clean stainless steel bowl, beat the egg whites and salt until stiff peaks form. Scoop about one-quarter of the egg whites into the bowl with the nut mixture and fold it in with the spatula. Add half of the remaining egg whites, carefully folding rather than stirring to prevent them from deflating too much. The batter will still be thick and sticky. Finally, add the last of the whites and continue folding with a firm but gentle hand until they are fully incorporated. The batter will be thick but spreadable. Scrape it into the prepared pan and smooth out the top.

6 · Bake the cake until puffed and browned on top and the center is no longer jiggling (a cake tester inserted in the center should come out clean), 40 to 45 minutes. Be careful not to jostle the cake when you're checking for doneness or the center might fall. (This won't affect the texture or taste of the cake but it won't be quite as pretty.)

7 · Let the cake cool in the pan on a wire rack for 10 minutes. Remove the outer ring and let the cake cool for an additional 20 to 30 minutes. Invert the cake onto a plate or another rack. Remove the bottom of the cake pan and peel off the parchment. Re-invert the cake onto the rack and let it cool completely.

8 · Transfer the cake to a serving plate. With a serrated knife, cut the cake horizontally through the middle. Set aside the top half and gently spread the preserves over the bottom half. Cover with the top half of the cake. Dust with confectioners' sugar just before serving.

COOK'S NOTE · To toast almonds, spread them out on a rimmed baking sheet and bake at 350°F until lightly golden and fragrant, about 7 minutes. Let cool to room temperature before stirring into the conserva.

CALCIONETTI

There are as many versions of this stuffed half-moon cookie, a specialty of Abruzzo, as there are cooks in the region—and almost as many variations on the name. Some versions are baked; some are fried. My mom's, which she calls calcionelli, meaning "stuffed little socks," are filled with ground nuts and honey. She would make a big batch of them every year for Christmas and we would eat them while we opened our gifts. I've swapped out her filling for one that combines the ground nuts with thick, rustic grape jam, bittersweet chocolate, and cocoa powder. This filling recipe comes from my friend Fabrizio Lucci's mother, Anna Maria, who calls her version of this cookie celli ripieni ("stuffed little birds").

FOR THE DOUGH

2¾ to 3 cups (325 to 350 g) unbleached
   all-purpose flour

½ cup (100 g) sugar

Pinch of fine sea salt

Finely grated zest of 1 orange

Finely grated zest of 1 lemon

8 tablespoons (1 stick/113 g) cold unsalted
   butter, cut into cubes

3 large eggs

1 to 2 tablespoons Punch Abruzzo or other
   sweet liqueur (see Cook's Note)

FOR THE FILLING

1 cup (340 g) Rustic Grape Jam (page 98), or
   substitute Blackberry-Apple Jam (page
   94) or good-quality blackberry jam

½ cup (70 g) almonds, toasted and finely
   chopped (see Cook's Note, page 93)

½ ounce (15 g) bittersweet chocolate, grated

1½ tablespoons unsweetened cocoa powder

½ teaspoon instant espresso powder

Vegetable oil, for frying

Confectioners' sugar, for serving

EQUIPMENT

Deep-frying thermometer (optional)

1 · **Make the dough:** Combine 2¾ cups (325 g) of the flour, the sugar, salt, and orange and lemon zests in the bowl of a food processor fitted with the metal blade; pulse briefly. Distribute the butter in the bowl and pulse until it is incorporated and the mixture is crumbly. Add the eggs and pulse until they are just incorporated. With the motor running, drizzle in the liqueur and process just until the mixture clumps together.

(recipe continues)

2 · Turn the dough out onto a lightly floured work surface and knead until a smooth ball forms. The dough should be soft but not sticky. Work in more flour by the tablespoon if it seems too sticky. Wrap tightly in plastic wrap and refrigerate for 1 hour or up to overnight.

3 · **Make the filling:** In a small bowl, combine the jam, almonds, chocolate, cocoa powder, and espresso powder and mix thoroughly.

4 · **Make the *calcionetti*:** Dust a rimmed baking sheet or a clean tablecloth with flour. Have on hand a 2¾-inch round cookie cutter, a small bowl of water, and a fork, for cutting, shaping, and sealing. Remove the dough from the refrigerator and cut in half. Rewrap and refrigerate one half. Roll the other half out on a lightly floured work surface into a large thin circle between ¹⁄₁₆ inch and ⅛ inch thick. Cut out as many circles as possible. Mound ½ teaspoon of the filling in the center of each circle. Dip a finger in the water and moisten the edges of the circle. Fold each circle into a half-moon. Press the tines of the fork along the edges to seal. Transfer the *calcionetti* to the baking sheet or tablecloth. Reroll the scraps to cut out more circles; fill, shape, and seal. Repeat with the remaining piece of dough. You may have leftover filling. Store it in a jar in the refrigerator; it's delicious on toast.

5 · Pour oil to a depth of 1 inch in a high-sided saucepan. Heat over medium-high heat to about 375°F on a deep-frying thermometer. Or test by dropping a scrap of dough into the hot oil; if it sizzles and floats to the surface, the oil is ready.

6 · Place a baking sheet or tray lined with paper towels near the stove. Carefully add 6 to 8 *calcionetti* to the hot oil. They will sizzle and begin to brown almost immediately, so keep an eye on them. Fry for about 30 seconds, using a skimmer to move them about. Transfer them to the paper towel–lined baking sheet. Continue to fry the *calcionetti* a few at a time until you have fried them all. Transfer them to a cooling rack to cool completely. To serve, dust with confectioners' sugar. The *calcionetti* will keep in an airtight container at room temperature for up to 5 days.

COOK'S NOTE · Punch Abruzzo is a sweet liqueur made from caramelized sugar and the zest of lemons and oranges. It is sometimes available at well-stocked liquor stores or online (see Sources, page 292). If you can't find it, substitute Cointreau, Grand Marnier, or dark rum.

Classic Meat Sauce, page 122

TOMATOES
AND
SAUCE

Tomatoes may have been brought to Italy from the New World, but it was Italians who divined their true purpose: sauce. A nice dish of pasta with tomato sauce is one of life's pleasures, and if you have a jar or two of your own sauce on hand, so much the better. I can't even begin to tell you how often a jar of homemade sauce has saved me at dinnertime.

Italians are serious about their tomato canning. From mid-August into September, extended families come together to harvest, mill, and can countless thousands of pounds of perfectly ripe tomatoes. It is an exceedingly messy and time-consuming task, often performed outdoors. But, oh, the satisfaction of seeing those jars and bottles lined up in rows like chorus girls.

San Marzano tomatoes, cultivated around Mt. Vesuvius, near Naples, have earned a reputation as the world's best sauce tomato. They have a meaty texture and excellent flavor. If you have a garden, you can grow San Marzano variety tomatoes. They are generally larger than plum tomatoes, somewhat pear-shaped, with a point on the end. The tomatoes I get at my local farmers' market are basic plum tomatoes and I'm happy to say they make excellent *passata* and sauce. They are also ideal for drying or making *conserva*, glossy tomato paste that is nothing like the aggressive commercial stuff.

Although this chapter starts with tomatoes, it does not end there, for where there are tomatoes and sauce there is also pasta, and where there is pasta there are beans, and where there are beans there is broth. The Italian larder is always stocked with these staples and so is mine. Here you will find techniques for making and preserving all of them. With these basics in your pantry, you always have the makings of a good home-cooked meal.

Special Equipment

- **Food mill:** This device turns tomatoes into puree, separating out the skin and seeds in the process. Mills can be hand-crank or electric, and they vary greatly in size, capacity, and price—from about $20 to $650. When processing fewer than 5 pounds, I use a small Italian hand-crank mill given to me by my mom years ago. For anything larger, I use a large hand-crank mill by Squeezo (made in the U.S.A.). If I were processing hundreds of pounds of tomatoes, I would probably switch to an electric mill.

- **Pasta machine:** I use a hand-crank Marcato Atlas pasta machine to roll out sheets of pasta and to cut noodles.

Tomato Essentials

- Most people think of tomatoes as acidic, but their pH level can vary depending on a number of factors, including the type of tomato and when it was harvested. To ensure that the acidity level in your tomatoes is suitable for canning, always add citric acid or lemon juice to the jar prior to processing. I prefer lemon juice and use 2 tablespoons per 1 pint of tomatoes.

- Certain recipes in this chapter call for water-bath processing (see page 15) or pressure canning (see page 18). Be sure to read those sections before proceeding with the recipes.

BOTTLED WHOLE TOMATOES

Bottling tomatoes only makes sense if you use good, ripe summer tomatoes that are meaty and flavorful. If you are a gardener, growing your own tomatoes is your best bet. Otherwise, look for ripe, unblemished plum tomatoes at your local farmers' market. Some markets now offer San Marzano–style tomatoes, which are typically longer than plums with a point on the bottom. They are the classic Italian tomato for sauce and canning.

2 pints Passata di Pomodoro (page 117), or best-quality commercial tomato puree

8 pounds (3.6 kg) ripe plum tomatoes

8 tablespoons freshly squeezed or bottled lemon juice

EQUIPMENT

4 sterilized 1-quart jars and their lids

Basic water-bath canning equipment (see page 15)

1 · Bring a large stockpot of water to a rolling boil, and have ready a large bowl of ice water. In a small saucepan, bring the *passata* to a simmer over medium heat. Reduce the heat to low and cover to keep warm.

2 · Cut a small "X" in the bottom of each tomato. Plunge the tomatoes, in batches if necessary, into the boiling water and boil for 1 minute. Use a large skimmer or slotted spoon to transfer them to the bowl of ice water. Drain the tomatoes, then peel and discard the skins.

3 · Add 2 tablespoons lemon juice to each jar. Pack the tomatoes tightly into each jar, fitting in as many as possible without squishing them. Funnel the hot *passata* into the jars, dividing it evenly.

4 · Screw the lids on tightly and process for 45 minutes in a boiling-water bath (see Water-Bath Canning, page 15). Remove the jars and set them upright on a clean kitchen towel. Let the jars cool to room temperature before storing in a cool, dark place for up to 1 year. Refrigerate after opening and use within 1 week.

BOTTLED DICED TOMATOES

Once the tomatoes have been blanched and peeled, gently split them open with your fingers and push out the seeds. Do this over a bowl to catch the seeds and juice. Cut the tomatoes into large pieces and pack them into the prepared jars as directed, taking care to add the lemon juice to the jars before filling. Strain the seeds and juice through a fine-mesh sieve. Discard the seeds and add the juice to the jars, dividing evenly. Ladle the hot *passata* into the tomatoes, dividing evenly. You should end up with about 3 quarts. Process as directed for bottled whole tomatoes.

Preserving Tomatoes and Traditions

It's hard to keep up with Sabato Abagnale. For one thing, he is a tall guy, with long legs and strides to match. For another, it seems he is being propelled forward by the unstoppable force of his own enthusiasm.

I follow him through rows of staked vines on a steep, terraced hillside across the valley from Mt. Vesuvius, south of Naples. He stops and parts a curtain of prickly green leaves to show me the subject of his ardor: tomatoes. They aren't ripe yet and won't be for another month. Still, I can tell from their elongated teardrop shape and pointed end that they are the famed San Marzano variety, sweet and meaty and purported to make the best sauce in the world. These are called *antico pomodoro di Napoli*, a variety of San Marzano—but better, Abagnale says, because they are not cultivated for industrial production.

This is a subject about which Abagnale knows a lot. He grew up right down the hill from these tomatoes, in Sant'Antonio Abate, a gritty suburb of Naples, where he still lives. He comes from a family of large-scale tomato producers and used to be in the business himself. About 15 years ago, he made a switch after becoming disillusioned with the process.

"Industrial machines ruin tomatoes," he says. "So producers cultivate tomatoes with thicker skins and less juice. That's progress? I decided that I had to go backward."

Abagnale started experimenting with family heirloom seeds, saving and propagating the best specimens. He and his wife, Concetta D'Anillo, a professor of industrial chemistry at the University of Naples, began working with the Slow Food Foundation for Biodiversity, which supports efforts to preserve local plant varieties and traditional processing methods around the world. Now they run a local Slow Food office in Sant'Antonio Abate, where they produce and sell high-quality canned and bottled whole tomatoes, *pomodorini* (small tomatoes), and tomato puree.

It took a while, Abagnale says, to establish his small company. "For the first three or four years the only thing I brought home was poetry," he jokes, using a local expression. Supermarkets were not interested in canned artisanal tomatoes. Now he sells to chefs and international food importers such as New York–based Gustiamo.com. But the business remains small by design. Abagnale collaborates with about a dozen farmers who grow his tomatoes on 7½ acres of the lower slopes of the Monti Lattari, the mountain range to the south of Vesuvius. The soil, the breeze from the nearby Mediterranean Sea, and the cooler mountain air all contribute to the quality of the crops grown here.

"Agriculture was what our grandparents did," Abagnale says. "It was the economic foundation of this area until 40 years ago, when industrialization took hold and people began to abandon the countryside. We want to revive the agricultural economy and traditions as a way of building a future for our children. Sometimes we have to go back to go forward."

PASSATA DI POMODORO

Tomato passata, or puree, is, for many Italians, the most essential item in the pantry. It is the beginning of a good sauce (see Cook's Note) and the foundation for countless soups and stews. For a quick weeknight meal, I sauté peppers, such as the sweet-and-sour peppers on page 38, in passata and then fry eggs in the mixture. When cooked down slowly in the oven, passata becomes another pantry staple: conserva (tomato paste; page 119). Yes, you can buy canned or bottled tomato puree, but it will never have that fresh flavor of passata canned at the end of summer. Even if I sometimes skip the canning of whole tomatoes, I always make sure to put up a few quarts of passata. I just like knowing that they are there, at the ready.

20 pounds (9 kg) sauce tomatoes, such as San Marzano, Roma, or other plum tomatoes

8 to 10 tablespoons freshly squeezed or bottled lemon juice

4 to 5 teaspoons fine sea salt

EQUIPMENT

Tomato or food mill

4 or 5 sterilized 1-quart jars and their lids (if using a pressure canner, you can skip the step of sterilizing the jars and lids and simply wash them with hot soapy water)

Basic water-bath canning equipment (see page 15) or pressure-canning equipment (see page 19) (see Cook's Note)

1 · Set up the tomato mill according to the manufacturer's instructions. For this amount of tomatoes, I recommend a larger mill with a hopper, such as the Squeezo Strainer. Position a bowl to catch the tomato puree.

2 · Slice the stem end off the tomatoes. Cut the tomatoes into quarters and put them into a large nonreactive saucepot. Use two pots if they don't all fit; or simmer in batches. Cover and bring the tomatoes to a simmer over medium-high heat. They will soon begin to release liquid. Cook, stirring a few times to prevent scorching, until the tomatoes are *spappolate*, which means until their pulp just begins to soften and break down, 15 to 20 minutes. With a slotted spoon, transfer the tomatoes to a large colander set in the sink and let drain for 10 to 15 minutes to release excess liquid. This step will keep your *passata* from being watery.

(recipe continues)

3 · Pass the tomatoes through the mill, catching the puree in a large bowl. Discard the skins and seeds. Transfer the puree to a large saucepot and bring to a simmer over medium-high heat. Boil for anywhere from 5 to 15 minutes, depending on how thick the puree is. The consistency should be thinner than sauce but not watery. Take care not to overcook or you will lose the fresh flavor of the *passata*.

4 · Place 2 tablespoons lemon juice and 1 teaspoon salt into the bottom of each jar. Ladle the hot *passata* into the jars, leaving ½ inch headspace. Screw the lids on tightly. If using a boiling-water bath, process the jars for 45 minutes (see Water-Bath Canning, page 15). If using a pressure canner, follow the manufacturer's instructions, and process at 10 pounds of pressure for 15 minutes (see Pressure Canning, page 18).

5 · Remove the jars and set them upright on a clean kitchen towel. Let the jars cool to room temperature before storing in a cool, dark place for up to 1 year. Refrigerate after opening and use within 1 week.

COOK'S NOTE · Tomato *passata* can be processed either in a boiling water bath or a pressure canner. Be sure to follow the proper instructions according to the method you choose.

COOK'S NOTE · To make simple tomato sauce from *passata*, sauté a clove or two of garlic in olive oil in a saucepan until fragrant. Pour in the *passata* (watch for spattering) and bring to a simmer over medium-high heat. Reduce the heat to medium-low and cook at a gentle simmer for about 30 minutes, until thickened to a sauce consistency. Season to taste with salt. Remove from the heat and stir in a little chopped fresh basil.

TOMATO CONSERVA

··· MAKES ABOUT 1 PINT ···

When made with the puree of ripe summer tomatoes, homemade tomato conserva, aka tomato paste, has a deep and savory tomato flavor. In southern Italy, where the Mediterranean heat of August is dry and intense, conserva is made outdoors. Large, shallow bowls or pans of passata are set outside and left to "cook" in the sun. In Virginia, where I live, and in much of the United States, it's impossible to string together a series of summer days without humidity or overcast skies. So I have moved the operation indoors, making conserva in my oven. I always keep a jar on hand in the refrigerator to use as a flavor booster for sauces, soups, and stews. Be sure to use conserva judiciously; it is quite salty.

2 quarts Passata di Pomodoro (page 117)
2 tablespoons fine sea salt
Extra-virgin olive oil

EQUIPMENT
2 sterilized ½-pint or four 4-ounce jars and
  their lids

1 • Preheat the oven to 200° F.

2 • Pour the *passata* into a large nonreactive saucepan and stir in the salt. Bring it to a boil over medium-high heat. Stir from time to time to prevent the bottom from scorching. Once the *passata* comes to a boil, reduce the heat to medium or medium-low and let it simmer until it is thickened to the consistency of sauce and reduced by about half, about 1 hour.

3 • Lightly coat an 11- by 17-inch rimmed nonreactive (non-aluminum) baking sheet with olive oil. Carefully spread the cooked *passata* on the baking sheet. Bake for 30 minutes. Remove from the oven and stir with a silicone spatula. Bake for another 30 minutes, and then stir again. It will be somewhat thickened

and may no longer fill the pan. Spread it out evenly and return it to the oven. Continue to bake the *passata*, stirring and re-spreading it every 30 minutes (be careful not to spread it too thin or you may end up with some overcooked spots), until it has reduced markedly in volume and turned into a deep red paste, 3 to 4 hours. Watch it closely, especially toward the end, to prevent burning or caramelizing.

4 • Lightly coat the inside of the jars with olive oil. Spoon the *conserva* into the jars, leaving about ¾ inch headspace. Press down on the surface with the back of the spoon to eliminate any air bubbles. Smooth out the top and pour in enough oil to completely cover the *conserva* by at least ¼ inch. Screw the lids on tightly and refrigerate.

5 • The *conserva* will keep in the refrigerator for at least 6 months. After each use, top off with more oil; this will help to prevent the growth of mold. For longer conservation, store jars in the freezer and thaw before using.

TOMATOES AND SAUCE
··· 119 ···

SMALL-BATCH TOMATO SAUCE

· · · MAKES 2 QUARTS · · ·

*Who says you have to put up a gazillion jars of tomato sauce? A couple
quarts may be all you need to see you through the winter doldrums. If even
this is too much, you can easily cut the recipe in half to yield 2 pints.*

8 pounds (3.6 kg) ripe plum tomatoes

½ cup extra-virgin olive oil

4 cloves garlic, lightly crushed

2 teaspoons fine sea salt, or to taste

8 fresh basil leaves

4 tablespoons lemon juice

EQUIPMENT

2 sterilized 1-quart jars or 4 sterilized 1-pint
 jars and their lids

Tomato or food mill (optional)

Basic water-bath canning equipment
 (see page 15)

1 · Bring a large stockpot of water to a rolling
boil over high heat and have ready a large
bowl of ice water. While the water is heating,
cut a small "X" in the bottom of each tomato.
Plunge the tomatoes, in batches if necessary,
into the boiling water and cook for 1 minute.
Use a large skimmer or slotted spoon to transfer them to the ice water.

2 · For a smooth sauce, drain the tomatoes
and then pass them, in batches, through a
food mill fitted with the disk with the smallest
holes into a bowl; discard the solids. Or, for
a pulpier sauce, drain the tomatoes and then
peel off the skins, which should slip off easily.
Cut the tomatoes in half lengthwise, remove

the core, and scoop out and discard the seeds.
Coarsely chop the tomatoes.

3 · In a large heavy-bottomed saucepan or
Dutch oven, warm the olive oil and garlic over
medium heat. Cook, stirring often, until the
garlic is fragrant, 1 to 2 minutes, but do not
let it brown. Carefully pour in the tomatoes—
they will spatter—and stir to combine them
with the oil. Raise the heat to medium-high
and bring the tomatoes to a boil; reduce the
heat to medium-low and simmer gently until
the tomatoes have deepened in color and lost
their raw flavor but still have a fresh tomato
flavor, 30 to 40 minutes. Season with the salt
and continue to cook until thickened to a
sauce consistency, 10 to 15 minutes more.
Remove and discard the garlic cloves. Turn off
the heat and stir in the basil.

4 · Pour 2 tablespoons lemon juice into each
quart-size jar or 1 tablespoon into each pint-
size jar. Funnel the hot sauce into the jars,
leaving ½ inch headspace.

5 · Screw the lids on tightly and process for
35 minutes in a boiling-water bath (see Water-
Bath Canning, page 15). Remove the jars and
set them upright on a clean kitchen towel. Let
cool to room temperature before storing in a
cool, dark place for up to 1 year. Refrigerate
after opening and use within 1 week.

CLASSIC MEAT SAUCE

··· MAKES ABOUT 2 QUARTS ···

*Honestly? I'm not sure there exists such a thing as "classic" Italian meat sauce.
Ragú di carne recipes vary from region to region, from town to town, and of
course, from cook to cook. I think of them as a sort of culinary fingerprint.
But if there were a classic version, surely it would be this one, long-simmered
on the stovetop and richly flavored with beef, pork, and sausage.*

3 tablespoons extra-virgin olive oil, plus
more as needed

6 ounces (170 g) boneless beef chuck roast,
cut into large pieces

6 ounces (170 g) boneless pork shoulder, cut
into large pieces, or half a slab of meaty
pork ribs, about 1 pound (454 g)

Fine sea salt and freshly ground black
pepper

2 hot or sweet Italian sausages (page 220) or
store-bought Italian sausages, cut in half
crosswise

2 quarts Bottled Whole Tomatoes (page 115)
or 2 (28-ounce/800 g) cans whole peeled
tomatoes

1 large yellow onion, finely chopped

1 carrot, finely chopped

1 celery stalk, finely chopped

1 cup (237 g) dry white wine

EQUIPMENT

2 clean 1-quart jars or four 1-pint jars and
their lids (optional; for pressure canning)

Tomato or food mill (optional)

Basic pressure-canning equipment (optional;
see page 19)

1 · Warm the olive oil in a large Dutch oven or
other heavy-bottomed pot over medium heat.
Season the beef and pork lightly with salt and
pepper. Add them to the pot, along with the
sausages. Brown the meat for 4 minutes; turn,
and brown the other side for about 4 minutes.
Transfer the meat to a bowl and set aside.

2 · Pass the tomatoes through a food mill
fitted with the disk with the smallest holes.
Discard the solids. (If seeds don't bother you,
you can skip this step and just mash the tomatoes with a potato masher or squeeze them
with your hands to break them up.)

3 · Reduce the heat to low. Add another tablespoon or so of oil if the bottom of the pot is dry. Stir in the onion, carrot, and celery and cook until the vegetables are beginning to soften, about 5 minutes. Return the meat to the pot, raise the heat to medium-high, and pour in the wine. Let it bubble for a minute or two and then stir in the tomatoes. Cover partially and bring to a boil, then reduce the heat to low to maintain a gentle simmer, and cook, stirring every so often, until the meat is very tender and the sauce is thickened, about 2 hours or more. Taste and adjust the seasoning with more salt, if you like.

4 · Remove from the heat and let cool briefly. Transfer the beef and pork shoulder to a cutting board and shred coarsely. Return the meat to the pot.

5 · **To refrigerate or freeze the sauce:** Let the sauce come to room temperature. Ladle it into containers of your choice with tight-fitting lids. The sauce may be refrigerated for up to 3 days or stored in the freezer for up to 3 months.

To pressure-can the sauce: Ladle the sauce into the jars. Following the instructions on page 19 and the canner manufacturer's instructions, process at 10 pounds pressure, 60 minutes for pints and 70 minutes for quarts. Remove the jars and set them upright on a clean kitchen towel. Let the jars cool to room temperature before storing in a cool, dark place for up to 1 year. Refrigerate after opening and use within 1 week.

BOTTLED BEANS IN TOMATO SAUCE

· · · MAKES 4 QUARTS · · ·

It was my friend, canning maven Cathy Barrow, who persuaded me to start canning my own beans. Previously, I'd always gone through the rigmarole of soaking and cooking dried beans each time I used them, which is often! The beauty of canning them is that you only have to go through that process once. After that, no more exertion is necessary beyond unscrewing a lid. I like to salt my beans just a little before processing them, but that's just my personal preference. You can omit the salt and just season the beans when you use them.

2 pounds (907 g) dried beans, such as borlotti or cannellini (I usually bottle two varieties at once)

2 gallons (7.6 kg) water

2 bay leaves

4 teaspoons fine sea salt (optional)

2 cups (454 g) Small-Batch Tomato Sauce (page 120), or best-quality store-bought sauce, heated to a simmer

EQUIPMENT

8 clean 1-pint jars and their lids

Basic pressure-canning equipment (see page 19)

1 · Rinse the beans thoroughly in a colander. If you're canning more than one variety, do this separately—unless you want to mix your beans, which is also fine. Remove and discard any shriveled beans or little stones. Put the beans in a large bowl (or bowls) with water to cover by 2 inches and soak them overnight.

2 · Drain the beans in a colander, separately if necessary, and rinse well. Place the beans in a large pot (or pots) with water to cover by

2 inches. Add the bay leaves and bring to a boil over medium-high heat. Lower the heat to medium and boil gently for about 20 minutes, skimming any foam from the surface. Remove from the heat and discard the bay leaves.

3 · Drain the beans, separately if necessary, in a colander set over a bowl to catch the cooking liquid. Reserve the cooking liquid.

4 · Pour ½ teaspoon of the salt, if using, into each jar. Ladle the beans into the jars, filling them two-thirds of the way. Ladle ¼ cup (57 g) of the tomato sauce over the beans, and then ladle in the cooking liquid, leaving 1 inch headspace. Use a bubble remover or a clean chopstick to dislodge any air bubbles. Screw the lids on tightly.

5 · Following the instructions on page 19 and the canner manufacturer's instructions, process the jars at 10 pounds of pressure for 75 minutes. Remove the jars and set them upright on a clean kitchen towel. Let the jars cool to room temperature before storing in a cool, dark place for up to 1 year. Refrigerate after opening and use within 1 week.

VARIATION · You can omit the tomato sauce to make simple canned beans. You can also can chickpeas in the same way, with or without the tomato sauce. Just substitute an equal amount of dried chickpeas for the beans.

HOMEMADE MEAT BROTH

Think of this brodo di carne *as a beefed-up version of chicken broth; in fact, that's exactly what it is. Adding beef bones to classic chicken broth ingredients contributes body and depth of flavor. This is an all-purpose broth in the Italian kitchen, used as a base for soups, braises, and sauces. You can freeze the broth or, for longer keeping, pressure-can it.*

1 whole chicken, about 4½ pounds (2 kg)

6 beef short ribs or beef marrowbones

4 carrots, ends trimmed, cut into 2-inch pieces

3 large celery stalks, preferably with leafy tops, cut into 2-inch pieces

4 whole cloves

2 large yellow onions, quartered

Stalks from 1 small fennel bulb, cut into 2-inch pieces (optional)

1 teaspoon whole black peppercorns

Generous handful flat-leaf parsley sprigs, coarsely chopped, stems included

6 quarts water

Fine sea salt

EQUIPMENT

Four clean 1-quart jars and their lids (optional; if pressure-canning)

Tight-weave cheesecloth

Basic pressure-canning equipment (optional; see page 19)

1 · Put the chicken, beef ribs, carrots, and celery into a 12- to 15-quart stockpot. Stick the cloves into 4 of the onion quarters and put the onions into the pot, along with the fennel, if using. Add the peppercorns and parsley, and enough water to cover by 2 to 3 inches, about 6 quarts.

2 · Bring the liquid to the boiling point over medium-high heat, then lower the heat to medium-low to prevent it from boiling rapidly. Cook the broth at a gentle simmer, skimming the foam off the top as it forms during the first hour or so. Continue to simmer, uncovered, until the broth is reduced by nearly half and has developed a rich, meaty taste, 4 hours or longer. Season to taste with salt and simmer for a few minutes more.

3 · Strain the broth through a colander lined with tight-weave cheesecloth into a large container with a tight-fitting lid. Discard the solids, or see the cook's note for how to repurpose some of them. Let the broth cool to room temperature, then cover and refrigerate until completely chilled. The fat will separate, rise to the top, and solidify, and the cold broth will be gelatinous. Skim off and discard that layer of congealed fat.

4 · Transfer the broth to a large saucepan and bring to a boil over medium-high heat. Boil vigorously for about 5 minutes. If freezing, let the broth cool, then ladle it into quart-size plastic containers with tight-fitting lids. Cover tightly and store in the freezer for up to 3 months.

5 · **To pressure-can the broth:** Ladle the hot broth into clean 1-quart jars, leaving 1 inch headspace. Use a damp paper towel to wipe any drops of broth from the rims, and screw the lids on tightly. Following the canner manufacturer's instructions, and the guidelines on page 19, process the jars at 10 pounds of pressure for 25 minutes. Remove the jars and set them upright on a clean kitchen towel. Let the jars cool to room temperature before storing in a cool, dark place for up to 1 year. Refrigerate after opening and use within 5 days.

COOK'S NOTE · My mother never threw out the meat from homemade broth, and I can't bring myself to do it either. Besides, it's delicious, either simmered in soup or served with a drizzle of good olive oil and a sprinkle of sea salt. Remove the meat from the chicken and beef rib bones. Discard the bones, skin, and any pieces of cartilage or inedible bits. Set aside the carrots and celery and serve those with the meat. Discard the onions and fennel stalks.

ZUPPA DI PASTA E FAGIOLI

··· MAKES 4 TO 6 SERVINGS ···

Wherever you go in Italy, you will always be able to find a good bowl of soup, whether a gentle homemade broth with egg noodles, or a hearty mix of vegetables and beans like this soup. I almost never make pasta e fagioli *the same way twice. It all depends on what's in season and what's in my pantry. The Pesto Abruzzese is optional, but if you have a jar in your fridge, it adds an additional layer of flavor to the soup.*

1 tablespoon extra-virgin olive oil

4 ounces (113 g) Slab Pancetta (page 226) or store-bought pancetta, diced

2 rounded tablespoons Pesto Abruzzese (page 172; optional)

1 cup diced carrots (4 ounces/113 g)

1 cup diced yellow onion (4 ounces/113 g)

½ cup diced celery (2 ounces/56 g)

1 tablespoon minced fresh rosemary

1 tablespoon minced fresh sage

1 fresh chile pepper, minced, or 1 dried chile pepper, crumbled

1 clove garlic, minced

2 medium Yukon Gold potatoes, peeled and cut into ½-inch cubes

3 to 4 cups chicken broth or vegetable broth

1 pint Bottled Beans in Tomato Sauce (page 124), or 1 (14.5 ounce) can borlotti or kidney beans

2-inch piece Parmigiano-Reggiano rind (optional)

1 cup small dried pasta, such as ditalini, cavatelli, or small shells

Best-quality extra-virgin olive oil, for drizzling

Freshly grated Parmigiano-Reggiano or Pecorino Romano, for serving

1 · In a large Dutch oven or other heavy pot, heat the oil and pancetta over medium-low heat. Cook the pancetta, stirring a few times, until it has begun to render its fat and brown, about 10 minutes. Stir in the pesto, if using. Cook, stirring, until the pesto is fragrant, a minute or two; then stir in the carrots, onion, celery, rosemary, sage, chile pepper, and garlic. Cook, stirring often, until the vegetables are softened, 8 to 10 minutes.

2 · Stir in the potatoes and 1 cup of the broth. Bring to a simmer and cook, stirring often to keep the potatoes from sticking, until the potatoes have begun to soften, about 15 minutes. Add the beans and stir gently to combine. Pour in 2 more cups of the broth and toss in the Parmigiano rind, if using. Cover the pot partially, raise the heat to medium, and bring the soup to a boil. Reduce

(recipe continues)

the heat to keep a gentle simmer and cook, stirring from time to time, until the vegetables are completely tender, about 30 minutes. Break up a few of the potatoes with the back of a wooden spoon; they will help to thicken the broth.

3 · Add the pasta and raise the heat to medium-high. Cook the soup at a lively simmer, adjusting the heat as necessary and stirring often, until the pasta is al dente. This will take a while, as cooking pasta in thick broth takes longer than cooking it in water. Add more broth if necessary to thin out the soup.

4 · Remove from the heat, cover, and let sit for 5 minutes. Ladle the soup into bowls, drizzle with a little olive oil, and sprinkle with cheese.

COOK'S NOTE · You can make this soup vegetarian by omitting the pancetta. Just add 2 more tablespoons oil to the pot before adding the Pesto Abruzzese or vegetables.

OVEN-DRIED TOMATOES

· · · MAKES ABOUT 2½ OUNCES (71 G) · · ·

It's always useful to have dried tomatoes on hand. They are easily reconstituted by pouring hot water on them, and they add a burst of flavor to grain salads, sauces, and dips. Making dried tomatoes is easy, even if you don't have the hot sun of Calabria or Sicily to do the work for you. I've often thought about buying a dehydrator but can't bring myself to purchase yet another kitchen appliance that will then have to be stored somewhere. Instead, I use my oven or the warming cupboard that is part of my range. Just be sure to keep an eye on them to make sure they don't scorch, and note that cooking times may vary depending on your oven.

2½ pounds (1.1 kg) ripe Roma (plum) tomatoes, about 10 large

1 · Turn the oven on to its lowest setting, anywhere from 150 to 200°F, no higher. If your range is equipped with a warming cupboard, you can use that instead.

2 · Cut the tomatoes in half lengthwise; scoop out and discard the seeds. Line a rimmed baking sheet with aluminum foil and set a rack with a grid over it. Arrange the tomato halves, cut side up, on the rack so that they are not touching each other.

3 · Let the tomatoes dry slowly in the oven, for as long as 24 hours. Check them after the first hour and again periodically when you happen to be around the kitchen. If they seem to be cooking rather than drying, or they are scorching in places, the heat is too high. Open the oven door a crack if necessary to keep the heat low.

4 · You will know when the tomatoes are done by the way they look and feel. They will be dark red, flattened, and crinkled, and they will feel leathery but still pliable. At this point, remove them from the oven and let them cool completely. They will have lost most of their weight and should weigh only 2 to 4 ounces (57 to 113 g).

5 · Pack the tomatoes into a clean glass jar with a tight-fitting lid and store in the pantry. They will keep in a cool, dark place for up to 1 year but are best used within 6 months; after that they will begin to lose their color and flavor.

OVEN-ROASTED TOMATOES IN OIL

Roasting tomatoes in a slow (low-heat) oven deepens their flavor and enhances that delicious savory quality known as umami. This technique can turn even anemic out-of-season tomatoes into something special. Even if all you have on hand is a box of pasta and a jar of these tomatoes, you have the fixings for a delicious dinner. I also use these as a topping for bruschetta or crostini, as a sauce for grilled or sautéed fish, or as a flavor booster for soups and stews. Because these tomatoes retain some juice, they won't keep as long as those that are dried completely in the sun or in the oven. Store them in the fridge and be sure to keep them submerged in olive oil to prolong their freshness.

2½ pounds (1.1 kg) ripe Roma (plum) tomatoes, about 10 large

3 tablespoons extra-virgin olive oil, plus more to cover

½ teaspoon fine sea salt

Freshly ground black pepper

A few thyme sprigs and/or crushed fennel seeds (optional)

1 · Preheat the oven to 275°F.

2 · Cut the tomatoes in half lengthwise and arrange them on a large rimmed baking sheet lined with parchment paper or aluminum foil. Drizzle the olive oil over the tomatoes and season with the salt and a generous grinding of pepper. Scatter the thyme and fennel seeds over the top, if using.

3 · Slow-roast the tomatoes until they are partially collapsed, crinkled, and somewhat dried out, but still soft and juicy, even a little caramelized, about 3 hours. Be sure to check on them from time to time to make sure they are cooking evenly and are not developing any scorched spots. Rotate the pan if necessary for even cooking. Let the roasted tomatoes cool completely.

4 · Pack the tomatoes into a glass jar with a tight-fitting lid. Pour in enough olive oil to cover them and store in the refrigerator for up to 2 months. As you use the tomatoes, top off those in the jar with oil to keep them covered.

HOMEMADE PASTA

Where there is homemade sauce there ought to be homemade pasta, right? The truth is, nobody—not even an Italian nonna—has to make pasta from scratch anymore. Plenty of supermarkets and gourmet food shops sell "fresh" noodles, ravioli, and lasagne sheets, in Italy and here in the United States. Shelves are filled with boxes of dried pasta shapes, mass-produced and artisan alike.

And yet, for many Italian cooks, making fresh noodles remains a frequent, if not daily, ritual, and a satisfying and rewarding endeavor. I still get a little thrill when I look at a batch of noodles, coiled into "nests" on a semolina-dusted baking tray, that I have just finished cutting; maybe that's why it tastes better to me. My pasta is never perfect; my noodles are not completely uniform. But that is the beauty of making your own pasta.

There are probably as many recipes for homemade pasta as there are cooks in Italy. Some call for nothing more than flour and eggs (or even just the yolks); some add semolina to the mix, or a dribble of olive oil; and some are made with only flour and water—no eggs at all.

It's best to start simply, with a good, all-purpose egg dough, and this is mine. What's great about it is its versatility. You can use it to make sturdy noodles such as trenette, or delicate pasta sheets for cannelloni. It can be mixed by hand or in the food processor—my preferred method for its ease. What's more, it stores well. I almost always make pasta ahead of time and freeze it. At cooking time, it goes straight from the freezer to the pot of boiling water (see Storing Pasta, page 139, for more).

These days, it's easy to find the soft wheat flour known as "00" flour that most Italians use for egg dough. It is similar to unbleached all-purpose flour, though it is finer and, in my opinion, turns out dough that is both slightly silkier and maintains a more appealing chewiness when cooked. But one can easily be substituted for the other, and I often make pasta using unbleached all-purpose flour.

I add a sprinkle of semolina flour to my dough because I like the body it gives to the pasta. I also use semolina, rather than flour, to dust my work surface and to sprinkle over freshly rolled or cut noodles. It prevents the noodles from sticking to one another but isn't as easily absorbed. I always use fine sea salt to flavor my dough. Coarse salt of any kind is not absorbed as readily and will affect the smooth texture of the dough. Last, I add a pinch of freshly grated nutmeg, which imparts a delicate sweetness.

I've included instructions for mixing the dough in the food processor and by hand. Either way turns out lovely, silky sheets. Just remember that when mixing the dough in a food processor, always start with the smaller amount of flour listed in the recipe. If the dough is too sticky, you can always work in more flour as you knead.

2 to 2¼ cups (255 to 285 g) Italian "00" flour or unbleached all-purpose flour

2 tablespoons semolina flour, plus more for dusting the work surface and dough

½ teaspoon fine sea salt

Pinch of freshly grated nutmeg

3 extra-large eggs

1 to 2 tablespoons extra-virgin olive oil

EQUIPMENT

Pasta machine

1 · **To mix the dough in a food processor:** Put 2 cups of the flour, the semolina, salt, and nutmeg into the bowl of a food processor and pulse briefly to combine. Break the eggs into the bowl and drizzle in 1 tablespoon of the oil. Process the mixture until it forms crumbs that look like small curds. Pinch together a bit of the mixture and roll it around. It should form a soft ball. If the mixture seems dry, drizzle in the remaining 1 tablespoon oil and pulse briefly. If it seems too wet and sticky, add additional flour, 1 tablespoon at a time.

Sprinkle a work surface lightly with semolina flour. Turn the dough out onto the work surface and press it together with your hands to form a rough ball. Knead the dough: Using the palm of your hand, push the dough gently but firmly away from you, and then fold it

over toward you. Rotate the dough a quarter turn (90 degrees), and repeat the pushing and folding motion. You are aiming for dough that is quite firm but still pliable and not dry. If the dough seems soft, sprinkle in a little flour or semolina. Continue kneading for several minutes until the dough is smooth and silky. Form it into a ball and wrap it tightly in plastic wrap. Let the dough rest at room temperature for 30 minutes before stretching it.

To mix the dough by hand: Mound the flour on a clean work surface and sprinkle the semolina over it. Make a wide well in the center of the mound. Break the eggs into the well and sprinkle in the salt and nutmeg. Add 1 tablespoon olive oil. Whisk the eggs with a fork to break them up and combine the eggs with the oil. Using the fork, gradually draw the flour from around the inside wall of the well into the egg mixture and whisk it to a batter-like consistency. Continue to whisk, adding more flour, until the mixture is too thick to work with the fork. Work carefully to avoid breaking the wall of flour and causing the egg mixture to run out. (If this happens, just use your hands to scoop up the mixture and work it back into the flour.)

Press the mixture into a rough ball and begin kneading it as directed above. Use a dough scraper to sweep away any excess

flour that doesn't get worked into the dough. Continue kneading until the dough is smooth and silky. Form it into a ball and wrap it tightly in plastic wrap. Let the dough rest at room temperature for 30 minutes before stretching it.

2 · **To stretch the dough:** Set up your pasta machine with the rollers on the widest setting (#1 on my standard Marcato Atlas hand-crank machine). Scatter a little semolina flour on the work surface around the machine and have more on hand for sprinkling on the dough.

3 · Cut the dough into 4 equal pieces and rewrap 3 pieces. Knead the remaining piece briefly. Using a rolling pin or patting it with the heel of your hand, form the dough into an oval 3 to 4 inches long and about 3 inches wide. Feed the dough through the rollers of the pasta machine, and then lay the strip on the work surface. Fold the dough into thirds, as you would a business letter, sprinkle with a little semolina, and pass it through the rollers again.

4 · Repeat the folding and rolling process a few more times, until the strip of dough is smooth. Move the roller to the next narrower notch and feed the strip through twice, sprinkling it with semolina if necessary to keep it from sticking. Continue to pass the dough through the rollers twice on each setting, until it is about $\frac{1}{16}$ inch thick or slightly thicker or thinner, depending on what kind of noodles you are cutting. Lay the sheet of dough out on a semolina-dusted surface and cover it lightly with plastic wrap or a clean kitchen towel while you stretch the remaining pieces.

5 · Once you have stretched all the dough into sheets, uncover them and let them dry slightly—just long enough so that the dough no longer feels tacky, but not so much that they will crack and split when you cut them into noodles. (The timing will depend on a variety of factors, such as how dry the atmosphere is in your kitchen, whether it's summer or winter, and so on.)

6 · **To cut the dough into noodles using the machine:** Stretch the dough to the desired thickness, anywhere from $\frac{1}{8}$ to $\frac{1}{16}$ inch, depending on the noodle. Attach the roller with the preferred cutter and feed each sheet through it, catching the noodles as they feed out the other side. Roll each cut sheet of noodles into nests and place them on a semolina-dusted work surface, tablecloth, or kitchen towel. Sprinkle a little more semolina on top.

To cut noodles by hand: Sprinkle each sheet generously with semolina and, starting at a short end, roll it up jelly-roll-style. Cut the rolled-up sheets crosswise into ribbons anywhere from $\frac{1}{8}$ wide, for thin noodles, to $\frac{1}{4}$ inch wide, for fettuccine, to $\frac{3}{4}$ inch wide, for pappardelle. Carefully unravel the noodles and wrap them around your hand to form a nest as above. Or uncoil them by fluffing them with your fingers and forming them into a loose mound. This is not as neat but is easier.

To cut trenette (for Trenette with Pesto Genovese and Prescinseua, page 211): Stretch the dough to a thickness of about $\frac{1}{8}$ inch. Roll the sheets up jelly-roll-style and cut them into noodles about $\frac{1}{8}$ inch wide or a little wider.

To cut *spaghetti alla chitarra* (for Spaghetti alla Chitarra with Classic Meat Sauce, page 140): Stretch the dough to a thickness of about ⅛ inch. If using a traditional *chitarra* (see page 140, and Sources, page 292), cut the pasta sheets into 12-inch lengths. Lay a sheet on top of the *chitarra* strings and use the small rolling pin that comes with the *chitarra* to roll over the sheet. Roll back and forth gently but firmly to press the sheet of pasta through the wires. The noodles will fall onto a wooden plank designed to catch them. Retrieve the noodles, form them into a nest, and set them on a semolina-dusted tray before proceeding with the next sheet. Repeat until you have cut all the sheets.

If using the *chitarra* cutting attachment to your pasta machine, attach it to the machine and dust the work surface around the machine with semolina flour. Cut the pasta sheets into 12-inch lengths. Feed the sheets through the cutters, catching the noodles as they fall. Form the noodles into nests and set them on a semolina-dusted tray.

STORING PASTA

Pasta can either be dried at room temperature, or frozen. I find that pasta left out to dry will sometimes crack, break, or curl. There are just too many variables, such as how hot or cold it is outside and in the kitchen, and whether the weather on a particular day is dry or humid. For that reason, I generally prefer freezing, as I find it more reliable. That said, I have had success with drying noodle nests, so I am including that information.

To dry pasta nests: Wrap the cut noodles loosely around your hand to form a nest. Set it on a semolina-dusted tablecloth or kitchen towel for several hours or overnight to dry completely. Once dry, carefully place the bundles in a container with a tight-fitting lid and store in the pantry. Dried pasta keeps for at least 3 months.

To freeze pasta: Freeze soon after cutting. Arrange the noodle nests on a semolina-dusted rimmed baking sheet and freeze for at least 1 hour, or until firm. For flat shapes, such as lasagne, arrange them in layers separated by a sheet of waxed paper. Once frozen, transfer the pasta to tightly lidded containers or zipper-lock bags and return to the freezer. Use within 1 month. When cooking frozen pasta, transfer it straight from the freezer to a pot of boiling water.

SPAGHETTI ALLA CHITARRA
with Classic Meat Sauce

One of my most prized kitchen possessions is the chitarra *my mother gave me a few years back when my book* The Glorious Pasta of Italy *was published. This rectangular wooden instrument, called a "guitar," is strung with thin wires that cut sheets of pasta into long, square-cut noodles, a specialty of Abruzzo.* Chitarra *noodles, cut thicker than other types of fresh pasta, pair especially well with hearty sauces, like meat ragù. You can find a traditional* chitarra *at some kitchenware stores and online (see Sources, page 292). Some pasta machines also have roller attachments that cut pasta sheets into square-cut noodles. Otherwise, a regular spaghetti attachment will do fine.*

2 quarts Classic Meat Suace (page 122), thawed if frozen

2 pounds (907 g) Homemade Pasta dough, cut into spaghetti alla chitarra according to the instructions on page 139 (may be made ahead and dried or frozen)

Kosher or sea salt

Freshly grated Parmigiano-Reggiano or Pecorino Romano, for serving

Dried peperoncini (page 148), crushed, or crushed red chile pepper, for serving

1 · In a large Dutch oven or heavy-bottomed saucepan, bring the sauce to a simmer over medium heat. Reduce the heat to low and cover to keep warm.

2 · Have the noodles ready to cook. If you have made them ahead of time and frozen them, leave them in the freezer until it's time to cook them. Thawing fresh pasta will make it clump together, with disastrous results.

3 · Bring a large (10- to 12-quart) stockpot of water to a rolling boil over high heat, and salt it generously. Carefully drop the pasta nests into the boiling water and stir to separate the strands. Cover the pot for about a minute to bring the water back to a boil. Uncover and cook the spaghetti until al dente, 2 to 5 minutes—homemade pasta cooks quickly, and fresh or frozen pasta will be done sooner than dried pasta. Taste to be sure.

4 · Drain the pasta in a colander, reserving about 1 cup of the pasta water. Return the spaghetti to the pot and ladle a generous amount of sauce over it. Gently toss the noodles with the sauce until thoroughly coated. Add a little of the cooking water if necessary to loosen the sauce. Transfer the dressed pasta to a warmed serving bowl or individual bowls and spoon more sauce on top. Sprinkle a little grated cheese on top. Serve, along with additional cheese and the peperoncini.

SPAGHETTI
with Anchovies and Tomato Conserva

Do you have a favorite dish that you turn to after a long workday, or maybe on reentry from vacation? Something that requires next to no effort but still delivers? This is mine. Good olive oil, good anchovies, garlic, and a dollop of tomato conserva *together make one of the quickest but most flavorful sauces for pasta. If you don't feel like boiling a pot of water, try tossing the warm sauce with greens or spoon it on bread for an easy supper or snack.*

Kosher or fine sea salt

½ cup (110 g) extra-virgin olive oil

1 large clove garlic, minced

8 best-quality anchovy fillets in olive oil

1 to 2 tablespoons Tomato Conserva (page 119)

1 or 2 dried peperoncini (page 148), crumbled, or a generous pinch of crushed red chile pepper

1 pound (454 g) dried spaghetti

1 · Bring a large pot of water to a rolling boil and salt it generously.

2 · While the water is heating, combine the olive oil and garlic in a large skillet and cook over medium-low heat until the garlic is fragrant, about 2 minutes. Don't let it brown or it will turn bitter. Reduce the heat to low and add the anchovies and a spoonful or two of their oil, then stir in the *conserva* and peperoncini. Cook over low heat until the anchovies have more or less dissolved, about 2 minutes. Turn off the heat and cover to keep warm.

3 · Cook the spaghetti according to the manufacturer's instructions until al dente. Drain in a colander set in the sink, reserving about ½ cup of the cooking water. Transfer the drained pasta to the skillet and toss with the sauce until well coated. Add a splash of the reserved cooking water to loosen the sauce if necessary. Toss once more, and serve immediately.

Salt-Cured Olives, page 177

INFUSED OILS, VINEGARS, AND CONDIMENTS

The word *condiment* still conjures images in my mind of ballpark food: foot-long hot dogs and giant pump dispensers of ketchup, yellow mustard, and garish green relish. But of course the category encompasses so much more, and in Italy it refers to everything from a dollop of spicy jam to accompany cheese to certain pasta sauces, such as pesto.

Simply put, condiments add flavor to food; they liven it up. They can be sweet, salty, spicy, or mellow—sometimes in the same jar. Glossy, spicy tomato jam has it all; it's savory and sweet, a little vinegary, and a little fiery. It goes beautifully with almost any cheese, and also with grilled or roast pork.

Condiments are by nature versatile. I always keep a selection of seasoned salts in my pantry to dress up meat or fish, or even roasted vegetables. I use infused oil and vinegar for the same purpose—not merely to toss with salad. Classic Pesto Genovese (page 171) may have been invented as a pasta sauce, but it also adds a bright note to vegetable soups. And you can use it as a spread for mozzarella and tomato sandwiches, or as a topping for crostini.

Pesto is convenient; it comes together quickly, even if you are making it the old-fashioned way with a mortar and pestle. On the other side of the spectrum is *cotognata*—quince paste. It takes time to wrestle quince into edible shape; cooking, pureeing, cooking some more. But what a transformation. A gorgeous russet slice of sweet quince paste set out with a wedge of aged sheep's milk cheese is as lovely and nostalgic as autumn itself.

Time (plus salt) also transforms raw olives from hard, bitter, inedible fruits into the plump, flavor-packed antipasto staple so many of us adore. You might not have considered curing your own olives—I hadn't until just a few years ago. Now it is an annual ritual; I love watching, and tasting, the changes that take place over a period of weeks. Also, there is nothing like putting out a bowl of your own cured olives for friends to enjoy. Success never tasted so . . . briny.

CITRUS SALT

· · · MAKES ABOUT ½ CUP (125 G) · · ·

This is a delicate salt, good for seasoning roasted fish or a classic seafood stew. I also sprinkle it on roasted asparagus and artichokes. Beyond that? Try just a few flakes on top of bittersweet chocolate gelato.

½ cup (125 g) coarse sea salt
1 tablespoon finely grated orange zest
1 tablespoon finely grated lemon zest

1 · Combine the salt and zests in a bowl and rub them together with your fingers to distribute the citrus throughout the salt crystals.

2 · Line a rimmed baking sheet with parchment paper and spread the salt out on it. Let air-dry at room temperature until the fine shavings of citrus are completely dry and crumble when you roll them between your fingers, 2 to 3 hours or up to overnight.

3 · You can leave the salt coarse, if you like. Or, for a finer grind, pulse it in a food processor a few times to break down the salt crystals into smaller grains.

4 · Store at room temperature in a tightly lidded jar. It will keep indefinitely, though the citrus will lose its aroma over time.

PORCHETTA SALT

··· MAKES A SCANT 3/4 CUP (165 G) ···

Fennel and rosemary were made for pork. This makes sense when you think about it. Fall is the season of pig butchering, and it is also when these aromatics can be found in profusion in the Italian countryside. This salt conveniently combines all the flavors found in Italy's iconic porchetta (spit-roasted pig). I use it to make the Oven-Roasted Porchetta Sandwiches on page 183. But it's also great for seasoning roast chicken or roast potatoes. Here are the basic ingredients, followed by a list of optional additions. I've been known to add all of them for a really lavishly seasoned salt.

2 tablespoons fennel seeds

½ cup (125 g) coarse sea salt

2 tablespoons finely grated lemon zest

2 tablespoons minced fresh rosemary

2 tablespoons whole black peppercorns

1 · Preheat the oven to 200°F.

2 · Spread the fennel seeds in a small skillet and set over medium-high heat. Toast, stirring often, until the seeds are fragrant and have turned a shade darker, 1 to 2 minutes. Transfer to a bowl and let cool.

3 · Add the salt, zest, rosemary, and peppercorns to the bowl and mix well. Spread the mixture out on a rimmed baking sheet or pizza pan. Bake until the lemon zest and rosemary have dried out, about 30 minutes. Let cool to room temperature.

4 · Pulse the mixture briefly in a food processor, just enough to achieve a coarse grind. Store the seasoned salt at room temperature in a jar with a tight-fitting lid. For best flavor, use within 6 months.

OPTIONAL ADDITIONS
Crushed peperoncini, crushed bay leaf, fennel pollen, finely grated orange zest, minced fresh sage

PEPERONCINO GARLAND

··· MAKES ABOUT 4 OUNCES (113 G) COMPLETELY DRIED ···

In September and October, long strands of bright red chile peppers bloom all over Abruzzo, Puglia, Calabria, and other parts of Italy. They adorn the stalls at farmers' markets and roadside stands, and they hang from the ceiling in restaurants and in home kitchens. Not only are these garlands pretty to look at, but they are also the best way to dry peppers for using throughout the year. Placed in a dry spot with good air circulation, the peppers dry evenly over a period of weeks and months, turning first soft, then leathery, and finally crispy. Just snip a pepper or two from the garland when you want to use it; or grind an entire batch into flakes or powder.

1 pound (454 g) or more ripe fresh red horn-shaped chile peppers, such as cayenne

EQUIPMENT
Sturdy waxed cotton thread
Sewing needle

1 · Discard any peppers that have blemishes, soft spots, or other flaws.

2 · Thread the needle through the base of the stem of a pepper and knot the thread. Continue to thread and knot until you have a string of peppers about 1 yard long. Hang the garland on a hook in a dry, well-ventilated spot. In September, if the weather is sunny and dry, I hang the peppers outside on a hook under the eaves outside my family room. When the weather isn't cooperating, I simply bring the garland inside and hang it from the ceiling in my kitchen.

3 · Let the peppers hang for several weeks, or longer, until they are completely dried and crunchy.

4 · To make ground chile pepper, remove the peppers from the garland and cut off the stems. Blitz the peppers in a food processor until finely ground (the seeds will stay whole, which is fine). Or leave them on the garland and snip them off as needed.

VARIATION · You can use the same stringing and hanging method to dry sweet red horn-shaped peppers, such as Jimmy Nardello. The peppers must be thin-skinned; regular sweet bell peppers have too much juice and will not dry properly this way. It may take several months for the larger peppers to dry completely. Check them now and again to make sure they are not turning moldy as they dry.

PEPERONCINO CREAM

··· MAKES 1½ CUPS (345 G) ···

*In spite of its genial orange color, this hot pepper paste is wicked, and by that
I mean fiery. Of course, the spiciness will depend on what type(s) of chile
peppers you use. I like cayenne, which remind me of the long peperoncini
grown in Abruzzo; or the pepper Super Chili, which is smaller but hotter.
Use crema di peperoncino to spice up all sorts of dishes: tomato sauce, plain
spaghetti with garlic and olive oil, seafood stew, scrambled eggs, and so on.*

8 ounces (227 g) medium-hot to hot fresh
   chile peppers, such as cayenne

1 large red bell pepper, about 8 ounces (227 g)

¼ cup (70 g) fine sea salt

3 cups (710 g) white wine vinegar

1 cup (237 g) spring or filtered water

4 to 6 tablespoons (55 to 73 g) extra-virgin
   olive oil, plus more for topping off the jars

EQUIPMENT

3 sterilized 4-ounce jars and their lids

Disposable kitchen gloves (such as Playtex)

Stand blender or immersion blender

1 · Wearing kitchen gloves to protect your
hands, cut the stems off the chile peppers and
slice them in half lengthwise. Remove and
discard the seeds and any white pith. Cut
the halves crosswise into large pieces. Do
the same with the bell pepper. Put the chile
pepper and bell pepper pieces in a colander
set over a bowl. Sprinkle the salt over them
and toss to coat. Let stand overnight to release
liquid, then pat dry (discard the liquid).

2 · Combine the vinegar and water in a
medium saucepan and bring to a boil over
medium-high heat. Add the pepper pieces.
Raise the heat to high and, once the liquid
returns to a boil, boil the peppers for
1 minute. Drain in a colander set in the sink.

3 · Line a rimmed baking sheet with a clean
kitchen towel (use an old kitchen towel, as the
peppers might stain it). Wearing gloves, spread
the peppers out on the towel so they are not
touching. Let them dry for several hours or up
to overnight.

4 · Using a stand blender or immersion
blender, puree the peppers with 4 tablespoons
olive oil until they have become a coarse paste.
Add up to 2 tablespoons more oil if necessary
to achieve a thick paste consistency. Spoon the
paste into the jars, leaving ½ inch headspace.
Top off each jar with a little more olive oil to
cover the paste completely. Screw the lids on
tightly and refrigerate or freeze. I store one jar
in the refrigerator to use immediately and the
others in the freezer for later.

5 · Use the refrigerated *crema* within
3 months. Be sure to top it off with more oil
each time you use it so that the remaining
crema in the jar is completely covered.

OLIO SANTO (HOT PEPPER OIL)

··· MAKES 2 CUPS ···

No matter where you sit down for a meal in Abruzzo, whether at a restaurant or at someone's kitchen table, there will almost always be peperoncino—chile pepper. In summer it is likely to be a single fresh peperoncino, red or green, served on a plate with a knife or a pair of little scissors next to it for snipping. Sometimes it's a small bowl of dried, crushed peperoncini.

And sometimes it's *olio santo*. Sainted oil, holy oil. Hot oil. *Olio santo* is a staple all over southern Italy, made by infusing extra-virgin olive oil with chile pepper and letting it steep until the oil is tinged red and fiery hot. "It should be called *olio diabolico*," a friend of mine says. It's meant to be employed with care, spooned judiciously on roasted fish, issued in droplets over boiled escarole or rustic soups. I like a few drops on fried or scrambled eggs in the morning. You don't douse a dish with *olio santo*, you anoint it.

Olio santo is easy to make, and worth having in your pantry. There's a vendor at my farmers' market who sells a compact, bushy plant called Super Chili, and I buy one every year. It produces all summer long and well into fall, in spite of aggressive neglect by me. The peppers are plump, 1 to 2 inches in length, and about as spicy as a cayenne pepper, rating 50,000 on the Scoville heat unit scale. They dry beautifully and are perfect for making *olio santo*. Cayenne peppers are an excellent substitute.

25 to 50 thoroughly dried chile peppers, depending on how hot the peppers are and how spicy you like your oil

2 cups (439 g) good-quality extra-virgin olive oil

1 · Use a sharp paring knife or scissors to snip the stem end off the peppers. Cut the peppers crosswise into small pieces. Corral any seeds that try to escape. You may want to use kitchen gloves for this task to avoid getting pepper residue on your fingers.

2 · Put the snipped peppers and their seeds into a clean swing-top bottle or jar, then pour in the oil. Close tightly with the stopper or lid and set in a cool, dark place for 2 to 3 weeks to allow the heat of the peppers to infuse the oil. The oil will get spicier over time and will keep in a cool, dark place for up to 1 year.

COOK'S NOTE · Be sure to use unblemished peppers that are thoroughly dried, with no moisture. Discard any that have even one or two moldy seeds inside.

LEMON OLIVE OIL

Real lemon olive oil is a sort of by-product of olive oil production. In Abruzzo and Molise, whole lemons are put through the olive oil presses to clean them at the end of the season. The process yields a bright oil infused with lemon flavor. Since I don't have an olive oil press in my home in suburban Virginia, I rely on this cheater's method, which works quite nicely. This oil is a lovely condiment to have in your pantry; its uses are nearly endless. Toss it with baby greens for the simplest of salad dressings. Use it on fish, pasta, grilled chicken, roasted cauliflower, or shaved fennel. One of my favorite quick lunches on a busy workday is to split open an avocado, add a dollop of cottage cheese, and finish with a drizzle of lemon oil and a sprinkle of Citrus Salt (page 145). Because the lemon peel is fresh and not dried, this oil must be stored in the refrigerator.

1 cup (220 g) good-quality extra-virgin olive oil

3 large lemons, organic or untreated if possible

1 · Pour the olive oil into a heavy-bottomed saucepan. Using a vegetable peeler, remove the zest of the lemons in strips, avoiding any white pith. Let them drop right into the oil. (Reserve the lemons for another use.)

2 · Turn the heat on low and let the peels steep for 15 to 20 minutes. You're not really cooking the peels, but rather letting them infuse the oil with their aroma and flavor. The oil may sizzle a bit as the peels release their oils. Remove from the heat if necessary to keep the oil from getting too hot.

3 · Let the lemon oil cool to room temperature. Remove and discard the peels. Strain the oil into a jar and refrigerate. Bring to room temperature before using.

SEASONED VINEGARS

Vinegars flavored with herbs, spices, or fruit, or sometimes all three, are a nice way to enliven a weeknight salad or add a burst of flavor to other dishes. I never thought of them as typically Italian, but I have been seeing more of them on store shelves in Italy in recent years. They are easy to make and certainly less expensive than good-quality balsamic vinegar—Italy's true flavored vinegar. Balsamic vinegar is made from grape must that has been fermented and aged in barrels made from a variety of woods—cherry, chestnut, oak, and so on. The best balsamic vinegar is prohibitively expensive. I'm not suggesting that adding some dried figs or cherries to your vinegar will produce something as refined as balsamic vinegar aged for 12 years, but you will end up with a really tasty condiment. Here are two of my favorites. Be sure to use good-quality white wine vinegar and note that the fruit will turn the vinegar darker as it steeps.

FOR HERBED FIG VINEGAR

1 cup (125 g) chopped dried Mission figs

3 small lemon thyme sprigs

2 cups (473 g) white wine vinegar

FOR TART CHERRY VINEGAR

1 cup (125 g) fresh sour cherries, with pits

½ cup (70 g) dried sour cherries

2 cups (473 g) white wine vinegar

EQUIPMENT

1 sterilized 1-quart jar or wide-mouth
  bottle, with lid

1 sterilized 1-pint vinegar bottle or two
  ½-pint vinegar bottles, and caps

Tight-weave cheesecloth

Narrow funnel

1 · Place the figs and lemon thyme sprigs, or the fresh and dried cherries, in the jar or wide-mouth bottle.

2 · In a medium saucepan, bring the vinegar to a simmer without letting it boil. Pour the hot vinegar into the jar and cap with the lid. Let cool to room temperature. Set the vinegar in a cool, dark spot and let it steep for at least 2 weeks and up to 4 to develop the flavor.

3 · Strain the vinegar through damp tight-weave cheesecloth and then funnel it into the bottle. Store the vinegar in a cool, dark spot in your pantry, where it will keep for at least 3 months. If the vinegar develops mold or shows signs of fermentation such as bubbles, cloudiness, or sliminess, throw it and the bottle away without tasting.

APPLE AND PEAR PASTE

Since I enjoy making cotognata *(Quince Paste, page 158), I was inspired to try the same technique with the fruit's milder cousins, apples and pears. The result is this beautiful paste, which is perfumed with bay leaf. The paste glows like amber and, like quince* cotognata, *it makes an excellent accompaniment to cheeses. I like to serve this paste with good, pungent runny cheeses like Taleggio, robiola, and La Tur.*

2 pounds (907 g) Gold Rush or other dense-fleshed, sweet-tart apples

1 pound (454 g) ripe but firm Bosc pears

Peel and juice of 1 small lemon

1 cup (237 g) apple cider

½ cup (118 g) water

About 3 cups (680 g) sugar

½ vanilla bean

2 bay leaves

Vegetable oil or butter, for coating parchment paper

EQUIPMENT

Standard or immersion blender

Kitchen scale

1 · Peel and core the apples and pears, and remove the seeds. Cut the flesh into 1-inch pieces and put them in a large Dutch oven or heavy-bottomed pot. Add the lemon peel and juice, and pour in the cider and water. Bring to a boil over medium-high heat, reduce the heat to maintain a gentle simmer, and cook, stirring often, until the fruit is completely tender, about 1 hour. Let the mixture cool slightly, and then puree with an immersion blender. Or puree it in a standard blender, in batches if necessary.

2 · Weigh the fruit puree; you should have about 2 pounds (907 g). If you have more, measure out 2 pounds (907 g) and set aside the rest for another use (you can enjoy it as pear-applesauce). Return the puree to the pot.

3 · Weigh out three-quarters of the weight in sugar—1½ pounds (680 g), or 3 cups. Add it to the pot with the puree and stir to combine. Split the vanilla bean and scrape the seeds into the pot. Add the pod as well, along with one of the bay leaves. Cook over medium-low heat, stirring, until the sugar is completely

(recipe continues)

dissolved. Continue to cook, stirring often to prevent burning, until the puree is very thick and has turned several shades darker—an hour or longer. Watch out for spattering, and lower the heat if it gets volcanic. The paste is done when it pulls away from the sides of the pan as you stir. It will be a glorious, translucent golden-brown color and will smell like heaven. Remove and discard the bay leaf and the vanilla bean pod.

4 • Preheat the oven to 175°F. Line an 8-inch square baking pan with parchment paper, leaving an overhang on two opposite sides. Lightly coat the paper with a thin film of oil. Pour in the apple and pear paste and smooth out the top. Set the remaining bay leaf on top in the center. Bake until the paste is nicely set and firm to the touch, about 1 hour. Let cool to room temperature, then cover with plastic wrap and let it sit out overnight to set completely.

5 • When the paste is completely firm and set, remove it from the pan. Slice into squares or rectangles; or use lightly oiled cookie cutters to cut out decorative shapes. Wrap the pieces of paste tightly in plastic wrap and store them in the refrigerator. Stored this way, they will keep for at least 6 months. (Store in the freezer for up to 1 year.) Bring the paste to room temperature before serving.

QUINCE PASTE

Quince seems left over from another era: It's not a grab-and-go fruit; it can't be packed in a lunch box. With its round, slightly knobby shape, its beauty is unconventional. It bears some similarity to the apple and the pear, but retains a wild streak. Quince cannot be eaten raw; even when ripe the fruit is hard and unappealingly tart. But cooking transforms it completely; the tannins soften and the fruit's pale, off-white flesh turns a gorgeous russet. We had a quince tree in our yard, planted by my dad at my mom's request. She tamed the fruit into preserves every year. In southern Italy, the fruit is cooked down into this sweet, firm paste known as cotognata. *It's an excellent accompaniment to sharp cheeses.*

4 pounds (1.8 kg) ripe quince

Zest of ½ lemon, in strips (no white pith), plus the juice

About 4 cups (900 g) sugar

½ vanilla bean

Vegetable oil or butter, for coating parchment paper

EQUIPMENT

Kitchen scale

1 · Peel and core the fruit, and remove the seeds. Work carefully, as quince can be tough to cut. Cut the flesh into 1-inch pieces and put them in a large Dutch oven or heavy-bottomed pot. Add the lemon zest and enough water to cover the quince. Bring to a boil over medium-high heat, reduce the heat to maintain a gentle simmer, and cook, stirring often, until the fruit is completely tender, an hour or longer. Drain the quince in a colander set over a bowl, reserving the cooking liquid. Puree the fruit in a food processor. (You may need to do this in batches.) Add a splash or two of the cooking liquid to loosen the puree, if necessary.

2 · Weigh the fruit puree; you should have about 2 pounds (907 g). At this point your puree will be pale orange, but it will turn a beautiful rustic red-brown as it cooks down. Return the puree to the pot.

3 · Weigh out an equal weight of sugar—2 pounds (907 g), or 4 cups. Add it to the pot with the puree and stir to combine. Split the vanilla bean and scrape the seeds into the pot. Add the pod as well, and the lemon juice. Cook over medium-low heat, stirring, until the sugar is completely dissolved. Continue to cook, stirring often to prevent burning, until the puree is very thick and thin has turned several shades darker—about 1½ hours. Watch out for spattering, and lower the heat if it gets volcanic. The paste is done when it pulls away from the sides of the pan as you stir. It will be a beautiful red-brown in color and deliciously fragrant. Remove and discard the vanilla bean pod.

4 · Preheat the oven to 175°F. Line an 8-inch square baking pan with parchment paper, leaving an overhang on two opposite sides. Lightly coat the paper with a thin film of oil. Pour in the quince paste and smooth out the top. Bake until the paste is nicely set and firm to the touch, about 1 hour. Let cool to room temperature, then cover with plastic wrap and let it sit out overnight to set completely.

5 · When the paste is completely firm and set, remove it from the pan. Slice into squares or rectangles; or use lightly oiled cookie cutters to cut out decorative shapes. Wrap the pieces of paste tightly in plastic wrap and store them in the refrigerator. Stored this way, they will keep for at least 6 months. (Store in the freezer for up to 1 year.) Bring the paste to room temperature before serving.

Preserving the Flavors of Piedmont

❧ ❧ ❧ ❧ ❧ • • • ❧ ❧ ❧ ❧ ❧

Paolo Anselmino and Noemi Lora's shop is hidden in plain sight, a low-slung red stucco structure next to a bank on a stretch of the *strada statale* (state road) between Alba and Bra, in Piedmont.

Inside is a treasure trove of sweet and savory preserves; long tables stacked with jars in meticulous rows: *antipasto Piemontese*, a mixed vegetable pickle in tomato sauce; bite-size cherry peppers stuffed with tuna; marinated anchovy fillets; truffle cream; fruit mustards; nuts in honey and more. Each jar is positioned in such a way that its colorful, carefully packed contents are easily visible. Clearly, pride and passion are at work here.

Passion is what drove Anselmino and wife Lora to quit their jobs a decade ago and acquire I Frutti della Mia Langa (The Fruits of My Langa), the small food production company, from its original owner. It was a radical change; Anselmino had a successful niche career building sterile rooms for technology and pharmaceutical companies, and Lora, an avid bowler, was co-owner and manager of a bowling arcade.

"We were a little reckless," says Anselmino.

He and Lora make all of their products—48 in total—by hand with the help of one assistant, using only in-season ingredients from the surrounding Langhe and Roero hills. Everything is processed in the small but spotless stainless-steel kitchen at one end of the shop. The room is efficiently equipped, with a large food processor for slicing and chopping, a range, and a vat pasteurizer. There is no refrigerator. Everything they preserve, much of which comes from Lora's brother's farm, goes straight from the field to the jar.

Anselmino estimates that he and Lora fill close to 50,000 jars each year. Most of what they make is sold right in the shop, to long-time clients and locals and to passersby and tourists meandering around the hills of Barolo and Barbaresco in summer or during the fall grape harvest, or headed to the annual white truffle festival in Alba in October.

Preserving starts in May and goes full tilt through summer, winding down after the holidays (a busy time for gift baskets). One morning when we meet, Lora and assistant Marta Tosa are in the kitchen, up to their elbows in 40 kilos (88 pounds) of torpedo-shaped red onions, which they are peeling by hand. They will be chopped in the large processor, then marinated overnight in wine, sugar, brandy, and spices. The following day, golden raisins will be added and the mixture cooked down to a thick jam, enough to fill 400 small jars. The jam is popular, and once it sells there will be no more until next year.

It's the same with all of the foods they preserve. "We only do what we have the capacity to do, and we do it all locally," says Lora. "We could buy Spanish or Dutch produce, but then we would be like everyone else."

MIXED NUTS IN HONEY

This is one of the simplest condiments to serve with a cheese platter, especially with bold cheeses such as Pecorino Romano, Gorgonzola Dolce, Taleggio, and aged Asiago. Whole shelled almonds and hazelnuts, along with walnut halves, are suspended in honey as though in amber. The quality of ingredients is key here. Use freshly shelled nuts, and honey from a local purveyor if possible. Just be sure the honey isn't too dark. You want to be able to see the pretty mix of nuts in the jar. These honey nuts are also delicious on crostini: Spoon some fresh ricotta (page 203) on toasted or grilled bread. Coarsely chop up some nuts in honey and spoon them on top of the ricotta; add a few droplets of the honey and a grinding of black pepper.

⅔ cup (100 g) shelled skin-on almonds

⅔ cup (100 g) shelled hazelnuts

⅔ cup (100 g) shelled walnut halves

1 cup (340 g) honey

1-inch piece vanilla bean

EQUIPMENT

2 sterilized ½-pint jars and their lids

1 · Preheat the oven to 350°F. Spread the nuts on a large rimmed baking sheet, keeping the hazelnuts separate from the others. Bake until the nuts are fragrant and the hazelnut skins are beginning to crackle, 7 to 10 minutes.

2 · Carefully transfer the hot hazelnuts to a clean kitchen towel and wrap them in it. Let them sit for 1 minute, then roll the towel back and forth vigorously; this will help to loosen and remove the skins. Not all of the skins will come off; this is fine. Let all of the nuts cool to room temperature.

3 · Measure the honey into a heavy-bottomed saucepan and add the vanilla bean. Bring to a boil over medium heat and boil for 5 minutes. Remove from the heat and stir in the nuts.

4 · Pour the hot nuts and honey into the jars, packing them as tightly as possible and leaving about ½ inch headspace. Screw the lids on tightly and let the nuts sit overnight before serving. Store in the pantry for up to 6 months.

PEAR MOSTARDA

Most of the recipes in this book celebrate the frugal nature of Italian cooks, their desire to minimize waste and to preserve as much as possible from the bounty of the seasons. They are examples of cucina povera, *or peasant cuisine, at its best. Not so with fruit mostarda. This sweet and ultra-spicy condiment, a somewhat odd mix of syrup-poached fruit and potent mustard essence, is a traditional accompaniment to boiled or roasted meats. In the past, it was reserved for the tables of the wealthy, the noble, and the powerful and has a long and illustrious history in the cuisine of Emilia-Romagna and the Veneto. In recent years, mostarda has become newly popular among aficionados of Italian cooking. Although it is often served with classic bollito misto—a traditional stew of mixed boiled meats— I like this served with a wedge of good, sharp pecorino.*

Making mostarda is an art and a process. It requires poaching fruit—either whole, large pieces, or sliced—in syrup over the course of several days, until it is saturated and beautifully translucent. Once this candying process is completed, mustard essence is stirred in drop by drop until the mostarda is sufficiently spicy—spicy enough to make your eyes water! The type of fruit depends on what's in season, but quince, pears, apples, melon, and figs are all good candidates. Of all those, I prefer pears, which take beautifully to the candying process without (by some miracle) turning mushy at all. Although traditional mostarda is made with small whole or halved fruits, I cut the pears into thin slices, as I find the large pieces unwieldy.

Mustard essence is not an easy ingredient to find. In Italy it is sold in small bottles with dropper caps at old-fashioned pharmacies called *drogherie*, places where you will also find an eclectic mix of preserves, coffees, cake-decorating confections, and the like. Mustard essence is strong stuff and you need to be careful using it, as it can sting your eyes and your nostrils. If you don't have access to mustard essence (I have yet to find a reliable source for it here in the United States, though it is sometimes available on eBay), you can use ground mustard to spice up your mostarda, though the resulting mixture will be cloudy rather than translucent. In any case, be extra safe and wear gloves to protect your hands, and do not touch your face or eyes.

2½ pounds (1.1 kg) ripe but firm pears

1 pound (454 g) vanilla sugar (see page 57)

½ vanilla bean

Juice of ½ lemon

About 1 tablespoon mustard essence (see opposite page)

EQUIPMENT

1 sterilized 1-pint swing-top jar with rubber gasket

Disposable kitchen gloves (such as Playtex)

1 · **Day 1:** Peel the pears and quarter them lengthwise. Cut out the core and seeds. Slice the quarters into chunks, or cut them crosswise into thin slices. Place the pieces in a shallow bowl and add the sugar. Scrape the seeds from the vanilla bean and add them to the pears. Add the lemon juice and fold everything together gently so as not to break up the pears. Set a plate on top of the fruit and weight it down with a heavy object. Cover with plastic wrap and let the pears macerate overnight.

2 · **Day 2:** Drain the pears in a colander set over a bowl to catch the syrup. Transfer the syrup to a heavy-bottomed saucepan and bring it to a boil over medium-high heat. Boil for 5 minutes, then add the pears. Raise the heat to high and boil the pears for 1 minute. Then remove from the heat and pour the pears and the syrup into a shallow heatproof bowl. Cover with a plate and weight it down with a heavy object. Cover with plastic wrap and leave overnight.

3 · **Day 3:** Drain the pears in a colander set over a bowl to catch the syrup. Return the fruit to the heatproof bowl. Transfer the syrup to a heavy-bottomed saucepan and bring it to a boil over medium-high heat. Boil for 5 minutes. Pour the hot syrup over the pears. Set a plate on top and weight it down with a heavy object. Cover with plastic wrap and leave overnight.

4 · **Day 4:** Repeat the process one more time, draining the fruit in a colander and boiling the syrup. The syrup should be thickened like maple syrup rather than honey. If it becomes too thick, add a splash of water and boil briefly.

5 · At this point you need to determine whether the pears are sufficiently candied. Taste a piece. It should be dense, slightly sticky, and tender, and not raw at all. (If the pears still have an uncooked texture, pour the hot syrup over them, weight them down, cover with plastic, and leave overnight.)

6 · Once they are properly candied, let the pears and syrup cool to room temperature. Wearing kitchen gloves, add about 1 teaspoonful of the mustard essence to the pears in syrup and stir to combine thoroughly. Taste to determine the spiciness, and add more as desired. I find that 1 tablespoon of mustard essence is about right, but I like it daringly spicy. Carefully spoon the mostarda into the jar. Store it in the refrigerator, where it will keep for at least 6 months.

TROPEA ONION JAM

··· MAKES 1¼ PINTS ···

I first tasted this sweet, garnet-hued jam as part of a cheese antipasto at Osteria Morini, in Washington, D.C., with extra-aged Parmigiano-Reggiano, Pecorino Toscano, and pungent Gorgonzola. I'm grateful to executive sous chef Ben Pflaumer for sharing the recipe. Tropea is an ultra-sweet red onion. If you're a gardener, you can grow your own (see Sources, page 292). Otherwise, choose good, firm, young red onions. This jam is fantastic on beef burgers with blue cheese (see page 193).

1 pound (454 g) Tropea or other red onions, cut into small dice

2 cups (400 g) sugar

1 cup (237 g) Sangiovese or other sturdy red wine

½ to ¾ teaspoon kosher or fine sea salt

10 whole peppercorns

1 whole clove

1 bay leaf

1-inch piece vanilla bean

½ cinnamon stick

2 tablespoons red wine vinegar

EQUIPMENT

4-inch square of cheesecloth and a length of kitchen twine

Instant-read thermometer (optional)

2 sterilized ½-pint jars and 1 sterilized 4-ounce jar, and their lids

Basic water-bath canning equipment (see page 15)

1 · Combine the onions, sugar, wine, and salt in a wide, heavy-bottomed saucepan. Use the cheesecloth to make a sachet for the peppercorns, clove, bay leaf, vanilla bean, and cinnamon stick and tie it up with the kitchen twine. Put the sachet in the pot with the other ingredients.

2 · Bring the onion mixture to a boil over medium heat, stirring to dissolve the sugar. Cook at a simmer, stirring often, until the jam has thickened and reaches 220 to 225°F and you can drag a path along the bottom of the pot with a silicone spatula, about 20 minutes. Or use the freezer plate method to test for doneness as described on page 83. Stir in the vinegar and remove from the heat.

3 · Ladle the jam into jars, leaving ¼ inch headspace. Wipe the rims with a clean, damp cloth, if necessary, and screw the lids on the jars. Process in a boiling-water bath for 10 minutes (see Water-Bath Canning, page 15). Remove the jars and set them upright on a clean kitchen towel. Let cool to room temperature before storing in a cool, dark place for up to 1 year. Refrigerate once opened, and use within 6 months. If any jars have failed to seal properly, store them in the refrigerator and enjoy those first.

SPICED TOMATO JAM

··· MAKES 2½ PINTS ···

A little spicy, vinegary, and sweet, this is one of my favorite condiments to serve with cheese. Beyond that, it's wonderful on crostini (page 194) and also on a smoked turkey sandwich.

5 pounds (2.3 kg) ripe red plum tomatoes

2 large lemons

2 cups (200 g) vanilla sugar (see page 57)

2 tablespoons good-quality aged balsamic vinegar

1 teaspoon fine sea salt

8 whole cloves

2 bay leaves

2 fresh chile peppers, minced

EQUIPMENT

5 sterilized ½-pint jars and their lids

Basic water-bath canning equipment (see page 15)

1 · Cut off the stem end of the tomatoes and peel them with a vegetable peeler. Cut them in half lengthwise and scoop out and discard the seeds. Cut the tomatoes in half again lengthwise into quarters, and cut the quarters into 2 or 3 pieces. Put them in a large nonreactive heavy-bottomed saucepan or preserving pot as you work.

2 · Zest the lemons with a vegetable peeler, taking care to get just the thin outer skin and no pith. Chop the zest finely and juice the lemons, discarding the seeds. Add the zest

and juice to the pot with the tomatoes. Stir in the sugar, vinegar, salt, cloves, bay leaves, and chile peppers. Bring to a simmer over medium heat, stirring to dissolve the sugar. Continue to cook at a lively simmer until the jam is glossy and thick enough that you can drag a path along the bottom with a silicone spatula. When the jam is ready, fish out and discard the bay leaves and cloves.

3 · Ladle the jam into the sterilized jars, leaving ½ inch headspace. Wipe the rims clean, if necessary, with a clean, damp cloth and screw the lids on the jars.

4 · Process for 15 minutes in a boiling-water bath (see Water-Bath Canning, page 15). Remove the jars and set them upright on a clean kitchen towel. Let the jars cool to room temperature before storing in a cool, dark place for up to 1 year. Refrigerate after opening.

VARIATION · Using yellow tomatoes instead of red yields a lovely, deep golden-colored jam. Look for yellow plum tomatoes or medium yellow globe tomatoes such as Lemon Boy. Follow the same instructions using white balsamic vinegar in place of red.

SAVORY MINT SAUCE

··· MAKES 1⅓ CUPS ···

This is one of the simplest sauces to make, and one of the most versatile. In Sicily it is known as zogghiu and is believed to be Maltese in origin. It is used to dress grilled fish, meat, and vegetables (page 197). It is also delicious spooned onto grilled bread and topped with fresh summer tomatoes. In this version, I've added some chopped walnuts to the basic sauce for a little extra body. See the variations that follow for more ways to switch up this spunky, garlicky sauce.

2 lightly packed cups (28 g) fresh mint leaves

2 lightly packed cups (28 g) fresh flat-leaf parsley leaves

2 large cloves garlic, coarsely chopped

1 teaspoon fine sea salt

¼ cup (28 g) coarsely chopped walnuts

3 tablespoons white wine vinegar

¾ cup (165 g) extra-virgin olive oil, plus more to cover

1 • Place the mint and parsley leaves, garlic, and salt in the bowl of a food processor fitted with the metal blade. Pulse briefly to chop the leaves. Add the nuts and pulse again until everything is coarsely chopped. With the motor running, add the vinegar, 1 tablespoon at a time. Turn off the motor and scrape down the sides of the bowl if necessary. Then, with the motor running, drizzle in the oil. You should end up with a sauce that is somewhat thinner than classic basil pesto, but thick and spoonable nonetheless.

2 • Scrape the sauce into a jar or container and top off with a thin layer of olive oil. Store in the refrigerator for up to 1 week, or in the freezer for up to 6 months. If you like, divide the sauce between two or three containers before storing.

VARIATIONS

Add 3 or 4 anchovy fillets and 1 tablespoon capers.

Substitute almonds for the walnuts.

Add a handful of finely chopped olives and a generous pinch of dried peperoncini flakes or minced fresh peperoncini.

Preserving Pesto

Roberto Panizza did not intend to become the Ambassador of Pesto. It just happened, the way these things sometimes do when you are trying to rescue an iconic food from its own success.

And pesto, according to Panizza, a restaurateur and specialty foods shop owner in Genoa, was in need of rescuing. After all, until fairly recently in history, this aromatic green sauce of basil, olive oil, salt, pine nuts, and cheese, traditionally made with a mortar and pestle, was confined to the city and its surrounding region, Liguria, a rugged coastal sweep of northwestern Italy. Now it is known the world over and its iterations are countless: spinach pesto, parsley pesto, sun-dried tomato pesto, cilantro pesto, garlic scape pesto, stinging nettle pesto, pumpkinseed pesto, and more.

It's not that Panizza minds those variations; even basil pesto, he acknowledges, has evolved over the centuries from a coarse paste of garlic and basil to a more refined, creamier sauce with pine nuts and Parmigiano cheese. His aim is to make sure that this quintessential version, *pesto alla Genovese*, does not get lost in the shuffle.

"The word *pesto* refers specifically to that sauce, which is made with specific ingredients," says Panizza. "For example, there are hundreds of types of basil, but only one is right for pesto." Panizza travels the globe, mortar and pestle in hand, giving classes and demonstrations on how to make traditional pesto. In 2007 he helped to launch an international pesto-making competition that takes place every other year in Genoa's Palazzo Ducale. Over the course of one (long) day, a field of 100 contestants, each wielding a marble mortar and wooden pestle, is whittled down to a single winner. The 2008 winner was Danny Bowien, co-founder of Mission Chinese Food in San Francisco; the 2014 champion was an 85-year-old woman from Montoggio, north of the Genoa.

Traditional pesto, Panizza says, stars the young, tender leaves (no larger than a teaspoon) of a variety of basil called *basilico Genovese*, known for its sweet perfume. Like San Marzano tomatoes and prosciutto di Parma, true Genovese basil carries a DOP (*Denominazione di Origine Protetta*) designation, which means that it is grown in a specific way, in a specific geographic area, in this case on hillsides above the city that face the sea.

The other essential ingredients for the sauce are garlic (preferably mild, even more preferably from nearby Vessalico); pine nuts (all the better if they are the sweet variety grown around Pisa); coarse sea salt; olive oil (mild, buttery oil from Liguria is best); and a mix of grated Parmigiano-Reggiano and Pecorino Fiore Sardo cheeses.

To appreciate Panizza's devotion, it is important to understand the role that pesto plays in Ligurian cuisine and culture. It is not just a sauce, it is *the* sauce—for dressing pasta, for seasoning soup, for layering in lasagne—a staple of the daily diet dating back to at least the mid-nineteenth century, probably longer. Pesto's bright flavor and intense herbal aroma are as familiar to the people of Genoa as the sparkling blue Ligurian Sea into which the city spills or the warren of narrow streets called *carrugi* that make up its historical center.

If Panizza seems more devoted than most, it is because he has spent much of his life immersed in the art of the sauce. Since the 1970s, his family has owned a collection of gourmet food shops in Genoa that sell everything from caviar to candy. When the demand for pesto began to grow in the 1980s, they started producing fresh batches to sell in their shops. Now Panizza's company produces fresh and bottled pesto, both made with DOP basil and Parmigiano-Reggiano—though, he concedes, not with a mortar and pestle. In 2010, he opened a restaurant called Il Genovese, which serves pasta with the family's pesto, as well as other typical Ligurian dishes.

On a blistering July day, Panizza and I drive into the hills to see where the basil is grown, in terraced greenhouses, as it has been for at least a century. We stop at the farm of Ruggero Rossi, who cultivates the herb year-round, according to DOP specifications. Rossi, who has been growing DOP basil for Panizza and other clients since 1998, staggers the seeding and harvesting so that there is always basil ready to be picked. In summer, he says, it takes about 20 days for the plant to reach the harvest stage; in winter, up to 50.

We walk along a ledge that runs the length of one of the greenhouses, an emerald carpet at our feet. The air is saturated with the perfume of the herb. There are narrow planks positioned at intervals over the vast bed of basil, like bridges. On each plank is a person lying on his or her side, propped up on one elbow, carefully pulling up the basil plants one at a time, roots and all, and arranging them in small bunches. There are no more than four concave leaves on each plant, and the largest leaves are no bigger than my thumbprint.

The plants are plucked out with the roots attached to increase the shelf life of the leaves. Plus, you can't make pesto from second-growth leaves; they would not meet DOP criteria and would be too mature and aggressive in flavor. Once all the first-growth basil in a greenhouse has been harvested, the soil is turned and remixed and a new crop is planted.

On the drive back to the city, Panizza reflects on the campaign to preserve pesto. "We Italians can be a little bit obsessive with our rules," he allows. "But we feel it's important to save these traditions." His efforts seem to be paying off. The biannual championship now attracts contestants from around the world, from Russia to the United States and from South Africa to South America, and they are getting better at making the sauce.

"In the beginning there were lots of different sauces, but they weren't pesto," Panizza says. "Now it is becoming difficult to choose a winner because people have learned the technique, they know how to work with the mortar and pestle, and they are perfecting their recipes."

CLASSIC PESTO GENOVESE

· · · MAKES ABOUT 1 CUP (200 G) · · ·

This recipe is based on one shared by Roberto Panizza, Genoa's own Pesto Ambassador (see page 169). Making it with a mortar and pestle yields a creamier sauce than using a food processor. However, either technique works.

2 medium cloves garlic (peeled)

2 ounces (57 g) pine nuts

2 to 3 lightly packed cups (60 to 70 g) fresh, preferably young, basil leaves

1½ teaspoons coarse sea salt

1 cup (100 g) freshly grated Parmigiano-Reggiano

½ cup (30 g) freshly grated Pecorino Fiore Sardo; substitute Pecorino Romano if you can't find Fiore Sardo

¼ to ⅓ cup (55 to 73 g) extra-virgin olive oil, plus more for topping off the jars

EQUIPMENT

Mortar and pestle, or a food processor

Clean 1-pint jar and its lid

1 · To make the pesto using a mortar and pestle: Place the garlic cloves and pine nuts in the mortar and mash them with the pestle until creamy. Scoop the mixture out and set it aside in a small bowl. Add the basil leaves to the mortar and sprinkle the salt over them. Grind the basil leaves by gently moving the pestle around the interior of the mortar in a circular motion. Return the garlic-nut mixture to the mortar and gently stir everything together until well combined. Sprinkle in the cheeses and stir to combine. Finally, drizzle in the oil and stir until well incorporated.

To make the pesto in a food processor: Pack the basil into the bowl of a food processor and sprinkle in the pine nuts, garlic, and 1 teaspoon salt. Pulse until coarsely chopped. With the motor running, drizzle 2 tablespoons of the oil through the feed tube, until the mixture forms a thick paste. Stop and scrape down the sides of the bowl. Resume adding olive oil until the paste has thinned out to a sauce consistency (you may not use it all). Scrape the pesto into a bowl and stir in the cheeses. Taste and stir in a little more oil or salt if you like.

2 · For both methods: Scoop the pesto into the jar and smooth out the top. Cover completely with a thin film of olive oil, cap tightly, and, if not using immediately, store in the refrigerator for up to 3 days. Be sure to top off with oil each time you use the pesto to prevent it from turning dark.

Alternatively, store in the freezer for up to 6 months. If you like, divide the sauce between two or three small containers and refrigerate or freeze. Or, for even smaller portions to flavor soups, stews, and sauces, spoon the sauce into ice cube trays and freeze. Once the cubes are solid, pop them out of the trays, place them in a zipper-lock freezer bag, and return them to the freezer.

PESTO ABRUZZESE

· · · MAKES ABOUT 1 PINT · · ·

Don't let the word pesto confuse you. This raw vegetable paste is not for tossing with cooked pasta. It's a flavor base, an ingenious little shortcut that I learned from my friend Giulia Scappaticcio and her mother-in-law, Francesca. Together with the rest of their family they operate Casale Centurione, a guest house in the Abruzzo countryside. Francesca keeps a large container of this pesto in the refrigerator and adds generous dollops of it to skillets and saucepans as a starter for soups, sauces, and stews. When I'm short on time, I use it in place of the Italian "holy trinity" of flavor bases—minced carrot, celery, and onion. When I'm cooking more leisurely, I use both to create an extra layer of flavor.

4 medium carrots, cut into pieces or coarsely chopped

2 celery stalks, plus a handful of leaves if you have them, coarsely chopped

1 small yellow onion, cut into large dice

3 cloves garlic, coarsely chopped

Handful of fresh flat-leaf parsley leaves

2 teaspoons fine sea salt

½ cup (110 g) extra-virgin olive oil, plus more as needed

1 · Combine the carrots, celery, onion, garlic, parsley, and salt in the bowl of a food processor fitted with the metal blade. Pulse to break up the vegetables. With the motor running, drizzle in as much of the olive oil as needed to make a thick, coarse paste.

2 · Spoon the paste into a clean (or sterilized) wide-mouth jar and press it down with the back of a spoon. Top off with more oil (the paste doesn't have to be completely submerged).

3 · Store the pesto in the refrigerator and spoon out as needed. Use only in recipes that call for cooking the pesto; it doesn't taste good raw, but it makes a great starting point for almost any Italian soup, stew, or sauce. Just sauté the pesto in a little olive oil over low heat until fragrant and slightly softened; then proceed with the recipe (see Classic Meat Sauce, page 122, or Zuppa di Pasta e Fagioli, page 129). Use the pesto within 2 weeks.

CAPONATA

One summer when I was a teenager, my family spent some time visiting friends on the western coast of Sicily. Among the culinary highlights I still remember: freshly caught sea urchins seasoned only with fresh lemon juice; heavenly gelato-stuffed brioches; and this sweet-and-sour eggplant salad. I love caponata for its versatility: You can serve it as a topping for crostini, or as a side to roast chicken, grilled lamb, or sausages (page 220), or you can top it with a fried egg and call it a meal. Caponata keeps for at least a week in the refrigerator, but for longer keeping, divide it up into small containers and freeze.

2 pounds (907 g) firm eggplant (choose smaller ones, which are less likely to have lots of seeds)

Fine sea salt

¼ cup (55 g) sunflower oil or other vegetable oil, for frying

4 to 6 tablespoons extra-virgin olive oil

1 large onion (about 6 ounces/170 g)

1 celery heart or 3 stalks, cut crosswise into ¼-inch pieces

1 cup (227 g) Small-Batch Tomato Sauce (page 120) or best-quality store-bought tomato sauce

1¼ cups (200 g) meaty green olives, pitted and chopped into large pieces

2 tablespoons capers in salt or brine, rinsed and patted dry

Freshly ground black pepper

3 tablespoons sugar

6 to 8 tablespoons white wine vinegar

2 tablespoons white balsamic vinegar (optional)

3 tablespoons coarsely chopped fresh flat-leaf parsley

1 · Trim and peel the eggplant and cut crosswise into ¾-inch-thick rounds, then cut the rounds into ¾-inch cubes. Put the eggplant in a colander set over a bowl and sprinkle with salt. Set a plate on top and weight it down with a heavy object. Let sit for 1 hour to release the eggplant's bitter juices. (The salted and pressed eggplant will also absorb less oil during frying.)

2 · Heat the sunflower oil in a large skillet over medium-high heat and line a plate with paper towels. When the oil is shimmering, add one-third of the eggplant, taking care not to crowd the skillet. Fry, stirring every so often, until the cubes are browned, about 4 minutes. Transfer to the prepared plate. Fry the remaining eggplant in two more batches and let drain on the paper towels.

3 · Carefully drain off any excess oil and wipe the skillet clean (or use a clean skillet). Pour in the olive oil and heat over medium heat.

(recipe continues)

Add the onion and cook, stirring often, until softened and beginning to brown around the edges, about 5 minutes. Stir in the celery and cook until just beginning to soften, about 5 minutes. Pour in the tomato sauce and bring to a simmer. Simmer for 5 minutes; then add the olives and capers and season with a few grindings of pepper. Stir in the sugar and cook for a couple of minutes to dissolve. Stir in 6 tablespoons of the white wine vinegar and the balsamic vinegar, if using (or stir in 8 tablespoons white wine vinegar if not using the balsamic), and simmer for an additional 5 minutes to allow the flavors to mingle and the sauce to thicken.

4 • Add the reserved eggplant and the parsley to the pan and stir gently to coat with the sauce. Taste and adjust the seasoning with more salt or sugar if you like. Cook just until the eggplant is heated through. Remove from the heat and let the caponata cool completely. Store in the refrigerator. Caponata will keep for at least a week in the fridge; for longer keeping, spoon it into pint-size containers and freeze for up to 6 months.

CURING OLIVES

Never did I imagine that I would one day cure my own olives. I don't own or even live near an olive grove (though I have some lucky friends who do). But the deeper I got into research for this book, the more curious I became about whether it would be possible to make good home-cured olives.

The answer? An emphatic yes! All you really need is some salt and a few weeks of your (mostly hands-off) time. And olives, of course.

Procuring raw, uncured olives is easier than you might think. Although I travel to Italy often, I live in Virginia, and as far as I know there are no olive groves anywhere near my suburban home. I found my solution at Chaffin Family Orchards, in Oroville, California (www.chaffinfamilyorchards. com). This third-generation family farm in the Sacramento Valley produces award-winning olive oil and grass-fed beef, and, lucky for me, sells raw olives online.

In California, like in Italy, olives are harvested in fall, usually from mid-September through November. They can be picked green (unripe), purple-black (ripe), and anywhere in between. But no matter how ripe, an olive picked right off the tree is inedible, hard, and extremely bitter due to a compound called oleuropein. It does a number on your tongue. Curing the olives is necessary to soften the fruit and tame the bitterness, in essence to make them palatable.

There are several simple methods for curing olives, including brining, salt-curing, and lye-curing. Olives cured in a lye (sodium hydroxide) solution are less bitter than those that are cured in salt or brine. But lye is a caustic substance that requires some extra precautionary measures, so I prefer to stick to the natural curing methods of salting and brining. Plus, I prefer olives that have something of a bitter bite to them; they have more character.

Curing olives in brine yields a plump olive that is pleasantly bitter. Both unripe and ripe olives can be brined successfully. Salt-curing gives you those black, shriveled, intensely flavored "Moroccan-style" olives that you sometimes see in olive bars. I grew up on these olives (my Italian mother used them often in cooking) and absolutely love their strong, appealingly bitter flavor and their soft texture. For salt-cured olives, you must start with ripe olives.

I have found home-curing olives to be a completely worthwhile project. I am one of those people who always has olives on hand to put out when company comes, as part of a family aperitivo offering on the weekend, or for tossing in salads or with pasta.

Beyond practical reasons, it is just really interesting, not to mention satisfying, to participate in the transformation of this bitter, hard fruit into something so savory and delicious, in just a few short weeks.

Whether you are harvesting your own olives or buying online, it is important to begin the curing process soon after they are picked. Use only fresh, unblemished olives; toss any with bruises, soft spots, or lots of little speckles.

SALT-CURED OLIVES

··· MAKES 5 PINTS (1.5 KG) ···

I enjoy salt-cured olives the way others enjoy peanuts; one after another after another. Also known as oil-cured or dry-cured olives, these are glossy, creased black olives, sometimes labeled Moroccan olives in stores, with soft flesh and a bitter finish. They pair well with other assertive flavors—anchovies, garlic, capers, and sharp cheeses—and bitter greens such as spicy arugula or crunchy radicchio or endive.

Curing olives with salt is a simple, mostly hands-off project. What you really need is cold weather, to keep the olives from spoiling, and patience to give the transformation time to happen properly, anywhere from 6 to 8 weeks. Once cured, the olives are rubbed with olive oil, which makes them shine and softens their skins. You can leave them as is or season them with additional flavors, from citrus zest to crushed red chile pepper or fennel seeds. Your choice. By the way, this recipe makes a lot of olives. You can easily cut this recipe in half. Or share your bounty with the olive lovers in your life.

6 pounds (2.7 kg) raw ripe black olives, such as Mission (see Sources, page 292)

3 to 4 pounds (1.4 to 1.8 kg) fine sea salt

About ½ cup (110 g) extra-virgin olive oil

Optional flavor additions: whole or crushed peperoncini (page 148) or crushed red chile pepper; whole fennel seeds; strips of lemon or orange peel; crushed dried oregano or rosemary

EQUIPMENT

2 clean 1-gallon wide-mouth glass jars or food-safe white plastic buckets

5 sterilized 1-pint jars and their lids

1 · Rinse the olives in cold water. Remove any stems and leaves, and discard any olives with blemishes or soft spots.

2 · Sprinkle a layer of salt in the bottom of the jars or buckets. Add a layer of olives. Continue to layer the salt and olives, ending with a layer of salt on top. The olives should be more or less submerged in the salt. Set the jars or buckets in a cold, dry spot; no need to cover them. I put mine on a shelf in my garage. Avoid cellars or basements where there is likely to be mildew, which could turn the olives moldy.

(recipe continues)

3 · After about a week, begin to check on the olives; within 2 weeks they will start to look shriveled, though if you taste one it will still be too hard and bitter to eat. There might be liquid at the bottom of the jar or bucket. You can drain it if you like, but it's not necessary.

4 · Continue to check the olives every few days, or at least once a week. You can mix them if you like, but it's not necessary. If there is a lot of liquid at the bottom of the jar or bucket, carefully pour it out, holding your hand over the mouth to keep any olives from escaping. If the amount of liquid is small, leave it be.

5 · Your olives should be ready within 6 to 8 weeks. Keep tasting each week, brushing the salt off and rinsing the olive before tasting. You will know when the olives are ready; they will be wrinkled but still plump, with a mellow flavor and pleasantly bitter finish.

6 · When the olives are ready, pour them out of the jar or bucket into a colander. Shake off as much excess salt as you can. Spread the olives out on rimmed baking sheets and let them dry overnight. You should end up with 3 to 4 pounds (1.4 to 1.8 kg) of olives, or 10 full cups.

7 · Transfer the olives to a bowl. Drizzle in the olive oil. Use your hands and fingers to work the oil into the olives so they are thoroughly coated in it. Pack the olives into the pint-size jars. At this point, you can add any of the optional flavors. Go easy on the flavoring, though; much of the appeal of these olives comes from their own rich, pleasantly bitter flavor. Store the olives in the refrigerator, where they will keep for up to 1 year.

BRINE-CURED OLIVES

I always keep a container of olives in brine in the fridge, whether store-bought or my own. Not only are they my go-to party snack for impromptu entertaining, but they are also pretty much part of my daily diet. I toss a few on my plate to go with an omelet or fried egg for lunch; I chop them up and make pasta puttanesca for dinner; I mash them to a coarse paste and spread them on crostini or in sandwiches. As with salt-cured olives, brined olives are easy to make. You just need time and a little patience.

3 pounds (1.4 kg) raw green, purple, or black (unripe or ripe) olives, about 9 cups (see Sources, page 292)

Distilled water

Fine sea salt

¼ cup (59 g) white wine vinegar, plus more as needed

Optional flavor additions: whole black peppercorns, whole coriander seeds, bay leaf, dried peperoncini, garlic cloves

EQUIPMENT

1 clean 1-gallon deep glass bowl or food-safe white plastic bucket

1 sterilized ½-gallon jar and its lid, or smaller jars with lids (quart- or pint-size)

1 · Rinse the olives in cold water. Remove any stems and leaves, and discard any olives with blemishes or soft spots. With a sharp paring knife, cut a vertical slice down one side of each olive.

2 · Combine 6 cups water and ⅓ cup (113 g) salt in a large bowl and mix gently to dissolve the salt. Place the olives in the clean bowl or pail and pour the brine over them. Place a plate on top of the olives and weight it down with a heavy object to keep them submerged. Set the olives in a cool spot or in a corner of your kitchen where they will not be in the way. I keep mine on a shelf in the garage. You can also put them in the refrigerator. Avoid cellars or basements where there is likely to be mildew, which could turn the olives moldy.

(recipe continues)

3 · Let the olives cure for 1 week, stirring them two or three times during this period. Drain the olives and discard the brine. Taste one; it's likely that the olive will still be much too bitter to eat. Mix up another batch of brine using another 6 cups water and ⅓ cup salt. Return the olives to the bowl or pail and pour the brine over them. Weight them down and let them cure for another week, stirring them two or three times.

4 · Continue to taste the olives and change the brine every week until the olives are to your liking, anywhere from 6 to 10 weeks. They will still be bitter, but pleasantly so.

5 · When the olives are ready, drain them once more. Mix up a new batch of brine, this time adding the vinegar to the water and salt. Place the olives in the jar or jars and pour the brine over them. Add any of the optional spices, but don't add a lot; the idea is to flavor the brine without masking the taste of the olives. I usually add 1 dried peperoncino and sometimes a garlic clove.

6 · Cap the jar or jars and let the olives cure in the refrigerator for at least 2 to 4 weeks before using. The olives will improve in flavor and in texture the longer they sit, and they will keep in the refrigerator for up to 1 year.

OVEN-ROASTED PORCHETTA SANDWICHES

··· MAKES 8 SERVINGS ···

Porchetta—generously seasoned, deboned, stuffed, and roasted whole pig—is sold in marketplaces all over central Italy, particularly the hill towns of Lazio, beyond Rome, out to Abruzzo, Le Marche, Tuscany, and Umbria. Making great porchetta is an art form; there are regional and national competitions and awards. For producers, it's a way of life. Porchetta trucks travel from town to town, setting up in piazzas and farmers' markets, purveyors deftly carving slice after slice and selling the spiced meat by the kilo or piled into large crusty rolls. The seasonings vary from place to place and from producer to producer, but you can almost always count on rosemary, garlic, and fennel being part of the mix. My simplified, home-cooking version of this iconic street food is based on the porchetta I grew up eating in Abruzzo. I have to brag that it tastes pretty darned authentic.

3 tablespoons extra-virgin olive oil, plus more for rubbing on the pork

1 small fennel bulb, coarsely chopped, about 1 cup (113 g)

⅓ cup (40 g) coarsely chopped garlic, about 12 cloves

3½ to 4 pounds (1.6 to 1.8 kg) boneless pork shoulder (Boston butt)

¼ cup (70 g) Porchetta Salt (page 146)

8 ciabatta rolls or other crusty rustic rolls

1 · Place the oil, fennel, and garlic in a medium skillet and cook, stirring, over low heat until the vegetables have begun to soften, 7 to 8 minutes. Remove from the heat and let cool.

2 · **Butterfly the pork:** Lay the shoulder on its side on a cutting board. Beginning at the top, make an incision about 1 inch from the edge and 1 inch deep. Continue to slice down the length of the pork, unfolding the meat as you go. Work slowly and deliberately, going no deeper than an inch and pulling back the meat as you work. Once you've cut the entire length of the roast, start at the top again and make another, deeper cut, again working down the length of the roast and pulling back the meat as you go. Continue to slice and unfold the shoulder from top to bottom, until you've cut your way through the roast. When

(recipe continues)

you're done it should be lying flat and open, more or less. Mine is never perfect. If you don't care to tackle the task yourself, ask your butcher to butterfly it for you.

3 · Sprinkle 1 tablespoon of the porchetta salt over the surface of the pork. Spread the fennel-garlic mixture on top, then sprinkle another tablespoon of the salt on top. Beginning at one of the short ends, roll up the pork as tightly as you can, arranging it seam side down on the cutting board. Tie the roast at 1-inch intervals with kitchen twine. Drizzle 1 tablespoon of oil over the meat and rub it in gently. Then sprinkle all over with the remaining 2 tablespoons salt.

4 · Set the porchetta on a rack inside a roasting or baking pan. Refrigerate, uncovered, for 24 hours.

5 · Remove the pork from the refrigerator and let it sit at room temperature for 1 hour. Heat the oven to 275°F.

6 · Roast the porchetta, uncovered, until the top is deeply browned and the meat is well cooked and fork-tender throughout, 3 to 4 hours. It should register 160 to 170°F on a meat thermometer. Remove the roast from the oven, tent with aluminum foil, and let sit for at least 15 minutes, preferably 30. Turn off the oven and place the rolls inside to warm up for a few minutes.

7 · Transfer the porchetta to a cutting board and remove the twine. Reserve the juices in the roasting pan. Cut the roast into thin slices, setting aside any crusty pieces.

8 · **Assemble the sandwiches:** Split the warm rolls and spoon some of the juices onto each bottom half. Pile the pork generously on top, making sure each sandwich has a piece or two of the crust. Top with the upper half of the rolls and serve.

BAKED WHOLE TROUT
with Citrus Salt

··· MAKES 4 SERVINGS ···

*Cooking whole fish can seem intimidating, even to an accomplished home cook.
But fishmongers and supermarket seafood departments have made it easy for us.
You can buy already cleaned, scaled, boned, and gutted fish—with heads and tails
still attached—at many well-stocked seafood markets and grocery stores today.
Just be sure the fish you buy is good and fresh. The flesh should be firm when you
poke it—and feel free to ask the clerk at the fish counter to poke it—and the eyes
should be clear, not cloudy. Fresh fish smells just that: fresh and clean and not at
all fishy. This recipe is one of the easiest ways to put an elegant dinner on the table
without much effort. All you have to do is open the fish up like a book, season,
close, and bake. I make this for my family with a side of wilted rapini or steamed
broccolini, and roasted or boiled new potatoes drizzled with lemon olive oil.*

4 small whole rainbow trout, about
  12 ounces (340 g) each; cleaned and
  gutted, heads and tails still attached

8 teaspoons Lemon Olive Oil (page 153)
  or extra-virgin olive oil, plus more for
  drizzling

½ cup (7 g) fresh flat-leaf parsley leaves

2 cloves garlic

Citrus Salt (page 145)

Freshly ground black pepper

½ lemon

1 · Preheat the oven to 450°F. Line a baking
sheet with parchment paper.

2 · With a sharp knife, make diagonal slashes
at 1-inch intervals along both sides of the fish.
Open up the fish and drizzle 2 teaspoons of
the lemon oil over the interior of each one.

3 · Chop the parsley and garlic together until
they are reduced to a fine mince. Sprinkle the
parsley mixture over the interior of the fish,
followed by a light sprinkle of citrus salt.
Close the fish and rub each one all over with
a drizzle of oil. Sprinkle lightly with more
citrus salt and a grinding of pepper.

4 · Arrange the fish on the prepared baking
sheet. Roast until the fish is cooked through
and the skin is browned in places, 15 to
20 minutes. Remove from the oven and
squeeze the lemon half over the fish. Garnish
each with a few more drops of lemon oil and a
pinch of citrus salt and serve.

VEGETABLE ZUPPA
with Olio Santo

Despite the fact that you see a written recipe before you, I rarely make this soup the same way twice. It all depends on what's in season, what's in my pantry, and what mood I'm in. One thing that never changes, though, is the way I cook the vegetables—low and slow. Cook them gently until they are meltingly tender and have given up all their flavors to the soup. You can serve this soup several ways: as is, with cooked farro stirred in, or pureed and topped with croutons (see Cook's Note).

3 tablespoons extra-virgin olive oil

3 small or 1 medium-large carrot, diced, about ¾ cup (113 g)

1 cup (113 g) diced red spring onion or regular red onion

1 large celery stalk, leaves included, diced, about ¾ cup (100 g)

1 large clove garlic, minced

2 tablespoons minced fresh flat-leaf parsley, or 1 tablespoon dried parsley

2 medium zucchini, diced, about 1½ cups (227 g)

8 ounces (227 g) green beans, cut into 1-inch pieces

1 yellow potato, such as Yukon Gold, peeled and diced, about 1 cup (170 to 227 g)

½ teaspoon fine sea salt, or to taste

Freshly ground black pepper (optional)

1 quart Homemade Meat Broth (page 126), or best-quality commercial vegetable or chicken broth

2-inch piece of Parmigiano-Reggiano rind (optional)

1 cup (227 g) Passata di Pomodoro (page 117), or best-quality commercial tomato puree (optional)

1¼ cups (170 g) cooked farro (optional; see Cook's Note)

1 tablespoon chopped fresh basil

4 to 8 tablespoons Olio Santo (page 150)

Freshly grated Parmigiano-Reggiano, for serving

1 · In a large Dutch oven or heavy-bottomed pot, heat the olive oil, carrots, onion, celery, garlic, and parsley over medium-low heat. Cook, stirring often, until the vegetables turn shiny and begin to soften, 8 to 10 minutes. Take care not to let them brown.

2 · Add the zucchini, green beans, and potato, and season with the salt and a few grindings of pepper, if desired. Stir to combine. Reduce the heat to low and cover the pot. Let the vegetables cook slowly until they are tender, about 20 minutes. Check and stir them every few minutes to prevent them from sticking to the bottom of the pot.

3 • Stir in the broth and toss in the Parmigiano rind. Add the *passata*, if using. Raise the heat to medium-high and bring the soup to a boil. Reduce the heat to medium-low and cook, partially covered, until the vegetables are soft enough to mash with a wooden spoon, 45 to 60 minutes. Stir in the cooked farro, if using, and cook until heated through, 10 to 20 minutes longer. Otherwise, remove from the heat and stir in the basil.

4 • Ladle the soup into bowls and drizzle 1 to 2 tablespoons Olio Santo over each serving. Serve with grated Parmigiano on the side.

COOK'S NOTE • To cook the farro, rinse ½ cup (85 g) farro under cold water and put it in a saucepan with water to cover by 2 inches. Add a generous pinch of salt. Bring to a boil over medium-high heat and boil until the farro is tender but still slightly chewy, 15 to 20 minutes. Drain and add to the soup as directed.

COOK'S NOTE • To serve the soup as a puree, use an immersion blender to puree the soup right in the pot, adding a splash of broth or water if necessary to thin it. Ladle into bowls and garnish with a drizzle of Olio Santo and a handful of croutons.

SPAGHETTINI AL LIMONE

· · · MAKES 4 SERVINGS · · ·

Sorrento and the towns along the Amalfi Coast spill out into the Bay of Naples in a riot of color. This slice of southern Italy, famous for its beaches, profusion of flowers, staggering cliffs, and narrow coastal roads with hairpin turns, is drop-dead gorgeous. The food is fresh and zesty—think tomatoes, garlic, seafood, and lemons. Lots of lemons. Sorrento's aromatic and sweet lemons are known the world over. And they appear in many dishes. This one, spaghettini al limone, *has become something of a tourist must-have for people visiting the region, but with good reason. It's simple, and simply delicious. You can make it with or without cream, but I like it with; the cream tames the lemon without overpowering it. Use the best organic lemons you can find to give this dish its due.*

¼ cup (55 g) Lemon Olive Oil (page 153)

Finely grated zest of 1 lemon, plus 2 tablespoons juice

1 cup (250 g) heavy cream

1 pound (454 g) spaghettini (thin spaghetti)

½ cup (50 g) freshly grated Parmigiano-Reggiano, plus more for sprinkling

1 tablespoon minced fresh flat-leaf parsley

1 tablespoon minced fresh basil

Freshly ground black pepper

1 · Bring a large pot of water to a rolling boil and salt it generously.

2 · While the water is heating, make the sauce. Heat the lemon oil and lemon zest in a medium heavy-bottomed saucepan over low heat. Cook, stirring now and again, until the zest starts to sizzle gently. Stir in the cream and raise the heat to medium-high. Bring to a boil. Cook, stirring, until the cream is thickened, 3 to 5 minutes. Gradually whisk in the lemon juice, 1 tablespoon at a time. Turn off the heat and cover to keep warm.

3 · Cook the spaghettini according to the package instructions until al dente. Drain, reserving 1 cup of the cooking water. Return the pasta to the pot and add the sauce. Toss gently to combine. Add the cheese, parsley, basil, and a few grindings of pepper and toss again. Add a splash or two of cooking water if necessary to loosen the sauce. Toss once more and serve, sprinkling a little more cheese on each serving.

SIMPLE GREEN SALAD
with Seasoned Vinegar

··· MAKES 4 TO 6 SERVINGS ···

My husband likes to punch up salads with lots of additions—sliced mushrooms, peppers, radishes, scallions, and such. I enjoy these salads, but I'm more about the greens. Give me a bowl of freshly picked greens—some bitter, some tender, some spicy—and a simple dressing of good olive oil and vinegar and I'm happy. Here is the salad you'll find on my dinner table on any given night. As with most Italian cooking, the quality of the ingredients makes the dish.

8 to 10 ounces (227 to 280 g) mixed greens, such as arugula, butter lettuce, radicchio, and red romaine

Optional additions: handful of fresh herbs, a couple tablespoons grated carrot, 1 ripe tomato

2 tablespoons Herbed Fig Vinegar or Tart Cherry Vinegar (page 154)

4 tablespoons best-quality extra-virgin olive oil

1 teaspoon honey

Fine or flaky sea salt and freshly ground black pepper

1 · Place the greens in a large salad bowl and add any of the optional ingredients.

2 · Measure the vinegar into a bowl or glass measuring cup. Vigorously whisk in the olive oil until emulsified. Add the honey and whisk to combine. Season with salt and pepper to taste and whisk once more. Drizzle the dressing over the greens and toss gently until well coated. Serve soon after tossing.

BAKED OLIVES AND SALAMI
with Citrus

*Heating olives in the oven really brings out their flavor. This antipasto
mix makes a welcoming appetizer for a casual dinner party, especially
in fall, when there is a chill in the evening air. It's nice with a wedge of
good aged pecorino or provolone cheese. You can, of course, substitute
good store-bought olives; use a mix of green, purple, and cured.*

2 cups (340 grams) Brine-Cured Olives
(page 179) or a mix of brine-cured and
Salt-Cured Olives (page 177)

8 ounces (227 g) good-quality salami, cut
into ½-inch cubes

2 strips lemon zest (no white pith)

2 strips orange zest (no white pith)

3 cloves garlic, lightly crushed

3 tablespoons extra-virgin olive oil

3 tablespoons dry white wine

1 small rosemary sprig

1 dried peperoncino (page 148), crushed,
or a generous pinch of crushed red chile
pepper

1 · Preheat the oven to 325°F (165°C).

2 · Combine the olives, salami, citrus zests,
and garlic in a small baking dish. Add the oil
and wine and toss gently to coat the olives.
Tuck in the rosemary and sprinkle in the
peperoncino. Bake, uncovered, for 10 minutes; toss and bake until the olives are heated
through, another 5 to 10 minutes. Remove
from the oven and toss gently.

3 · Serve warm.

BLUE CHEESE BURGERS
with Tropea Onion Jam

· · · MAKES 4 SERVINGS · · ·

I'm going to boast on behalf of my mom here. She was making fat, juicy, gourmet burgers topped with caramelized onions before most of the chefs doing it these days were even born. Of course back then, I wasn't so keen on her homemade burgers and would gladly have traded mine for a skinny one from a fast-food joint. Foolish. I finally saw the light, and I'm happy to say that both my kids have always preferred a good homemade burger to anything they might get from a drive-through. I knew the moment I tasted this red onion jam that it would be great on a burger, and it is, especially with blue cheese added to the mix. For a tasty variation, try the onion jam on lamb and feta burgers.

1½ pounds (680 g) freshly ground beef
   chuck or sirloin, or a mix

Freshly ground black pepper

4 tablespoons (80 g) Gorgonzola Dolce

Fine sea salt

4 burger buns, split

4 tablespoons Tropea Onion Jam (page 165),
   or to taste

1 • Prepare a hot fire in a charcoal grill or preheat a gas grill on high.

2 • Put the beef in a bowl and sprinkle generously with pepper. Mix gently but thoroughly (I use my hands). Divide into 4 equal portions and shape into balls. Make a deep depression into the top of a ball and press 1 tablespoon of the cheese into it. Press the beef around the cheese to enclose it and pat the ball into a patty. Repeat to make 3 more stuffed patties. Right before cooking, season the patties lightly with salt.

3 • Coat the grill grates with a thin film of oil. Grill the burgers on one side until seared, 4 to 5 minutes. Turn and sear on the other side until nicely charred on the outside and juicy and medium-rare to medium inside, 4 to 5 minutes more. A minute or two before the burgers are done, place the buns, cut side down, on the grill to lightly char them.

4 • Place the burgers on the bottom half of the buns and top each with a tablespoon (or more) of the jam. Top with the upper half of the buns and serve.

CROSTINI
with Spiced Tomato Jam and Ricotta

··· MAKES ABOUT 32 CROSTINI, ENOUGH FOR 8 TO 10 APPETIZER SERVINGS ···

Here is my go-to antipasto, the one I can quickly throw together for an impromptu dinner party or when a guest turns up unexpectedly. A slather of ricotta, a dollop of spiced tomato jam, a slice of bread. That's it. If you have a little extra time, you can make your own ricotta (page 203); otherwise use the best quality you can find from a reliable source. None of that grainy commercial supermarket stuff!

¾ cup (170 g) Buttermilk Ricotta (page 203), well drained, or store-bought fresh ricotta

1 thin baguette (ficelle), cut on the bias into ½-inch-thick slices

8 ounces (227 g) Spiced Tomato Jam (page 166) or Golden Tomato Jam variation (page 166)

1 · Position an oven rack 4 inches from the broiler and turn the broiler on.

2 · Spread 1 rounded teaspoon ricotta on each of the bread slices and top with a rounded teaspoon of the jam. Arrange the slices on a rimmed baking sheet and broil until the topping is just starting to bubble and the edges of the bread are nicely browned, 1 to 2 minutes.

3 · Transfer the crostini to a serving platter and serve warm.

GRILLED SUMMER VEGETABLES
with Savory Mint Sauce

Grilling is my favorite way to prepare vegetables in summer. All of them, from assertive peppers to mild zucchini, benefit from spending a few minutes on the hot grates, just enough for them to soften up and absorb the smoky flavor. While they are still hot, I dollop the vegetables with spoonfuls of Savory Mint Sauce. Its bright, herbaceous flavor stands up nicely to the smoky notes, and the splashes of green make for a pretty presentation. Serve this as a side to grilled steak or chicken, or alongside a platter of cheese and salumi.

2 or 3 long, slim eggplants, about 1 pound (454 g)

Fine sea salt

2 large bell peppers, red or yellow, or one of each, about 1 pound (454 g)

2 medium zucchini, about 1 pound (454 g)

6 portobello mushrooms, about 1½ pounds (680 g)

Extra-virgin olive oil

Freshly ground black pepper

About 1 cup (227 g) Savory Mint Sauce (page 168), at room temperature

1 · Slice the eggplants in half lengthwise, cutting right through the stem ends. Make a series of deep crisscross slashes on the cut sides. Sprinkle with about ½ teaspoon sea salt (total) and set, cut side down, on a plate or in a colander for 30 to 60 minutes.

2 · Trim and core the peppers. Cut them lengthwise into quarters. Scrape out any seeds and white pith on the ribs. Trim the zucchini and cut them in half lengthwise. Remove the portobello stems, and scrape out the gills.

3 · Squeeze the eggplants lightly to remove any bitter juices and pat them dry.

4 · Prepare a charcoal grill or heat a gas grill to medium-high. Brush the grate with vegetable oil or spray with high-heat cooking spray.

5 · Brush the vegetables all over with olive oil and season with a little salt and pepper. Place them, cut side down, on the grill grate and grill, turning several times, until they are charred here and there and somewhat softened but still a little firm, 15 to 20 minutes. If necessary, move the vegetables to the perimeter of the grill to keep them from charring too much. Transfer the vegetables, as they are done, to a large serving platter.

6 · Spoon the mint sauce over the vegetables while they are still hot, and serve.

Slab Pancetta, page 226

FRESH CHEESES AND SIMPLE CURED MEATS

In November 2004, my husband and I took our two children to Italy for the first time. For a variety of reasons we ended up in Umbria. I was working on my first cookbook, about Italian soups and stews, and Umbria, with its lush hills, chilly mists, and earthy country food, seemed like a good place to conduct research.

Nearly every meal began with platters of house-made or local *salumi* (cured meats and sausages) and cheeses. For someone who was researching soups and stews, I consumed an inordinate amount of tangy wild boar sausages and sheep's milk cheese.

This ritual of setting out local *salumi* and cheeses occurs daily all over Italy, from Alto Adige to Sicily. There are countless variations on sausages, both fresh and dried, from the massive yet delicately flavored pistachio-studded mortadella from Emilia-Romagna to the ultra-spicy, spreadable 'nduja sausage from Calabria. Cheeses range from milky burrata and fluffy ricotta to crumbly extra-aged Parmigiano. These products, to me, offer the truest expression of Italian regional cuisine, of the land and what grows on it, of local flavors and preserving traditions.

This chapter is not intended to turn you into a master cheese maker or *salumiere*, but rather to offer a window—a peek—into the centuries-old Italian art of meat and milk preservation, and to introduce you to some simple techniques that will give you a better understanding of, and appreciation for, these essential foods of the Italian table.

MAKING FRESH CHEESE

There is nothing quite like an Italian cheese-making room in the morning, when the process of turning fresh milk into mozzarella and ricotta or other fresh cheese is in full swing. The air is thick with the warm aroma of curds, sweet and a little sour, with a bit of barnyard mixed in. It is one of the most comforting scents I know. The tile floor is splashed with puddles of whey, and the cheese maker (or cheese makers), suited up in white, are neatly cutting curd, or pressing it into baskets, or stretching it into balls or braids at a steady clip.

Cheese in Italy, both fresh and aged, is not something to put out when guests come calling; it is an essential part of the daily diet: ricotta on bread in the morning, Parmigiano grated onto pasta at lunch, a selection of cheeses served with salad as a light *secondo* (second course) in summer.

Most Italians don't make their own cheese; just about everyone lives within walking distance of (or, at most, a short bike ride or drive from) a cheese shop or cheese-making operation of some sort. The countryside from Alto Adige to Sicily is dotted with caseifici—dairy farms that produce a spectrum of cheeses made with milk from cows, buffalos, sheep, or goats. With few exceptions, every small town and mountain village has at least one shop that brings in fresh cheese every day, and there is always at least one cheesemonger's truck at the local farmers' market. Good cheese is everywhere.

But if most Italians don't make cheese at home, why should you? For one thing, it's fun. It is also rewarding. I love ogling the little rounds of just-made *primo latte* (page 208), neatly imprinted with the pattern of the draining basket. Put a round of that out next time you entertain and I guarantee you will earn some wows. Presiding over the transformation of milk into cheese, even a simple fresh cheese like ricotta, will give you a better understanding of the cheese-making process in general, and a better appreciation of this culinary art that predates the Romans. You will become more curious and therefore more knowledgeable about cheese, about selecting it, tasting it, and enjoying it.

The recipes that follow are all fairly simple and produce fresh, unaged cheeses. Read the following section before you get started; it will help to make your cheese-making endeavors successful from the get-go.

Ingredients

Good cheese comes from good milk. Professional cheese makers start with the raw product; that is, milk that has not been pasteurized—heated to kill bacteria—or homogenized—treated to keep the cream from separating. Raw milk can be tough to source for the home cook, and it is not always legal, depending on state dairy laws. (Federal law bans the interstate sale or distribution of raw milk.)

Most supermarket milk has been ultra-pasteurized, meaning it has been heated briefly to 280°F, a process that kills nearly all the bacteria. While this makes it safe for drinking, it also alters the flavor of the milk and impedes its ability to transform into cheese. Most supermarket milk is also homogenized. This process of breaking down the fat globules so that they don't separate into cream interferes with milk's ability to separate into curds and whey, the first step in making cheese.

What's the alternative? I rely on whole pasteurized, non-homogenized milk from several local dairies that I buy at farmers' markets and at well-stocked grocery stores. This milk is often, but not always, sold in glass half-gallon bottles and has a telltale cap of thick cream milk at the top, which is why it is sometimes called "creamline" milk. It has been pasteurized, meaning it has been heated either to 145°F for 30 minutes or to 161°F for 15 seconds (high-temperature short-time pasteurization). Pasteurization, more gentle than ultra-pasteurization, kills harmful bacteria and increases the milk's shelf life without affecting its flavor or its ability to coagulate. You should be able to find good local milk without too much trouble; the DIY food movement, along with the proliferation of farmers' markets over the past few decades, has created a demand for it and made it more accessible.

To turn that milk into cheese, you need to introduce a coagulant, an ingredient that will transform it by forming curds. In the simplest cheeses, this is done by slowly heating the milk and then adding acid: typically lemon juice, vinegar, buttermilk, or calcium chloride. Any of those will work in making ricotta at home (page 203), but I use buttermilk because to me it tastes closest to the ricotta I buy in Italy.

Another coagulant is animal rennet, derived from enzymes found in the stomach lining of calves and other animals. It has been an essential ingredient in cheese making for thousands of years, and is commonly used to create a firmer, more solid curd. Commercial rennet is available in liquid or tablet form; I prefer liquid, as it is easier to measure and incorporate into milk.

Starter cultures and secondary cultures—molds and bacteria—have more specific roles in cheese making. Different strains contribute different characteristics, such as the blue veining and pungent flavor in Gorgonzola and other blue cheeses; or the bloomy white rind and creamy texture of, say, robiola. I mention these cultures only in passing, as they are integral to the craft of more advanced cheese making. For the recipes in this chapter, rennet is the most exotic ingredient you will need.

Salt is used to flavor Primo Latte (page 208). You can buy special cheese salt, which dissolves quickly, but I find that fine sea salt works well.

Equipment

Here is a list of equipment needed to make the cheeses in this chapter. With one or two exceptions, you probably already have most of it in your kitchen.

- Colander or large fine-mesh sieve for draining curds

- Tight-weave cheesecloth or butter muslin for draining soft cheese curds (see Sources, page 292)
- Stainless steel ladle for ladling curds into a colander or mold
- Large skimmer or kitchen spider for scooping curds
- Liquid measuring cups and measuring spoons
- Two 2½- by 5-inch plastic "basket" draining molds with slats (see Sources, page 292)
- Large wire whisk for stirring ingredients into milk
- Long palette knife (such as the kind used for frosting a cake) for cutting curd
- 11-by 17-inch baking sheet for holding molds

Tips and Techniques

- Make sure all your equipment is sanitized before you start. Wash your pots, ladles, measuring cups and spoons, and any other equipment in hot soapy water, rinse, and set everything to air-dry on a rack. Make sure your hands are also washed.

- Easy does it. Take your time and work carefully when making any of the cheeses in this chapter. Although simple to make, they can easily be ruined by inattention or heavy handling. Always stir the milk gently and never over-stir. Carefully monitor the temperature of the milk as it heats. Overheating the milk could render it unusable. Don't rush the process; enjoy it.

BUTTERMILK RICOTTA

··· MAKES ABOUT 2 CUPS (1 POUND/454 G) ···

This ricotta isn't true ricotta; real ricotta is made from the whey left over from cheese making, usually mozzarella or pecorino. It takes a lot of leftover whey to produce just a little ricotta, so this is a practical—and good—alternative for the home kitchen. It is adapted from Chef Michael Chiarello's book Casual Cooking: Wine Country Recipes for Family and Friends. *Many recipes for homemade ricotta use lemon juice, vinegar, or citric acid to curdle the milk. I've tried lots of different versions, but I always come back to this one. To me, it tastes closest to real fresh ricotta: sweet and creamy, with just the slightest tang. Use pasteurized rather than ultra-pasteurized milk for this recipe, as the ultra-pasteurization process affects the milk's ability to properly form curds.*

2 quarts (1.9 kg) whole pasteurized (not ultra-pasteurized) milk, preferably creamline (not homogenized)

1 pint (480 g) whole-milk buttermilk

EQUIPMENT

Wide colander

Tight-weave cheesecloth

Large (4-quart) stainless steel pot

Instant-read thermometer

1 · Line a wide colander with a double layer of damp cheesecloth (use a quadruple layer if the cheesecloth is not tight-weave).

2 · Combine the milk and buttermilk in the pot and set it over medium-high heat. Heat, stirring gently to prevent scorching, until warm. Stop stirring when the mixture is warmed through. As the milk heats up, curds will form. Use a wooden or silicone spatula to gently scrape the bottom of the pot to keep any curds from sticking.

3 · Bring the mixture to 180 to 190°F. At this point, the curds will form a billowy mass on the surface of the pot and the whey will be cloudy. Remove from the heat, cover, and let sit for 5 minutes. The whey should turn clearer, with a yellowish tint, and separate from the curds.

4 · Gently ladle the curds into the prepared colander, taking care not to break them up. Without pressing on the curds, let them drain for about 15 minutes, depending on how "loose" or "dry" you want your ricotta. (Keep in mind that it will firm up in the refrigerator.) Gather up the ends of the cheesecloth and squeeze very gently to release a little more whey, if you like.

5 · Spoon the ricotta into a clean container with a tight-fitting lid and refrigerate if you are not using it immediately. The ricotta will keep in the refrigerator for up to 1 week.

LIGURIAN PRESCINSEUA

· · · MAKES ABOUT 2 CUPS (1 POUND/454 G) · · ·

I have yet to encounter this fresh cheese outside Liguria, where I first tasted it. It hovers somewhere between ricotta and cottage cheese, with notes of buttermilk and yogurt. It has a clean, tangy flavor and a soft-curd texture. Prescinseua (roughly pronounced pray-shin-SEW-ah) dates back to the fifteenth century and has long been appreciated as a lighter, easily digestible alternative to richer cheeses. It is used as a filling for the region's famous cheese-stuffed focaccia (page 212), and in torta pasqualina, *a savory vegetable torte traditionally served at Easter. It is also mixed into ravioli stuffing. Purists will tell you that prescinesua can only be made with milk from Apennine cows, but if you can procure milk from a good local dairy you will do fine. Enjoy it for breakfast with sliced fresh fruit—I love it with sliced peaches—or spooned onto crostini.*

3 cups (720 g) whole pasteurized (not ultra-pasteurized) milk, preferably creamline (not homogenized)

1 cup (240 g) pasteurized (not ultra-pasteurized) heavy cream

3 tablespoons whole-milk yogurt

⅛ teaspoon liquid rennet (see Sources, page 292)

EQUIPMENT

Large (5-quart) stainless steel pot

Stainless steel ladle

Instant-read thermometer

Fine-mesh sieve or colander

Tight-weave cheesecloth

1 · In a large stainless steel pot, whisk together the milk, cream, and yogurt. Cover the pot and leave it at room temperature for 48 hours. During that time, the milk will sour and develop a thick skin on the surface.

2 · Without mixing, ladle out about ¾ cup of the curdled milk, breaking through the surface with your ladle. Pour the ladleful of milk into a small pot and heat it to 110°F. Add the rennet and then gently stir this mixture back into the rest of the milk. Take care not to over-stir. Cover and let stand for 4 to 5 hours.

3 · Line a fine-mesh sieve or colander with a double layer of cheesecloth and set it in the sink. Gently ladle or pour the milk mixture into the cheesecloth. Let it drain until the prescinseua has thickened a bit but is still soft, creamy, and spoonable, at least 1 hour. Spoon it into a container with a tight-fitting lid and store in the refrigerator for up to 1 week.

State-of-the-Artisan Mozzarella

→→→→→ · • • · ←←←←←

I'm standing on a platform overlooking a herd of water buffalo. The animals are in a barn, a cavernous structure that is open on all sides to allow for ventilation. The roof overhead has large open slats designed to let the sun in and draw hot air up and out.

On this mid-July morning, the buffalo appear content. A number of them are lined up at the far end of the barn at a long trough, in anticipation of their morning meal. Others are lounging on large padded rubber mats that are arranged in rows. A few more have queued up to take their turn at either of two massage stations—yes, massage stations. These are mechanical arms outfitted with enormous twirling bristle rollers. One at a time, the buffalo stand at a machine while a roller runs over their back and neck.

Welcome to Tenuta Vannulo, a 500-acre buffalo dairy just north of the famous ruins of Paestum, in Campania. The farm, which has four barns like the one I described, houses 600 (mostly female) water buffalo, half of which are giving milk at any one time. The animals, all raised on organic feed grown and mixed on the property, produce enough milk to make more than 800 pounds of hand-pulled mozzarella every day, plus ricotta, yogurt, and other dairy delicacies.

To say that this place is state-of-the-art is almost an understatement; yet the philosophy behind the operation is simple: "If the animals are well, if they are free of stress, then the milk they give us is high quality," says Antonio (Tonino) Palmieri, who owns and runs the farm with his wife, Caterina, and their three grown children.

The majority of Italy's buffalo mozzarella comes from two places: Caserta, north of Naples, and here, farther south, along the Cilento Coast. Buffalo milk, which is higher in butterfat than cow's milk, produces especially rich mozzarella that is both sweet and tangy. And the buffalo mozzarella at Tenuta Vennula is some of the best, made from raw organic milk and available only at the farm. In fact, all morning there has been a knot of people trying to get inside the already crowded cheese shop on the property. By 12:30 p.m. the last ball of mozzarella will have been sold.

As we make the rounds, daughter Teresa Palmieri fills me in on the farm's history, explaining that her great-grandfather bought the land and a few head of buffalo back in 1907. Each generation since has been raised here, in the salmon-colored stucco villa that stands at the front of the property.

"My first memory is of buffalo," she says. "The morning my sister was born, my father first took me to check on the buffalo; then we went to the hospital to see my sister."

For years the farm sold the milk from its buffalo to cheese makers in the area. That changed in 1988, when Tonino and Caterina Palmieri opened the dairy and began making mozzarella and ricotta. In 2000 they added yogurt and gelato, followed by buffalo milk pudding in 2002. The most recent addition is *crema spalmabile*—high-end Nutella-like spreads in hazelnut, gianduja, and pistachio.

Without a doubt, Vannulo's most impressive feature is the way the farm manages to seamlessly integrate high-tech and artisanal practices. Take the milking process. The buffalo are milked, one at a time, twice a day, by a machine with a mechanical arm. To access the milking machine, a buffalo passes through a turnstile in the barn. She does this at will, when her udder feels full. Thanks to a computer chip the animal wears, the mechanical arm—which has "memorized" the shape of each buffalo's udder—attaches itself to her and milks her. If, however, the buffalo has already given her daily allotment, the machine will divert her through another turnstile, back into the barn.

When it comes to breeding, however, the operation is decidedly old-school. Instead of high-tech artificial insemination, the farm relies on eight bulls, two in each barn.

All of the buffalo have names and profiles, kept on the computer. Everything about them is known—their age, their weight, their parentage, their medical history; how many times they've given birth, whether they are pregnant now and if so, when they're due; when they last gave milk, how much they gave, what their weekly average is, what their lifetime average is, and—if you can believe it—how much milk each teat produces.

"All of this information is important; it informs everything we do here," Teresa Palmieri says.

Inside the white tile and stainless steel dairy, the mozzarella at Vannulo is still pulled by hand, the process visible through a large picture window. Six cheese makers in white pants, white T-shirts, and white baseball caps tackle stainless steel tubs filled with large wobbly blocks of curd. Working in pairs, they expertly slice, stretch, and shape the curds into milky white balls, which they toss into an awaiting receptacle.

"The *mozzatura* (pulling and shaping) must be done by hand to get the right texture," Teresa Palmieri says.

I ask her why Vannulo products are only available at the farm. Her answer, like everything else here, is about quality. "If we start bringing in distributors and intermediaries, then our cheeses, our products, become something different," she says. "The only way we can be sure that the consumer is getting the product as we intend it to be is if it passes from our hand to theirs."

PRIMO LATTE

Primo latte *means "first milk." It is the freshest of cheeses, ready to enjoy as soon as it has set. This cheese has lots of appeal—a smooth, snow-white paste that slices beautifully and a fresh milky flavor enhanced by the salt. Enjoy the process of turning the cheese and letting it rest; this is what gives* primo latte *its silky texture and creates the pretty imprint from the slats in the basket mold. My favorite time to make and serve this cheese is in spring and summer, as it beautifully complements the vegetables of those seasons—asparagus, fava beans, tomatoes, and peppers.*

1 gallon (3.8 kg) whole pasteurized (not ultra-pasteurized) milk, preferably creamline (not homogenized)

⅓ cup (80 g) whole-milk yogurt

2 to 3 tablespoons fine sea salt

½ teaspoon liquid rennet (see Sources, page 292)

EQUIPMENT

Large stainless-steel pot

Instant-read thermometer

2 plastic "basket"-style cheese molds with slats, 5 inches wide by 2½ inches high (see Sources, page 292)

1 · Pour the milk into a large stainless-steel pot and set over medium heat. Heat, stirring gently a few times to prevent scorching on the bottom, to 108°F. Remove from the heat and gently but thoroughly whisk in the yogurt and salt. Let the milk cool to 100°F, then stir in the rennet. Cover the pot and let sit until the curd has formed a smooth, soft, solid mass on top, 50 to 60 minutes.

2 · Use a large offset metal spatula to cut the curd at 2-inch intervals into a grid pattern, making a series of slices in one direction and then in the other. Slice all the way to the bottom of the pot to cut completely through the curd. Cover the pot and let rest for 15 minutes. Cut the curd once more, cutting in one direction only, through the center of the large cubes to slice them in half. Cover the pot once more and let the curd rest for another 15 minutes.

3 · Place the cheese molds on a large rimmed baking sheet and place it near the pot of curds. Use a wire skimmer or spider to lift the curds from the pot and pack them into the cheese molds. They will be very soft, like a soft egg custard. Gently but firmly press out the whey with your hands and then add more curds to the molds, filling them to the top again. If too much whey accumulates on the baking sheet, tip it out into the sink (or into a bowl if you want to save it). Press out more whey to compress the curds into a solid mass. Keep pressing and adding until you have distributed all of the curds between the two molds—you might think they won't all fit, but they will. Let the cheese drain for 20 minutes.

4 · This is the tricky—but fun—part. Carefully turn one of the molds over into the palm of your hand. The *primo latte* should come out in one solid but wobbly round, like very soft tofu. (If you are reluctant to turn the cheese out into your hand, turn it out onto a clean plate.) Return the inverted cheese to the mold so that what was the top is now on the bottom. If the mold is flared, as mine is, you will have to carefully press the cheese in to fit. Turn the cheese in the second mold in

the same way. Let the cheeses rest for another 15 to 20 minutes, then carefully turn them again and return them to the molds. Let rest for 15 to 20 minutes, then repeat the turning and resting two more times. The cheese rounds will be more compressed and firm, but still a little soft, and they will bear the basket patterns of the mold. Set the baskets on a clean baking sheet or tray, cover the tops with plastic wrap, and refrigerate for about 2 hours to further set the cheese.

5 · To serve, unmold the cheese onto a plate. To store, place the cheese in a small plastic container with a tight-fitting lid and refrigerate for up to 5 days.

COOK'S NOTE · *Primo latte* is delicious on its own, or drizzled with olive oil and sprinkled with chopped fresh herbs or cracked black pepper. Serve it with good bread and good salami. Or slice it into thin wedges and serve on crostini along with a dollop of Spiced Tomato Jam (page 166). It is also delicious with Pickled Garlic Scapes in Oil (page 31), Sweet-and-Sour Roasted Peppers with Capers (page 38), and Grilled Zucchini in Oil (page 40).

TRENETTE
with Pesto Genovese and Prescinseua

··· MAKES 4 MAIN-DISH SERVINGS ···

*I was surprised, on a recent trip to Genoa, to find many restaurants offering
pesto with gnocchi or trofie, small, squiggly pasta. When I was growing up,
pesto was almost always served with trenette—noodles about the width of
linguine but slightly thicker in breadth. I happen to love the combination
of the silky noodles and creamy sauce, especially with tangy prescinseua
cheese stirred in, so I'm sticking with it here. But you should know that
the ricotta gnocchi on page 215 also pair beautifully with this pesto.*

Kosher or sea salt

Homemade Pasta dough, cut into trenette
(page 138) or 1 pound (454 g) dried
spaghetti or linguine

⅔ cup (150 g) Classic Pesto Genovese
(page 171) at room temperature

½ cup (113 g) Ligurian Prescinseua
(page 204) at room temperature, or
Buttermilk Ricotta (page 203) at room
temperature; or substitute high-quality
store-bought ricotta

Freshly grated Parmigiano-Reggiano,
for serving

1 · Bring a large pot of water to a rolling boil
and salt it generously. If you're using fresh
pasta, have all your other ingredients ready,
as the pasta will cook quickly.

2 · Gently drop the pasta into the boiling
water, and use a pasta fork or a serving fork
to swirl the noodles around. Cook fresh pasta
for 3 to 5 minutes, until tender but not too
soft (taste one to check). If using dried pasta,
cook according to the package instructions
until al dente.

3 · Drain the pasta, reserving about 1 cup of
the cooking water. Return the pasta to the pot
and add all but a couple of tablespoons of the
pesto. Toss gently until the noodles are well
coated. Add the prescinseua and toss again to
incorporate the cheese.

4 · Divide the noodles among warmed bowls
and spoon a little of the remaining pesto on
top of each serving. Serve with Parmigiano on
the side.

LIGURIAN-STYLE CHEESE FOCACCIA

The word focaccia probably conjures up images of pillowy rectangles of dimpled flatbread with a tender interior and crispy crust. This is not that focaccia, but it is just as good. If you have been to Cinque Terre, a popular destination in Liguria, you might be familiar with focaccia di Recco, *which lies somewhere between a flatbread and a cheese-stuffed pizza. Two layers of dough, made without yeast, are rolled out paper-thin; sandwiched between them are dollops of soft, tangy fresh cheese, either stracchino or prescinseua. The focaccia is baked in a superhot oven, yielding a stuffed flatbread that is tender and gooey and crispy all at once. Making this special stuffed bread takes some elbow grease and even a little agility in order to stretch the dough to the proper thinness—as in transparent. Stick with it. You will get better with each try, and this focaccia is worth it.*

3 cups (390 g) bread flour or Italian pizza dough flour such as Caputo "00" flour, plus more for the work surface

¾ cup (177 g) tepid water

2 tablespoons extra-virgin olive oil, plus more for the pizza pan and for brushing on the focaccia

1 teaspoon fine sea salt

⅛ teaspoon sugar

1 pound (454 g) Ligurian Prescinseua (page 204), or 1 pound (454 g) ricotta (homemade, page 203, or best-quality store-bought) mixed with 2 tablespoons yogurt

1 · Mound the flour onto a clean work surface and form a wide well in the middle. Carefully pour in the water and oil, and sprinkle in the salt and sugar. Take care not to "break" the walls of the mound. With your fingers or a fork, begin to incorporate the flour into the liquid in the well. When the mixture becomes too thick and sticky to stir, begin kneading it with your hands. Continue to knead the dough, incorporating flour, until it is about the consistency of pizza dough; that is, smooth and supple and no longer sticky. Scrape away any flour that remains on the work surface. Knead for a few more minutes, until smooth. Form it into a ball, wrap tightly in plastic wrap, and refrigerate for several hours or overnight. Let the dough come to room temperature before proceding.

2 · Position a rack in the upper third of the oven and preheat the oven to 500°F. If you have a pizza stone or a baking steel (see page 79), set it on the rack to preheat. Coat a large rimmed round or rectangular baking pan with olive oil (I use a 14-inch pizza pan).

3 · When the dough is at room temperature, lightly flour a clean work surface. Cut the dough in half; rewrap one half and set it aside. Knead the first piece of dough briefly, roll it into a ball, and let it rest for about 5 minutes. Using a rolling pin, begin rolling the dough out into a circle. Try not to add too much flour as you roll or you will end up with a grainy coating on the focaccia. The dough will spring back as you roll; this is fine. Just stop rolling and let it rest for a couple of minutes, then continue rolling. You may have to start and stop several times.

4 · Keep rolling until the dough is as thin as you can get it, thinner than for piecrust. When you think it's as thin as it will get, keep rolling, lightly flouring as necessary. You are aiming for a circle of dough that is as thin as strudel dough. Lift around the edges of the dough and gently pull it to stretch and extend it all around. If you want to be adventurous, gently lift the dough and drape it over your knuckles. Gently rotate the dough, inching it along your knuckles, just like a *pizzaiolo* would do. Stretching the dough in this way is the best way to get it as thin as it needs to be— about 1/16 inch thick. You should be able to see the work surface through it.

5 · Once you've finished rolling and stretching the dough, gently pick it up, taking care not to tear it, and drape it evenly over the prepared pan. The dough should be large enough that it drapes over the sides of the pan by a couple of inches all around. Gently press it into the pan, leaving the overhang.

6 · Dollop the cheese by the tablespoon onto the dough inside the pan, leaving about 1 inch between dollops and a 1½-inch border all around.

7 · Briefly knead the second piece of dough and roll it into a ball. Cover with plastic wrap and let it sit for 5 minutes. Then roll it out and stretch it as you did with the first piece.

8 · Carefully drape the dough evenly over the top of the focaccia, leaving the overhang. Then use a rolling pin or the palm of your hand to press down and cut off the overhang. Press the edges to seal the top and bottom crust. Brush the top of the dough with about 1 tablespoon olive oil. With a small paring knife, cut five or six slashes or holes into the top of the dough.

9 · Bake the focaccia for about 12 minutes, checking about halfway through to make sure the crust is not puffing up. If it is, quickly and carefully poke it into submission. The focaccia is done when the cheese is melted and bubbly and the top is well browned in spots.

10 · Let sit for a minute or two, then slice into wedges or squares and serve.

RICOTTA GNOCCHI
with *Simple Tomato Sauce*

Light and delicate, these cheese gnocchi are a lovely alternative to classic potato gnocchi, especially as part of a spring menu. They can be made ahead of time and frozen so that all you have to do is cook them when it's time to serve. Use your own homemade ricotta, or a high-quality commercial one from an Italian delicatessen or a good market. For years I used a regular table fork to shape my gnocchi, but a couple of years ago a friend gave me a small wooden gnocchi board that has vertical ridges on one side (see Sources, page 292). It's perfect for this dough, but a fork is fine, too.

About 1 cup (125 g) Italian "00" flour or unbleached all-purpose flour, plus more for the work surface and as needed to stiffen the dough

1 pound (454 g) Buttermilk Ricotta (page 203) or best-quality store-bought cow's milk ricotta, well drained

½ cup (50 g) freshly grated Parmigiano-Reggiano, plus more for serving

2 large eggs, lightly beaten

¾ teaspoon fine sea salt

Pinch of freshly grated nutmeg

Pinch of freshly ground white pepper

4 cups (907 g) tomato sauce, preferably homemade (page 120)

1 · Dust two large baking sheets with flour.

2 · In a large bowl, break up the ricotta with a fork and work it until it is smooth. Add the Parmigiano, eggs, salt, nutmeg, and white pepper and mix well with a spatula. Sprinkle the 1 cup flour over the top and fold it in. Scrape the mixture onto a well-floured work surface and sprinkle a little more flour on top. Knead the dough into a soft, pliable ball. It should feel slightly wet but not sticky.

3 · Cut the dough into 6 equal pieces. Work with one piece at a time and cover the rest with a clean kitchen towel. Sprinkle the work surface with a little more flour and roll the piece of dough into a rope about the thickness of your pinkie. Cut it crosswise into 1-inch pieces.

(recipe continues)

4 · Roll each piece of dough down the tines of a fork, using a finger to propel it and, at the same time, create a small indentation in it. When you are done, you should have the groove from your finger on one side and ridges from the fork tines on the other. (If you happen to own a gnocchi board, you can use that instead.) Place the gnocchi on the baking sheets as you roll them. You should end up with about 130 gnocchi.

5 · If cooking immediately, you can leave the gnocchi on the baking sheets. Otherwise, pop the baking sheets into the freezer and freeze until the gnocchi are solid, 1 to 2 hours. Transfer them to a zipper-lock freezer bag or a tightly lidded container and freeze for up to 1 month.

6 · To cook, bring a large pot of water to a rolling boil and salt it generously. In a saucepan, heat the tomato sauce to a simmer. Turn the oven on to a low setting. Spoon a little of the sauce into a serving bowl and place the bowl in the oven to keep warm.

7 · Gently drop the gnocchi into the boiling water. (If they are frozen, transfer them straight from the freezer to the boiling water.) In a couple of minutes, even before the water returns to a boil, the gnocchi will start to bob to the surface. Let them cook for about 3 minutes, then taste one; it should be soft and tender but cooked throughout, with no raw flour flavor. If not quite done, cook for another 2 minutes, then taste again.

8 · Transfer the gnocchi with a skimmer or slotted spoon to the serving bowl and spoon more sauce on top (don't toss the gnocchi with the sauce, as they are quite delicate). Sprinkle each serving with a little Parmigiano, and serve.

VARIATION · Serve the gnocchi with a sauce of melted butter and chopped sage in place of the tomato sauce. Sprinkle generously with Parmigiano. Or serve with Classic Pesto Genovese (page 171).

SAUSAGES AND SIMPLE SALUMI

I was a devoted vegetarian in high school— for about eight months. I passed on the Thanksgiving turkey and turned down the filet mignon on Christmas Day. I abstained from roast lamb on Easter and put a stop to our longtime family ritual of T-bone steaks and baked potatoes on Saturday nights.

Prosciutto was my undoing. As a young child I had earned the nickname Prosciutella, or "little prosciutto," from my Italian aunts. Every summer they would purchase a whole leg of prosciutto. From June through August, we would slice away at it, to eat as a snack with cheese or as a simple second course, or even draping it over fried eggs (my favorite). I loved that combination of creamy fat and tangy red meat. As a teenager I proved unable to resist it. Even today, I rarely crave a hamburger or steak; it's those tasty bits—sausage crumbled into pasta sauce, a flavor base of sautéed pancetta in Zuppa di Pasta e Fagioli (page 129), or rich strips of guanciale in Pasta alla Gricia (page 233)—that I can't do without.

Like cheese making, the art and craft of curing meat dates back centuries in Italy. And like most preserving techniques, it was born out of necessity. If you were fortunate to have a hog to butcher, especially in remote mountainous areas, you darned well better utilize every part, because you had to live off it for months. To this day, many *salumi* are named for the part of the pig used in their making: testa (head); coppa (back of the head and neck); spalla (shoulder); guanciale (jowl); pancetta (belly); and so on. Included in the *salumi* spectrum are also sausages and salami, made from ground or chopped meat.

The herbs and spices used to flavor these various cured meats differ from region to region. In Tuscany, where wild fennel grows in abundance, fennel is a predominant flavor. In Umbria, truffle is the star flavor, and in Calabria and other southern regions, some of the cured meats are a deep red from the addition of ground pepper—both sweet and hot.

As with the cheese section of this chapter, the recipes that follow are intended as an introduction to simple Italian meat-preserving techniques: You'll learn how to make fresh sausages and how to cure pancetta and guanciale. These are gateway recipes and techniques, and you may find yourself wanting to know, and do, more. You're not alone; the DIY food community in the United States has embraced the craft of meat curing in recent years. There are Web sites and Facebook pages devoted to it. For professional chefs and restaurateurs, having a house-made *salumi* or meat-curing program has become almost a requirement, and there are a handful of restaurants that have built their entire menus around the theme. For more in-depth information, techniques, and recipes, I recommend the books *Cooking by Hand*, by Paul Bertolli; *Charcuterie*, by Michael Ruhlman and Brian Polcyn; and *Dry-Curing Pork: Make Your Own Salami, Pancetta, Coppa, Prosciutto, and More*, by Hector Kent.

Before you start, carefully read the section introductions, as well as recipes and instructions; curing meat is a serious pursuit, even for a beginner, and proper preparation is essential. Keep in mind that your *salumi* will only be as good as the meat used to make them. Buy your pork from a reputable source. I rely on an organic butcher and a local farmer who raises a small number of pigs. The meat from these animals is deeply rosy and marbled with sweet, creamy fat. I may pay more per pound, but in the end I win because I am stocked with enough sausages, pancetta, and guanciale to last the better part of a year.

Making Italian Sausages

You don't always have to cross the ocean to find the right expert on Italian food. My friend Carolyn Van Damme is our local sausage maven. Every December she invites a bunch of friends and their kids over and together everyone grinds, mixes, and cranks out about 100 pounds of sausage—hot and sweet Italian, chorizo, merguez, and more. There is music, lots of food and wine, and at the end of the day we all go home with enough sausage to enjoy throughout the winter.

Carolyn's heritage is Italian and German, so sausage making is pretty much in her DNA; she has been doing it since she was a child, when she used to assist her maternal grandfather. The operation has grown in recent years, to the point where she recently graduated from using the sausage attachment on her stand mixer to employing a motorized meat grinder and a heavy-duty, 10-pound sausage stuffer.

My own sausage-making ambitions are more modest; with my hand-crank grinder and 5-pound stuffer I can turn out 8 to 10 pounds of sausage in a few hours. There is nothing like homemade sausage, especially if you start with good-quality meat and fresh, aromatic spices to punch up the flavor. Carolyn uses a mix of pork and beef in her sausages (2 parts pork to 1 part beef); she prefers the heartier flavor that beef imparts. I'm more of a traditionalist and so I make mine with all pork.

Don't be alarmed at the generous quantity of pork fat called for in the following recipes; good sausage requires a fair amount of fat to help bind the meat and produce an appealing texture, as well as to keep it from drying out when cooked. Look for good, fresh pork fatback, or ask the butcher in your supermarket's meat department to set some aside for you. You can also use more fatty cuts of pork shoulder. I sometimes set aside extra-fatty pieces of home-cured guanciale or pancetta and use those. Both Carolyn and I like our sausages highly seasoned with lots of black pepper and fennel. Carolyn's grandfather taught her that the best way to tell when enough pepper had been added was when you could see individual grains stuck to your hands after mixing.

To make sausages you need a couple of special pieces of equipment: one to chop or grind the meat, and one to stuff the mixture into casings. If you have a stand mixer that comes with the option of meat-grinding and sausage-stuffing attachments, you can use those. However, if you are planning to make sausages more than just once or twice I recommend investing in a stand-alone grinder and stuffer (see Sources, page 292). Most grinders come with two dies, one for a coarse grind and one for a fine grind, and some come with more. I have a small cast-iron grinder that clamps to my kitchen countertop and is perfect for churning out the amount of meat required in the following recipes. I also have a hand-crank sausage stuffer that fills up to 5 pounds of sausage at a time. Follow the manufacturer's instructions for setting up the grinder and stuffer, or for assembling the grinding and stuffing attachments for the stand mixer.

I use and recommend natural hog casings for stuffing sausages. You can buy them at butcher shops or special-order them from the supermarket meat department, but they are also available online, packed in salt and vacuum-sealed (see Sources, page 292).

Casings come in a variety of widths; those labeled "32-35 mm" are ideal for Italian sausages. If you have any left over after sausage making, pack them in salt water in a container with a tight-fitting lid and store them in the freezer.

Following are instructions for making typical "sweet" (that is, not spicy) Italian-style sausages, with a variation for "hot" (spicy) sausages, and a recipe for garlic, cheese, and wine sausages. Once you are familiar with the process, you will be able to come up with your own favorite flavor and spice combinations.

SWEET ITALIAN SAUSAGE

··· MAKES 4 POUNDS (1.8 KG) ···

These are what you think of when you think of Italian sausage: rich, juicy, and generously spiked with fennel. The addition of fennel pollen is optional; it's not that easy to find but it can be ordered online. I love the flavor it imparts to the sausages—it's more savory than fennel seed, with a hint of curry. As "sweet" (that is, not spicy) sausages go, these are pretty spicy—there's a generous amount of black pepper and fennel in the spice mix. Use less if you prefer.

About 20 feet of natural hog casings (see page 219)

3 pounds (1.4 kg) lean pork shoulder

1 pound (454 g) pork fatback or fat trimmed from shoulder

½ cup (57 g) whole fennel seeds

2 teaspoons fennel pollen (see Sources, page 292)

2 tablespoons coarsely ground black pepper

1 tablespoon fine sea salt

1 cup (237 g) apple juice

EQUIPMENT

Electric spice grinder

Manual or electric meat grinder, or stand mixer fitted with the meat-grinding attachment and coarse-grinding die (¼ inch)

Sausage stuffer, or stand mixer fitted with the sausage stuffing attachment and plastic stuffing nozzle

1 · Immerse the casings in a bowl of warm water and leave them to soak. This will soften them and remove the gritty salt they are packed in.

2 · **Prepare the meat:** Cut the shoulder and fatback into 1- to 2-inch-thick strips or pieces to fit into the grinder. Arrange the pieces on rimmed baking sheets and place them in the freezer to chill. Ideally they should be chilled to freezing temperature (32°F) or slightly above.

3 · **While the meat is chilling, prepare the spices:** Spread the fennel seeds in a small dry skillet and cook over medium-high heat, stirring often, until the seeds have turned a shade darker and are fragrant, about 3 minutes. Remove from the heat and let cool briefly. Grind the seeds in a spice grinder to a coarse or fine powder—your choice. If you like whole fennel seeds in your sausages, you can leave half the seeds whole and grind the rest.

4 · Combine the toasted fennel, fennel pollen, pepper, and salt in a small bowl and mix well.

5 · Assemble the meat grinder or stand mixer grinding attachment according to the manufacturer's instructions, using the coarse-grinding die (¼ inch). Fill the hopper with the chilled pieces of meat—as much as will comfortably fit—and grind into a bowl or

onto a rimmed baking sheet. Continue to feed the hopper and grind until you have ground all the meat. The meat should still be cold; if it has warmed up, return it to the freezer to chill for a few minutes.

6 · Sprinkle three-quarters of the spice mix over the ground meat and mix well with your hands for several minutes to bind the meat and to incorporate the spices. You really need to make sure the spices are evenly distributed throughout the meat and that there are no "pockets" of spice. Pour in the apple juice and continue to mix until it is all absorbed. Test the seasonings by pinching off some of the meat and making a small patty. Fry it in a skillet until cooked through and then taste. Mix in the rest of the spice mix if you want to punch up the flavor more. Refrigerate the ground meat until you are ready to stuff it.

7 · **Rinse the casings one by one:** Run the faucet at a gentle stream. Gently pull open the end of a casing and run water all the way through it to flush out any grit or debris. Set aside and continue until you have rinsed all the casings. This is a tedious but necessary task.

8 · Fill the sausage stuffer with the cold seasoned ground meat. Carefully thread two or three casings onto the nozzle of the stuffer, letting the end of the last one hang down about 3 inches. Set a clean rimmed baking sheet under the nozzle. Begin cranking the stuffer (or turn on the mixer) to fill

the first casing, guiding it with one hand to fill it evenly. This process is best done with two people, one to crank (if using a stuffer) and the other to move the casing along and guide and coil the sausage as it fills the tray. Try not to overfill the casings, or it will be difficult to twist and tie the sausages and they may rupture. Stop filling when there are still 2 to 3 inches of space left in the casing. Knot the sausage at both ends. Carefully pinch and twist the sausage at 4- to 5-inch intervals to create individual connected links. Continue to fill casings, threading them onto the nozzle as needed, until you have used up all the filling.

9 · Line a rimmed baking sheet with waxed paper and set the linked sausages on it. Refrigerate for 24 hours; then turn them over and refrigerate for another 24 hours. This curing time in the fridge dries the sausages out a bit and gives the flavors a chance to develop. Once cured, the sausages may be kept refrigerated for up to 2 days longer. Otherwise, wrap them in plastic wrap and put them in zipper-lock freezer bags. They will keep in the freezer for up to 1 year. For best results, vacuum-seal the sausages before putting them in the freezer.

VARIATION · To make Hot Italian Sausages, reduce the amount of black pepper in the spice mix to 1 tablespoon, and add 1 teaspoon crushed red chile pepper and 1 teaspoon ground cayenne (or other hot) pepper.

GARLIC, CHEESE, AND WINE SAUSAGE

··· MAKES ABOUT 4 POUNDS (1.8 KG) ···

Years ago, our local Trader Joe's sold packaged garlic and cheese sausages. They were delicious, but one day they disappeared from the shelves, never to return. Finally I took matters into my own hands and made my own. Getting the garlic right was the biggest hurdle. Raw garlic and garlic powder were both too aggressive. Then the lightbulb went on: roasted garlic. The creamy softened garlic cloves blend into the ground meat mixture beautifully, and their mellow flavor provides just the right amount of garlicky richness.

1 large head garlic

2 teaspoons extra-virgin olive oil

About 20 feet of natural hog casings (see page 219)

3 pounds (1.4 kg) lean pork shoulder

1 pound (454 g) pork fatback or fat trimmed from shoulder

¼ cup (5 g) dried parsley

1 tablespoon coarsely ground black pepper

1 tablespoon fine sea salt

2 cups (4 ounces/200 g) shredded Pecorino Romano

1 cup (237 g) dry white wine

EQUIPMENT

Electric spice grinder

Manual or electric meat grinder, or stand mixer fitted with the meat-grinding attachment and coarse-grinding die (¼ inch)

Sausage stuffer, or stand mixer fitted with the sausage stuffing attachment and plastic stuffing nozzle

1 · Preheat the oven to 400° F.

2 · Peel off the loose outer layers from the head of garlic but leave the head intact. Cut off about ¼ inch of the top to expose the cluster of cloves. Set the entire head on a piece of aluminum foil, drizzle the oil over the cloves, and wrap the head in the foil. Place it on a small baking sheet and roast until the cloves are soft and golden brown, about 45 minutes. Let cool slightly, then separate and pop the individual cloves out of their skins. Put them in a small bowl, mash them with a fork, and set aside.

3 · Immerse the casings in a bowl of warm water and leave them to soak. This will soften them and remove the gritty salt they are packed in.

4 · **Prepare the meat:** Cut the shoulder and fatback into 1- to 2-inch-thick strips or pieces to fit into the grinder. Arrange the pieces on rimmed baking sheets and place them in the freezer to chill. Ideally they should be chilled to freezing temperature (32°F) or slightly above.

5 · Assemble the meat grinder or stand mixer grinding attachment according to the manufacturer's instructions, using the coarse-grinding die (¼ inch). Fill the hopper with the chilled pieces of meat—as much as will comfortably fit—and grind it into a bowl or onto a rimmed baking tray. Continue to feed the hopper and grind until you have ground it all. The meat should still be cold; if it has warmed up, return it to the freezer to chill for a few minutes.

6 · Combine the parsley, pepper, and salt in a small bowl and mix well. Sprinkle the spice mix and the cheese over the ground meat. Drop the mashed garlic in small dollops on top to distribute it and mix well with your hands for several minutes to bind the meat and to evenly incorporate the spices, cheese, and garlic. You really need to make sure the spices are evenly distributed throughout the meat, and that there are no "pockets" of spice. Pour in the wine and continue to mix until it is all absorbed. Test the seasonings by pinching off some of the meat and making a small patty. Fry it in a skillet until cooked through and then taste. Adjust the seasonings if desired. Refrigerate the ground meat until you are ready to stuff it.

7 · **Rinse the casings one by one:** Run the faucet at a gentle stream. Gently pull open the end of a casing and run water all the way through it to flush out any grit or debris. Set it aside and continue until you have rinsed all the casings. This is a tedious but necessary task.

8 · Fill the sausage stuffer with the cold seasoned ground meat. Carefully thread two or three casings onto the nozzle of the stuffer, letting the end of the last one hang down about 3 inches. Set a clean rimmed baking sheet under the nozzle. Begin cranking the stuffer (or turn on the mixer) to fill the first casing, guiding it with one hand to fill it evenly. This process is best done with two people, one to crank (if using a stuffer) and the other to move the casing along and guide and coil the sausage as it fills the tray. Try not to overfill the casings, or it will be difficult to twist and tie the sausages and they may rupture. Stop filling when there are still 2 to 3 inches of space left in the casing. Knot the sausage at both ends. Carefully pinch and twist the sausage at 4- to 5-inch intervals to create individual connected links. Continue to fill casings, threading them onto the nozzle as needed, until you have used up all the filling.

9 · Line a rimmed baking sheet with waxed paper and set the linked sausages on it. Refrigerate for 24 hours; then turn them over and refrigerate for another 24 hours. This curing time in the fridge dries the sausages out a bit and gives the flavors a chance to develop. Once cured, the sausages may be kept refrigerated for up to 2 days longer. Otherwise, wrap them in plastic wrap and put them in zipper-lock freezer bags. They will keep in the freezer for up to 1 year. For best results, vacuum-seal the sausages before putting them in the freezer.

MAKING PANCETTA AND GUANCIALE

In some ways, making pancetta or guanciale is easier than making sausage: no chopping or grinding, no slippery casings to deal with, no concerns about overstuffing and sausage explosions. The basic process is simple, and essentially the same for both: The meat is rubbed with a "dry" brine of salt and spices, and put to cure in the refrigerator for a week. Then it is cleaned and hung in a cool spot to air-cure for several weeks (or longer).

On the other hand, this is true curing. You're hanging a slab of raw, brined meat out to dry with the expectation that it will transform into something not only edible (and not lethal!) but also delicious—spiced, salty, meaty, tangy. It's a little unnerving.

Read through the following section to familiarize yourself with ingredients, equipment, and techniques. Follow the directions in the recipes closely, but also use common sense. Know that problems can come up; you are trying to create conditions in which good bacteria will flourish and bad bacteria will be banished, but the bacteria may have other ideas. If the meat smells off at any point during curing, rancid or rotten rather than pleasantly tangy, discard it. Look carefully at any mold that develops. White bloomy patches of mold are a sign that conditions are good and the meat is curing as planned. If the mold is dark—red, black, or green—or fuzzy, or looks ominous to you, something is not right. Don't try to scrape the mold off; put on gloves and throw the whole thing away, then carefully clean any areas that may have been in contact with the meat.

Ingredients

Pancetta (pork belly) and guanciale (pork jowl) are whole-muscle cuts of meat, which is good because it means bad bacteria have fewer places to thrive. Buy your meat from a trusted source. Make sure the pieces you are curing are squared off, with no hanging flaps, nooks, or pockets that might encourage the growth of harmful bacteria such as botulism. If you are familiar with trimming meat, you can easily do this yourself; otherwise have a butcher do it for you. Both cuts vary in size, and the belly, which is larger, can weigh up to 10 pounds (4.5 kg). I usually ask the butcher for a 5-pound (2.25 kg) slab, which I divide in two and cure with two different spice rubs. Be sure to ask the butcher to remove the rind, which can be difficult to cut off neatly. The jowl is smaller, but usually still has glands attached to it. Make sure these are removed before you start the cure.

Salt has been used as a preservative since ancient times (as you no doubt learned in elementary school). Essentially it works by drawing moisture out of food, thus making the environment unfavorable for harmful bacteria. But it also adds flavor and firms up the texture of meat as it cures. The amount of salt typically used in a salt cure is calculated at 3 percent of the total weight of the meat in grams. If you are curing 2 kilograms (2,000 g) of pancetta, you will need 60 grams of salt. You can use either kosher or sea salt, but I prefer sea salt.

Pink salt, also called curing salt, is a mixture of salt and sodium nitrite. It is dyed bright pink so as not to be confused with regular salt. Pink salt isn't necessary for pancetta or guanciale, but its antimicrobial properties help to suppress the growth of dangerous bacteria. Consumed in large quantities, pink salt can be harmful. However, when used judiciously in very small quantities, it makes for a better product. Beyond its antibacterial use, it also contributes to that characteristic "cured" flavor—slightly tangy, slightly sweet—that we associate with bacon, ham, and pancetta. Always use gloves when working with pink salt, and store it safely away from children. To calculate the amount needed, weigh the trimmed meat. Multiply the weight by 0.25 percent. That's the amount of pink salt needed for the cure. In this case, 0.25 percent of 1 kilogram is 2.5 grams.

Spices have some preservative properties, but that is a secondary role; the mixture of pepper, fennel, bay leaf, sage, and other spices is what gives pancetta and guanciale their distinctive flavor profiles.

Equipment

- I recommend a digital scale so that you can accurately weigh the amount of pink salt required in the salt cure; you will also be able to keep accurate track of how much weight your meat has lost during the time it is air-drying.
- Use disposable kitchen gloves, such as Playtex, to coat the meat with the dry brine. Once coated, seal the meat in a large, heavy-duty zipper-lock freezer bag and set that on a rimmed baking sheet or shallow roasting pan. Heavy kitchen twine works well for hanging the meat once it has been brined.

Once it is done brining, the pancetta or guanciale will need a place to (literally) hang for a few weeks. This is known as the curing space. You want a cool, dark spot, with good air circulation, temperatures hovering around 60°F, and 60 percent humidity. I have used my garage as a curing space and I've also appropriated my husband's wine refrigerator and have found that both work well. (Check the conditions of your curing space with a thermometer-hygrometer, available at any hardware store.)

Finally, remember that cured meats are traditionally made in fall and winter, during butchering season, and this is still the best time to do it. (I don't even want to think about what would happen to my pancetta if I hung it in the garage during midsummer in Virginia.)

SLAB PANCETTA

Think of pancetta as bacon with an Italian accent: same cut, different treatment. Pancetta is cured with salt and lots of spices, but it is not smoked. It is an essential ingredient in countless Italian dishes, especially as a flavoring agent for soups, sauces, and stews. The spicy dry brine in this recipe is one I've tweaked to my liking over the years. I've also included a variation for a really peppery brine that I love. Most recipes don't call for it, but I like to "wash" my pancetta with wine before hanging it, not so much for preservation reasons but because I find it adds to the complex tangy flavor of the finished pancetta. Feel free to experiment with your own spice mix, but be sure not to change the ratios of salt and pink salt.

1 slab trimmed pork belly, rind removed, belly trimmed of excess flaps of meat and fat, and squared off at the edges (have the butcher do this for you); about 2.2 pounds (1 kg) after trimming

30 g (1 tablespoon plus 1¼ teaspoons) fine sea salt, depending on the exact weight of the pancetta; the weight of the sea salt should be 3 percent the weight of the trimmed meat (see page 224)

2.5 g (1 scant teaspoon) pink curing salt, depending on the exact weight of the pancetta; the weight of the pink salt should be 0.25 percent the weight of the trimmed meat

4 cloves garlic, minced

3 bay leaves, crumbled

3 to 4 tablespoons coarsely ground black pepper

2 teaspoons lightly crushed juniper berries

½ teaspoon lightly crushed fennel seeds

½ teaspoon dried rosemary leaves, lightly crushed

1 teaspoon ground sweet red pepper (optional)

¼ teaspoon crushed red chile pepper

Pinch of freshly grated nutmeg

1½ cups (355 g) dry white wine, such as Orvieto, Soave, or Pecorino

EQUIPMENT

Digital kitchen scale with metric weight measurements

Disposable kitchen gloves (such as Playtex)

Kitchen twine

1 · Place the trimmed belly on a cutting board. Put on kitchen gloves to make the dry brine. In a bowl, combine the sea salt, pink salt, garlic, bay leaves, black pepper, juniper berries, fennel seeds, rosemary, ground sweet pepper (if using), crushed red pepper, and nutmeg and mix well. Sprinkle the cure all over the meat and, wearing the gloves, rub it in well. Place the meat in a zipper-lock freezer bag. Scoop up any stray rub and add it to the

bag. Squeeze out the air and seal. Place the bag in a baking dish and refrigerate for 1 week. Turn the bag over once a day and give the meat a little massage as you turn it.

2 · After 1 week, remove the sealed bag from the baking dish. Pour the wine into the baking dish. Wearing gloves, remove the pork belly from the bag and use your (gloved) fingers to brush off as much brine as you can. Immerse the pork in the wine to dislodge more brine; then transfer it to a clean cutting board. Use a sharp paring knife to cut a hole in one corner of the belly, about 1 inch from the edge. Thread a length of kitchen twine through the hole and knot it where it meets the pork. Tie the ends together tightly to create a long loop for hanging.

3 · Weigh the meat and note the weight.

4 · Hang the pancetta in a secure curing space (see page 225) for 3 to 5 weeks, until it has lost 20 to 30 percent of its weight. If you don't have a separate curing space, place the pancetta on a rack set inside a shallow pan. Place in the refrigerator and let it cure, uncovered, for at least 1 week and up to 1 month or longer, until it has lost 20 to 30 percent of its weight. When it is done, it will feel firm but still a little supple and pliable.

5 · To store the pancetta, cut it into 4- or 8-ounce (113- or 227-g) pieces and vacuum-seal or wrap tightly in plastic wrap and seal in a zipper-lock bag. Store in the freezer for up to 1 year. Once opened, store the pancetta in plastic wrap in the refrigerator for up to 1 week.

VARIATION · To make Three-Pepper Pancetta, substitute the dry brine with a mixture of 30 g sea salt, 2.5 g pink curing salt, ¼ cup (28 g) coarsely ground black pepper, 1 to 2 teaspoons crushed red chile pepper, and 2 teaspoons crushed dried sweet peppers (page 148) or ground sweet paprika.

Salumi in the Family

Step inside the *salumeria* in the medieval town of Bevagna, Umbria, and inhale deeply. Take in the wonderful, rich, spicy, meaty, funky aroma that pervades the small space.

Just inside the arched doorway, is a row of guanciale—cured pork jowls, at least two dozen, hanging from hooks on a chain that runs from wall to wall. Each one is tagged with a square of butcher paper the color of spicy mustard on which is written the date that the jowl was hung.

Many other things hang in Macelleria and Norcineria da Tagliavento: pancetta, whole legs of prosciutto, dried sausages, salami, capocollo, coppa, lonza; each meticulously tagged and accounted for.

Two glass cases hold the day's offering of fresh meat—veal, pork, fresh sausages, chicken and more *salumi*, local cheeses, and the shop's renowned porchetta—whole pig, stuffed and seasoned, roasted, and ready to be sliced for sandwiches.

Behind the display cases, sporting a crisp red apron, white polo shirt, and (though you can't see them) metallic gold running shoes, is *salumiere* Marco Biagetti. He is salting a leg of pork, which will be cured and dried. At least two years will pass before he slices into it.

"I've been behind this counter since I was ten," says Biagetti, who owns the shop with his wife, Rosita Cariani. Both come from a long line of butchers and *norcini* (*salumieri* who specialize in the butchering and curing of pork). The two families were competitors for generations, until Biagetti and Cariani put an end to the rivalry in the 1980s by getting married. Now they make the *salumi* and run the shop together, along with a trattoria farther up the ancient cobbled street.

The shop's reputation has traveled far beyond this tiny stone village. Tagliavento has garnered mentions in *The New York Times* and *Food & Wine*, among other publications, something Biagetti attributes to *passa parola*—word of mouth. His father, Renato, opened the shop in its current spot in 1965. He named it Tagliavento (wind slicer), a nickname he earned for his quick knife skills. According to family lore, Renato Biagetti was so fast that he could butcher an entire steer in the time it took to smoke a cigarette.

But speed is not what sets Tagliavento's cured meats apart. Rather, it's the opposite. Biagetti and Cariani begin with top-quality meat from heritage breeds raised by farmers they know well. Everything is cured using traditional methods, without additives or chemical enhancements. The *salumi* are tagged and dated and left to air-dry, first in a cantina and then in the shop, for as long as is necessary—up to two years for prosciutto. The result is prosciutto that is darker in color than typical mass-produced Parma prosciutto, with a meatier, more intense flavor and a thick ribbon of creamy fat along the edge.

I ask Biagetti whether there will be a fifth generation in the business. He's optimistic. "Our son is a radiologist, but every day when he finishes work he still comes to work here, in the shop or in the restaurant." He shrugs his shoulders and smiles. Who knows?

GUANCIALE

· · · MAKES 21 TO 25 OUNCES (600 TO 700 G) AFTER CURING · · ·

Guanciale is generally a smaller and fattier cut than pancetta (page 226), and the meat is said to taste sweeter. Cured guanciale definitely has a discernible, appealing porkiness about it, and it is the central ingredient in several iconic pasta dishes, including Spaghetti alla Carbonara (page 234) and Pasta alla Gricia (page 233). Until a few years ago, pork jowl was not that well known in the United States, and it can still be hard to find. You may need to ask a butcher to special-order it for you. While you are at it, be sure to ask the butcher to remove the yellowish glands from the jowl. Use guanciale as you would pancetta, in pasta dishes and sautéed as a flavor base for sauces, soups, and stews.

1 hog jowl, glands removed, trimmed of excess fat and meat (have the butcher do this for you); about 2.2 pounds (1 kg) after trimming

30 g (1 tablespoon plus 1¼ teaspoons) fine sea salt, depending on the exact weight of the jowl; the weight of the sea salt should be 3 percent the weight of the trimmed meat (see page 224)

2.5 g (1 scant teaspoon) pink curing salt, depending on the exact weight of the jowl; the weight of the pink salt should be 0.25 percent the weight of the trimmed meat

3 cloves garlic, minced

4 tablespoons (28 g) coarsely ground black pepper

1 teaspoon dried crushed rosemary

1 teaspoon dried crushed sage

1½ cups dry white wine, such as Orvieto

EQUIPMENT

Digital kitchen scale with metric measurements

Disposable kitchen gloves (such as Playtex)

Kitchen twine

1 · Place the trimmed jowl on a cutting board. Put on kitchen gloves to make the dry brine. In a bowl, combine the sea salt, pink salt, garlic, pepper, rosemary, and sage and mix well. Sprinkle the cure all over the meat and, wearing the gloves, rub it in well. Place the meat in a zipper-lock freezer bag. Scoop up any stray rub and add it to the bag. Squeeze out the air and seal. Place the bag in a baking dish and refrigerate for 1 week. Turn the bag over once a day and give the meat a little massage each time you turn it.

(recipe continues)

2 · After 1 week, remove the sealed bag from the baking dish. Pour the wine into the baking dish. Wearing gloves, remove the pork jowl from the bag and use your (gloved) fingers to brush off as much brine as you can. Immerse the pork in the wine to dislodge more brine; then transfer it to a clean cutting board. Use a sharp paring knife to cut a hole in one corner of the jowl, about 1 inch from the edge. Thread a length of kitchen twine through the hole and knot it where it meets the pork. Tie the ends together tightly to create a long loop for hanging.

3 · Weigh the meat and note the weight.

4 · Hang the guanciale in a secure curing space for 3 to 5 weeks, until it has lost 20 to 30 percent of its weight. If you don't have a separate curing space, place the guanciale on a rack set inside a shallow pan. Place in the refrigerator and let it cure, uncovered, for at least 1 week and up to 1 month or longer, until it has lost 20 to 30 percent of its weight. Turn the guanciale over every few days to ensure that all sides are exposed to air.

5 · To store the guanciale, cut it into 4- or 8-ounce (113- or 227-g) pieces and vacuum-seal or wrap tightly in plastic wrap and seal in a zipper-lock bag. Store in the freezer for up to 1 year. Once opened, store the guanciale in plastic wrap in the refrigerator for up to 1 week.

GRILLED SAUSAGES
with Pickled Vegetables

··· MAKES 6 TO 8 SERVINGS ···

The tantalizing aroma of smoke is almost always detectable in the countryside and hill towns of Abruzzo, Tuscany, and Umbria. These regions take their grilled meats seriously, and a mixed grill platter always features sausages. When I serve grilled sausages at home, I put out a selection of pickles to go with them; the vegetables' bright colors dress up the platter and the vinegary flavors help to cut the richness of the meat. Gas grills are fine, but you'll get a more "authentic" smoky flavor if you use a charcoal grill (see Cook's Note).

Selection of pickled vegetables, such as Sweet-and-Sour Roasted Peppers (page 38), Pickled Rapini in Oil (page 41), Red Cabbage Pickle (page 47), and Cipollini in Agrodolce (page 60)

2 pounds (907 g) Garlic, Cheese, and Wine Sausages (page 222) or Sweet Italian Sausages (page 220)

Freshly squeezed juice of ½ lemon (optional)

Best-quality extra-virgin olive oil, for serving

1 · Remove the pickles from the refrigerator, if necessary, and arrange them on a large serving platter, leaving space for the sausages. Be sure to drain off any excess oil or vinegar before placing the vegetables on the platter.

2 · Prepare a medium-hot charcoal grill or heat a gas grill to medium-high. Be sure that the coals are not too hot or the sausages will split open from the excessive heat. When the coals are ready, or when the gas grill is preheated, arrange the sausages on the grate directly over the heat. Grill, turning occasionally, until the sausages are cooked through and nicely charred on the outside, about 10 minutes.

3 · Transfer the sausages to the platter. Squeeze the lemon juice over them, if using, then drizzle a thread of olive oil over the sausages and vegetables and serve.

COOK'S NOTE · I prefer hardwood lump charcoal to pressed carbon charcoal briquettes. The wood imparts a smokiness that nicely captures the classic flavor of the Italian grill. I also like the delicate tinkling-glass sound of the wood as it burns.

PASTA ALLA GRICIA

··· MAKES 4 SERVINGS ···

Four ingredients make up this classic Roman pasta dish, so success depends on the quality of those ingredients. Choose a good brand of dried pasta (I like Rustichella d'Abruzzo, Cocco, or De Cecco) and use freshly ground pepper and freshly grated cheese. If you have made your own guanciale, now is the time to enjoy your handiwork.

8 ounces (227 g) guanciale (page 229), cut into 1-inch strips or diced

Lots of freshly ground black pepper

1 pound (454 g) rigatoni, penne rigate, or spaghetti

1 cup (100 g) freshly grated Pecorino Romano

1 • Bring a large pot of water to a rolling boil and salt it generously.

2 • Put the guanciale in a large, dry cast-iron or heavy-bottomed skillet. Set over low heat and let the guanciale warm up gradually. After about 3 minutes, it will start to sizzle quietly. Continue to cook, stirring from time to time, until the guanciale is lightly browned and has rendered some of its fat, about 15 minutes. Shower the guanciale with freshly ground pepper—add more than you think you should. This is a peppery dish.

3 • Cook the pasta according to the package instructions until very al dente—slightly underdone. As the pasta is cooking, scoop out a ladleful of the cooking water and add it to the skillet with the guanciale. Stir well, scraping up any browned bits from the pan.

4 • Drain the pasta, reserving a little of the cooking water. Transfer the pasta to the skillet and stir gently but thoroughly to combine it with the guanciale and pan sauce. Add a splash or two more of the reserved cooking water, if necessary, and continue to cook for a minute or two, until the pasta has absorbed some of the liquid and is al dente.

5 • Spoon the pasta and sauce into bowls and sprinkle the cheese on top. Serve immediately.

SPAGHETTI ALLA CARBONARA

· · · MAKES 4 SERVINGS · · ·

What could be better than spaghetti with bacon and eggs? That is, essentially, what spaghetti alla carbonara is. But it's not as easy to pull off as you might think. It takes some elbow grease to achieve that luscious, creamy egg sauce. You must work quickly when adding the beaten eggs to the hot pasta, and stir, stir, stir. Otherwise you'll end up with spaghetti and scrambled eggs, and the Romans will feed you to the lions.

2 tablespoons extra-virgin olive oil

2 large cloves garlic, lightly crushed

7 ounces (200 g) pancetta (page 226) or guanciale (page 229), cut into strips or diced

⅓ cup (79 g) dry white wine

4 large eggs

2 tablespoons heavy cream

½ teaspoon fine sea salt

Freshly ground black pepper

½ cup (50 g) freshly grated Pecorino Romano, plus more for serving

1 pound (454 g) spaghetti

1 · Bring a large pot of water to a rolling boil and salt it generously.

2 · Combine the olive oil and garlic in a large skillet over medium heat. Cook for about 5 minutes, pressing down on the garlic to release its flavor. Remove the garlic before it starts to brown. Stir in the pancetta and cook until it has rendered some of its fat and is lightly browned, about 10 minutes. Raise the heat to medium-high and pour in the wine. Cook, stirring often, until most of the liquid has evaporated, 1 to 2 minutes.

3 · Crack the eggs into a bowl and beat lightly. Whisk in the cream, salt, and a generous grinding of pepper. Stir in the cheese.

4 · Cook the spaghetti according to the package instructions until al dente. Drain, reserving about 1 cup of the cooking water. Return the pasta to the pot and place it back on the stove, but do not turn the burner on. Gradually pour in the egg mixture in a steady stream, while stirring vigorously with a serving fork or pasta fork as you pour. This stirring is what will give the sauce its creamy, rather than scrambled, texture, so don't let up. Once all the egg mixture has been added, add a splash or two of cooking water to loosen the sauce if necessary. Then stir in the pancetta and any drippings from the pan. Toss well to incorporate.

5 · Serve the spaghetti hot, with additional cheese for sprinkling on top.

BUCATINI ALL'AMATRICIANA

This is not, strictly speaking, a Roman dish. It comes from the town of Amatrice, in the mountains of Lazio near the Abruzzo border. If you visit, you will be bombarded with signs from restaurants claiming to offer la vera pasta all'Amatriciana, *the "original" version. Who is telling the truth is anyone's guess. Bucatini are fat noodles, pierced through the center for even cooking. Guanciale is the traditional cured meat for this dish, but my kids like pancetta, which is meatier, so I've included both options.*

5 ounces (140 g) guanciale (page 229) or pancetta (page 226), diced into ½-inch pieces

1 tablespoon extra-virgin olive oil

1 clove garlic, lightly crushed

¾ cup (85 g) finely diced red onion

1 dried peperoncino (page 148), crushed, or a generous pinch of crushed red chile pepper

¼ cup (59 g) dry white wine

2 cups (340 g) Bottled Diced Tomatoes (page 115) or store-bought diced tomatoes

½ teaspoon fine sea salt, or to taste

1 pound (454 g) bucatini (also known as perciatelli)

Finely grated Pecorino Romano, for serving

1 · Bring a large pot of water to a rolling boil and salt it generously.

2 · Put the guanciale in a large, dry cast-iron or heavy-bottomed skillet over medium heat. Sauté until the meat has begun to render its fat and turn brown, about 10 minutes. Add the oil, garlic, onion, and peperoncino, and cook, stirring often, until the onion begins to soften, about 5 minutes. Raise the heat to medium-high and pour in the wine. Cook at a lively simmer until most of the wine has evaporated, 1 to 2 minutes.

3 · Pour in the tomatoes and season with the salt. Bring the sauce to a simmer, reduce the heat to medium or medium-low, and cook at a gentle simmer until the sauce is thickened, about 20 minutes. Turn off the heat and cover to keep warm.

4 · Cook the bucatini according to the package instructions until al dente. Drain, reserving about 1 cup of the cooking water. Return the pasta to the pot and spoon in about three-quarters of the sauce. Toss gently until the pasta is well coated with sauce. Add a splash or two of the reserved cooking water to loosen the sauce if necessary. Transfer the dressed pasta to a warmed serving bowl or individual bowls. Spoon the remaining sauce on top and sprinkle with a little cheese.

Sour Cherries in Boozy Syrup, page 267

SYRUPS, LIQUEURS, AND FRUITS PRESERVED IN ALCOHOL

My parents threw great dinner parties, serving their lucky guests homemade *spaghetti alla chitarra*, juicy roasts, and my mother's signature desserts—ricotta cake, frozen coffee soufflé, or her impossibly high lemon meringue pie. These meals were bookended with Italian liqueurs—aperitivi to start, and a selection of cordials, amari, and digestivi—characteristically bitter and potent after-dinner drinks—following dessert. As a child I was allowed to dip the tip of my tongue into my parents' cordial glasses, which may account for my lifelong taste for bitter things—and after-dinner drinks.

Over the years I've learned that the best Italian liqueurs are those made in-house, at a restaurant or in someone's home. I can still taste the creamy wild strawberry liqueur poured by the proprietor of a rustic mountaintop picnic spot in Abruzzo, and the dark, clove-scented nocino (green walnut liqueur) made by my friend Francesca's father-in-law, Vincenzo Gasbarro. In the following pages you'll find my versions of these, along with recipes for homemade limoncello, a luxurious coffee cream liqueur, and more.

Here is where you will also find the recipe that inspired this book—my nonna's *amarene sotto spirito*, sour cherries in boozy syrup. They are a most delicious adult spoon fruit.

You may not be familiar with *mosto cotto*—syrup made from cooking down grape must. It is sweet and tart with notes of spice and caramel. It is excellent on ice cream or for adding a sweet note to salad dressing.

Not everything in this chapter contains alcohol. Stir some almond syrup into a glass of soda water or milk and you have an Italian childhood favorite, orzata. Mint syrup in a glass of iced tea is a fine summer refresher. But cake with mint syrup stirred into the batter? Even better.

Essentials for Liqueurs, Fruit Syrups, and Alcohol-Preserved Fruit

- **Glass bottles and jars** in varying sizes. These can be bottles with swing-top lids fitted with gaskets or simply with tight-fitting lids. They are readily available at housewares stores such as Target or The Container Store or online (see Sources, page 292).

- For straining, draining, and filtering: a **narrow-neck funnel; coffee filters; tight-weave cheesecloth**; a **fine-mesh sieve**.

- Several types of alcohol and spirits are used in this chapter. The various liqueur recipes require a flavorless alcohol, such as grain alcohol or vodka. I use **Everclear**, which is distilled from corn. It is bottled at 151 proof (75.5 percent alcohol) and 190 proof (95 percent alcohol). Sale of the stronger version is banned in many states, so look for 151 proof or substitute 100-proof vodka. **Grappa** is a near-colorless Italian brandy made from the pulp, seeds, and stems left over from pressing grapes. **Cognac** is a distilled, aged brandy produced in western France. **Marsala**, named for a town in Sicily, is wine that has been fortified with brandy or neutral grape spirit.

MINT SYRUP

This syrup is not emerald green like commercial mint syrups. That's because it's completely natural, with no dyes or artificial flavors. So while the off-clear color may not be vibrant, the flavor is: pure, unadulterated, fresh. This syrup is the star ingredient in Gino's Mint Chocolate Chip Cake on page 272. It's also great in cocktails, drizzled on chocolate or vanilla ice cream, and tossed with fresh fruit. My son stirs it into his iced tea.

1 cup (237 g) water
1 cup (200 g) vanilla sugar (see page 57)
4 strips lemon zest (no white pith)
2 lightly packed cups (28 g) fresh mint leaves

1 · Combine the water and sugar in a heavy-bottomed saucepan and toss in the lemon zest. Bring to a boil over medium-high heat.

2 · When the syrup is almost at a boil, coarsely chop the mint leaves. Do this at the last possible moment so that you don't lose any of that wonderful mint aroma. As soon as the syrup starts to boil, turn off the heat and gently stir in the mint leaves. Cover the saucepan and let the syrup steep for 3 hours.

3 · Pour the mint syrup through a fine-mesh sieve into a clean glass jar or bottle. Cover and store in the refrigerator for up to 2 months.

ORZATA (ALMOND SYRUP)

Italian children are fond of orzata, ultra-sweet almond syrup, which they mix with sparkling water for a refreshing drink. When I was little, I was occasionally allowed to stir it into my milk. I liked it as much as chocolate milk, if not more. It's been a long time, but I've since rediscovered my favorite childhood drink, thanks to this homemade version of almond syrup. It's so much better than the commercial stuff. Orzata is also a key ingredient in my favorite kiddie cocktail, Tropicál, on page 269.

2 cups (280 g) whole raw almonds
3 cups (710 g) water
1 cup (200 g) sugar
1 teaspoon pure almond extract

EQUIPMENT
Tight-weave cheesecloth

1 · Place the nuts in the bowl of a food processor fitted with the metal blade. Pulse to chop the nuts a bit, then dribble in half of the water. Process until the nuts are very finely ground. Scrape into a bowl and stir in the remaining water. Let the mixture steep for several hours—3 to 4, if you have the time.

2 · Line a fine-mesh sieve with a piece of damp tight-weave cheesecloth and set it over a bowl. Pour the ground nut mixture into the sieve, collecting the liquid in the bowl. Press down on the nuts to extract as much liquid as possible. Dump the nuts back into the bowl with the liquid and let the mixture steep for another 2 to 3 hours.

3 · Once again, strain the almond liquid through a fine-mesh sieve lined with damp cheesecloth set over a bowl. Press down on the nuts to extract as much liquid as possible; then discard the nuts. You should have about 2 cups almond liquid.

4 · Pour the liquid into a saucepan and stir in the sugar. Set the saucepan over medium heat and bring the liquid to a boil. Reduce the heat to low or medium-low and simmer gently until the liquid has thickened slightly and is an opaque creamy pearl color, about 5 minutes. Remove from the heat and let cool for 10 minutes.

5 · Strain the syrup once more through a fine-mesh sieve (no need to use cheesecloth) into a bowl and stir in the almond extract. Let cool to room temperature. Funnel the syrup into a clean jar or bottle, cover, and refrigerate if not using immediately. The syrup will keep for up to 1 month. Shake well before using, as the syrup tends to separate as it sits.

ORZATA MILK
Pour 2 tablespoons of the syrup into a glass and fill with 1 cup cold milk. Stir and enjoy.

BLOOD ORANGE SYRUP

*My kids have always loved Italian Fanta orange soda, which they claim is
entirely different, and better, than the American version. They're right; it's less
sweet and pleasantly bitter. I have them to thank for giving me the idea to try
a homemade version using this jewel-toned syrup. As good as this syrup is in a
refreshing sparkling soda, it's even better on vanilla ice cream—think Creamsicle!*

2 cups (473 g) freshly squeezed blood orange
  juice, from 6 to 8 oranges
1½ to 2 cups (300 to 400 g) vanilla sugar
  (see page 57)

1 · Strain the orange juice through a fine-mesh sieve into a saucepan. Stir in 1½ cups of the sugar. Bring the juice to a simmer over medium-low heat, stirring often to dissolve the sugar. Taste and add the remaining ½ cup sugar if you prefer a sweeter syrup. Stir until dissolved. Remove from the heat, cover, and let cool to room temperature.

2 · Strain once more through a fine-mesh sieve and then funnel into a clean glass bottle or jar. Chill in the refrigerator before using. The syrup will keep, refrigerated, for up to 1 month.

ITALIAN BLOOD ORANGE SODA

Put a couple of ice cubes in an 8-ounce glass. Pour ¼ cup blood orange syrup into the glass and fill with soda water or sparkling spring water. Stir well, and enjoy.

MOSTO COTTO

My friend Marta Carrozza owns a small, beautifully appointed bed and breakfast in the historic heart of Sulmona. For much of the year, guests enjoy breakfast on the rooftop terrace, with the city's steeples and tile roofs and the surrounding mountains as their backdrop. Every morning, Marta sets out a selection of freshly baked cakes, bowls of seasonal fruit, and fresh ricotta accompanied by a small bowl of mosto cotto. *This thick, dark syrup is a prized condiment and ingredient throughout much of Italy, from Calabria to Emilia-Romagna, where it is known as saba.*

Mosto cotto is simply grape must—the freshly pressed and filtered juice of wine grapes—cooked down into syrup. But that description doesn't really do it justice. Once cooked, the syrup is put in bottles and left to age. It is here that the real transformation takes place. Over a period of weeks and months, the *mosto cotto* darkens in color to a deep, rich brown. It becomes smoother and more mellow, with notes of prune, raisin, fig, cherries, and spice. In Italy, *mosto cotto* was traditionally used as a sweetener in cookies and cakes before sugar was widely available, and it lends these sweets a rich, complex, fruity flavor (see Mostaccioli, page 270). There is really nothing like it. It is delicious drizzled over vanilla ice cream, fresh ricotta (page 203), or aged cheeses, as well as whisked into salad dressing and savory sauces.

Procuring fresh grape must will be your biggest challenge here, but I urge you to look for a source. Make friends with a winemaker. I have found them to be interesting, interested, and more than willing to help out. I have Michael Heny, the winemaker at Horton Vineyards, in Charlottesville, VA, to thank for providing me, over the last several years, with must from Cabernet Franc, Norton, Petit Verdot, Syrah, and Tannat grapes. Each variety yielded a slightly different flavor, with Norton being the most vegetal and Syrah the spiciest.

I got an unexpected bonus while working on this recipe: tasting real freshly pressed grape juice for the first time. Fresh grape must is bright and tart and sweet and, yes, thirst-quenching. I would drink it every day if I could. While I was tasting, I decided to mix myself a glass of homemade grape soda, which I did by adding a splash of sparkling spring water and a couple of ice cubes to half a glass of must. What a treat!

1 gallon fresh grape must

EQUIPMENT

Fine-mesh strainer

Tight-weave cheesecloth

Narrow funnel

1 sterilized 1-liter swing-top bottle with rubber gasket, or several smaller bottles

1 · Pour the must through a fine-mesh strainer lined with damp tight-weave cheesecloth into a large heavy-bottomed pot. Bring to a boil over medium-high heat. Reduce the heat to medium and cook at a lively simmer for 1½ to 2 hours. Skim any foam that rises to the top. As the must cooks, it will reduce in volume and begin to thicken slightly. It will start to smell "cooked." Here is where you need to be careful, as the must can go from perfectly cooked to overcooked very quickly. Reduce the heat to medium-low or low and continue to simmer gently until the must is reduced to about one-quarter its original volume, or even a little less. It will be thickened, but not too thick; it should coat a spoon but still pour easily. If you start to smell burnt caramel, remove the pot from the heat immediately.

2 · Let the syrup cool to room temperature. Strain it through a fine-mesh sieve lined with damp tight-weave cheesecloth and funnel it into the prepared bottle or bottles. Store in a cool, dark spot for up to 1 year. The *mosto cotto* will continue to improve in flavor as the months go by.

CLASSIC LIMONCELLO

· · · MAKES ABOUT 1½ QUARTS · · ·

Here's the beauty of limoncello: You make it in midwinter, when you can find good lemons at the market, and let it cure in your freezer. If you're smart you'll forget about it for a while. Then, on some sweltering summer night, you'll think to yourself: Aha! Limoncello! When you pull the bottle out of the freezer, it will frost up immediately. The liqueur inside will be cold and a little sluggish, a beautiful pearly yellow, and as inviting as the view from a balcony overlooking the blue Mediterranean.

What kind of lemon should you use for limoncello? In a perfect world, we would all have access to the large bumpy, thick-skinned lemons that grow around Sorrento and produce what many believe is the best-tasting limoncello (it's also where the drink originated). The Genoa lemon, brought to California by Ligurian immigrants, is a good variety, if you can find it. Otherwise, look for good organic lemons; those with thick, bumpy skins tend to have more oils, which is where most of the peel's fragrance and flavor resides.

10 large organic lemons

1 (750 ml) bottle 151-proof grain alcohol, such as Everclear, or 100-proof vodka

3 cups (600 g) vanilla sugar (see page 57)

3 to 4 cups (710 to 946 g) water

EQUIPMENT

2 clean 2-quart swing-top glass jars with rubber gaskets or Mason jars with screw-top lids

Fine-mesh sieve

Narrow funnel

2 coffee filters

1 clean 1-liter swing-top glass bottle and one 500 ml swing-top glass bottle, both with rubber gaskets, or three 500 ml swing-top glass bottles with rubber gaskets

1 · With a vegetable peeler, peel off the lemon zest in strips, removing only the thin top layer and leaving behind the white pith. Reserve the fruit for granita (page 275) or another use.

2 · Put the zest in a 2-quart glass jar. Pour in the alcohol and cover the jar tightly. Place it in a cool, dark spot and let it be for 2 months. Give it a shake from time to time to mix up the peels. As the alcohol sits, it will turn from colorless to a cheerful yellow, and the peels will lose their color.

(recipe continues)

3 · Combine the sugar and 3 to 4 cups water—depending on how strong you want to make your liqueur—in a heavy-bottomed saucepan. Cook, stirring, on low heat to dissolve the sugar. Raise the heat to medium and cook, stirring now and again, until the syrup reaches a boil. Remove from the heat and let cool completely. The syrup must be fully cool before it is mixed with the alcohol or the liqueur will be cloudy and opaque rather than translucent.

4 · Strain the lemon-infused alcohol through a fine-mesh sieve into the second 2-quart jar. Pour in the cool sugar syrup and swirl or stir gently to combine. Give the ingredients a few minutes to mingle. The liqueur will not be perfectly clear, but rather a pearly and translucent yellow.

5 · Line a narrow-neck funnel with a coffee filter and set it into the neck of one of the liqueur bottles. Filter the limoncello into the bottle, leaving 1 inch headspace. This process takes a little while, so just be patient and feed the funnel as needed. When the bottle is full, transfer the funnel to a second bottle. Check the filter; if it is clogged with debris, discard it and replace it with a new one. Filter the rest of the liqueur into the remaining bottle(s). Wipe the rims of the bottles and secure the lids. Let the bottles sit in a cool, dark spot for 2 to 4 weeks before using. Store the liqueur in the freezer for up to 1 year. Serve directly from the freezer.

THREE-CITRUS LIQUEUR

··· MAKES ABOUT 1½ QUARTS ···

The mix of lemons and oranges in this liqueur yields a lovely tangerine-colored liquid with bright citrus flavor. However, this recipe is just a guideline; the world of citrus is large, so feel free to experiment: Add in the peel of a sour Seville orange, or a grapefruit, or a many-fingered Buddha's Hand.

4 organic lemons

3 organic Meyer lemons

3 organic mandarin oranges

1 (750 ml) bottle 151-proof grain alcohol, such as Everclear, or 100-proof vodka

3 cups (600 g) vanilla sugar (see page 57)

3 to 4 cups (710 to 946 g) water

EQUIPMENT

2 clean 2-quart swing-top glass jars with rubber gaskets or Mason jars with screw-top lids

Fine-mesh sieve

Narrow-mouth funnel

2 coffee filters

1 clean 1-liter swing-top glass bottle and one 500 ml swing-top glass bottle, both with rubber gaskets, or three 500 ml swing-top glass bottles with rubber gaskets

1 • With a vegetable peeler, peel off the zest of the lemons and oranges in strips, removing only the thin top layer and leaving behind the white pith. Reserve the fruit for granita (page 275) or another use.

2 • Put the zest in a 2-quart glass jar. Pour in the alcohol and cover the jar tightly. Place it in a cool, dark spot and let it be for 2 months. Give it a shake from time to time to mix up the peels. As the alcohol sits, it will turn from clear to a pretty soft orange, and the peels will lose their color.

3 • Combine the sugar and 3 to 4 cups water—depending on how strong you want to make your liqueur—in a heavy-bottomed saucepan. Cook, stirring, on low heat to dissolve the sugar. Raise the heat to medium and cook, stirring now and again, until the syrup reaches a boil. Remove from the heat and let cool completely. The syrup must be fully cool before it is mixed with the alcohol or the liqueur will be cloudy and opaque rather than translucent.

4 · Strain the citrus alcohol through a fine-mesh sieve into the second 2-quart jar. Pour in the cool sugar syrup and swirl or stir gently to combine. Give the ingredients a few minutes to mingle. The liqueur will not be perfectly clear, but rather a pearly and translucent orange.

5 · Line a narrow-neck funnel with a coffee filter and set it into the neck of one of the liqueur bottles. Filter the liqueur into the bottle, leaving 1 inch headspace. This process takes a little while, so just be patient and feed the funnel as needed. When the bottle is full, transfer the funnel to a second bottle. Check the filter; if it is clogged with debris, discard it and replace it with a new one. Filter the rest of the liqueur into the remaining bottle(s). Wipe the rims of the bottles and secure the lids. Let the bottles sit in a cool, dark spot for 2 to 4 weeks before using. Store the liqueur in the freezer for up to 1 year. Serve directly from the freezer.

CREMA DI LIMONCELLO

*Adding cream to limoncello may seem like an unnecessary step toward
indulgence. But trust me, on those nights in midsummer when it's too hot
even to breathe, a little glass of this luxurious cordial, poured straight from
the freezer, is a life-saving measure. Okay, I exaggerate, but only a little.*

10 organic lemons

2½ cups (591 g) 151-proof grain alcohol,
such as Everclear, or 100-proof vodka

4 to 5 cups (800 g to 1 kg) vanilla sugar
(see page 57)

4 cups (960 g) whole milk

2 cups (480 g) heavy cream

EQUIPMENT

1 clean 2-quart swing-top glass jar with
rubber gasket or Mason jar with screw-
top lid

Fine-mesh sieve

Tight-weave cheesecloth

Narrow-mouth funnel

2 clean 1-liter swing-top glass bottles fitted
with rubber gaskets

1 · With a vegetable peeler, peel off the zest of
the lemons in strips, removing only the thin
top layer and leaving behind the white pith.
Reserve the fruit for granita (page 275) or
another use.

2 · Put the zest in the 2-quart jar. Pour in the
alcohol and cover the jar tightly. Place it in
a cool, dark spot and let it be for 2 months.

Give it a shake now and then to mix up the
peels. As the alcohol sits, it will turn from
colorless to a cheerful yellow, and the peels
will turn pale.

3 · To finish the liqueur, place the sugar (4 to
5 cups, depending on how sweet you want it),
milk, and cream in a large heavy-bottomed
saucepan. Cook, stirring, on low heat to dissolve the sugar. Raise the heat to medium and
bring to a boil. Remove from the heat and let
cool completely.

4 · Strain the lemon alcohol through a fine-
mesh sieve lined with damp cheesecloth into a
clean bowl, preferably with a spout. Pour the
cooled milk syrup through the lined sieve into
the bowl. Whisk to combine the syrup with
the alcohol, and give the ingredients a few
minutes to mingle.

5 · Funnel the liqueur into the bottles, leaving
1 inch headspace. If there is any left after the
two bottles are full, funnel it into a clean small
bottle. Wipe the rims of the bottles and secure
the lids. Place the bottles in the freezer. The
crema di limoncello is ready to serve after
1 week. Serve directly from the freezer, where
it will keep for up to 1 year.

STRAWBERRY CREAM LIQUEUR

My friend Marcello de Antoniis grew up in the foothills of Abruzzo's Gran Sasso d'Italia mountain range and truly knows the mountains like the back of his hand. One summer a few years ago, he drove my family and me up to La Baita della Sceriffa, a casual picnic spot. La Baita is where locals go to enjoy arrosticini, the delicious grilled lamb skewers that are a specialty of the region. After our al fresco lunch, we chatted with the owners and were treated to a selection of house-made liqueurs. I fell head over heels for a creamy but potent strawberry liqueur made from wild strawberries. Now I use tiny, deep red strawberries from my farmers' market to make this liqueur.

You really do need good local strawberries to make this liqueur successfully. The big cottony ones from the supermarket simply don't have enough flavor or fragrance to impart to the alcohol. For maximum enjoyability, store the liqueur in the freezer, where it will keep for at least 6 months. It is indescribably good served straight from the freezer—like an adult strawberry shake. Although you may be tempted to fill a parfait glass, serve the liqueur in small quantities, in cordial glasses.

1 quart ripe strawberries, hulled; about 1 pound (454 g)

2½ cups (591 g) 151-proof grain alcohol, such as Everclear, or 100-proof vodka

2 cups (480 g) heavy cream

2 cups (480 g) whole milk

2 cups (400 g) vanilla sugar (see page 57)

Seeds scraped from 1 vanilla bean, or 1 teaspoon pure vanilla extract

EQUIPMENT

1 clean 1-gallon glass container or jug with tight-fitting lid

Tight-weave cheesecloth

Narrow funnel

3 clean 500 ml swing-top bottles with rubber gaskets

1 · Place the whole hulled strawberries in the 1-gallon container. Pour the alcohol over the strawberries and cap with the lid so that no air can get in or out. Set the container on the counter out of the sun and let the strawberries steep for 2 to 3 days. Be sure to gently swirl the container a couple of times a day to mix things up. Within a day or two, you will notice that the liquid has turned a beautiful clear red and the strawberries have turned pale and anemic-looking.

2 · In a large saucepan, stir together the cream, milk, and sugar. Cook over medium heat until the sugar dissolves and the mixture just comes to a boil. Remove the pot from the heat and immediately stir in the vanilla. Let the mixture cool to room temperature.

3 · Strain the strawberry-infused vodka through a fine-mesh sieve lined with damp cheesecloth into a clean bowl. Don't press down on the strawberries or the liquid will turn cloudy. Discard the strawberries and rinse out the cheesecloth.

4 · Strain the cooled cream mixture through the cheesecloth-lined sieve into the bowl with the strawberry-infused vodka. Gently stir or whisk until thoroughly combined.

5 · Funnel the liqueur into the bottles, leaving 1 inch headspace. If there is any left after the two bottles are full, funnel it into a clean small bottle. Wipe the rims of the bottles and secure the lids. Place the bottles in the freezer. The *crema di fragole* is ready to serve after 1 week. Serve directly from the freezer, where it will keep for up to 1 year.

COOK'S NOTE · Whole strawberries freeze beautifully, so next time you see them at the farmers' market, get a couple of extra quarts. Hull them and spread them out on a rimmed baking sheet. Freeze until solid, and then transfer them to zipper-lock freezer bags and pop them back into the freezer.

ZABAGLIONE CREAM LIQUEUR

· · · MAKES 3 CUPS · · ·

*My Italian aunts had a small but well-chosen stash of liquor in their apartment
in Rome. Amid the Cognac, whiskey, and various amari there was always the
distinctive white bottle of Vov, a sweet liqueur made with egg yolks and Marsala
wine. The creamy liqueur (sort of an Italian version of eggnog) has a charming
backstory, one of typical Italian resourcefulness. In 1845, Gian Battista Pezziol,
a pastry chef in Padua, faced a daily dilemma: how to use up hundreds of egg
yolks left over from making torrone, Italy's famous nut-studded nougat (page
286). He hit on a liqueur based on zabaglione, a spoon dessert made from
yolks, sugar, and Marsala. He named it Vovi—Venetian dialect for "eggs."*

1 cup (240 g) whole milk

1 cup (240 g) heavy cream

2 cups (400 g) sugar

½ vanilla bean

4 large egg yolks

½ cup (118 g) dry Marsala wine

½ cup (118 g) 151-proof grain alcohol, such
as Everclear, or 100-proof vodka

¼ cup (59 g) Cognac

EQUIPMENT

Narrow funnel

1 clean 750 ml bottle with a swing-top lid
with rubber gasket

1 · Pour the milk and cream into a saucepan
and stir in 1 cup of the sugar. Scrape the seeds
from the vanilla bean into the saucepan. Bring
the mixture to a bare simmer over medium
heat, without letting it boil. Stir to make sure
the sugar dissolves completely. Remove from
the heat.

2 · Whisk together the egg yolks and remaining 1 cup sugar until thick and light in color.
Add a few driblets of the scalded milk mixture to the egg yolks, whisking vigorously to
prevent the yolks from curdling. Continue to
whisk in the milk mixture, a little at a time,
until you have added it all. Gently whisk in
the Marsala, alcohol, and Cognac.

3 · Pour the liqueur through a funnel into the
bottle. Refrigerate until thoroughly chilled.
The liqueur is ready to drink once it's cold. It
will keep for a month or longer in the refrigerator. Shake well before serving.

COFFEE CREAM LIQUEUR

· · · MAKES 1⅓ QUARTS · · ·

*Many restaurants in Italy—and increasingly here in the United States—
bring out a selection of house-made liqueurs after dinner. Over the years
I've tried numerous versions of coffee liqueur, and this one, made with
whole milk and cream, is my favorite. To make it successfully, you need
exceptionally strong brewed espresso that will stand up to the alcohol and still
shine through with its rich, bitter flavor. Brew your own, or buy it already
brewed from your local coffee bar, but make sure you request extra-strong.*

1 cup (240 g) whole milk

1 cup (240 g) heavy cream

1 cup (200 g) vanilla sugar (see page 57)

1¼ cups (177 g) double-strong brewed
espresso (see Cook's Note)

1¼ cups (177 g) 151-proof grain alcohol,
such as Everclear, or 100-proof vodka

EQUIPMENT

Stovetop espresso maker with 350 ml
(1½ cups) capacity, or electric espresso
machine (optional)

Fine-mesh strainer

Tight-weave cheesecloth

1 clean 1-liter swing-top bottle with rubber
gasket

1 · Combine the milk, cream, and sugar in
a large saucepan and bring to a boil over
medium heat, stirring to dissolve the sugar
completely. Once the milk boils, remove it
from the heat and stir in the espresso. Let cool
completely.

2 · Line a fine-mesh strainer with damp
cheesecloth and set it over a bowl. Strain the
milk-coffee mixture into the bowl. Gently
whisk in the alcohol, and give the ingredients
a few minutes to mingle.

3 · Funnel the liqueur into the bottle, leaving
1 inch headspace. Wipe the rim of the bottle,
secure the lid, and place in the refrigerator
or freezer (I prefer the freezer). The liqueur
is ready to serve after 1 week. Serve directly
from the freezer—it's like a delicious spiked
coffee slushie—where it will keep for up to
1 year.

COOK'S NOTE · To brew the coffee for this liqueur, I use a stovetop espresso maker with a 350 ml (1½-cup) capacity and run the brewed coffee through the espresso maker a second time to make double-strong coffee. Fill the bottom part of the espresso maker with enough water to come up to the notch. Fit the perforated coffee funnel into the opening and add 4 to 5 tablespoons freshly ground espresso, or as much as indicated by the manufacturer. Make the coffee on the stovetop. Pour the freshly brewed coffee into a heat-proof glass or liquid measuring cup. Rinse out the espresso maker (careful—it will be hot!).

Pour the brewed coffee into the bottom part of the machine and add enough water to reach the notch. Refit the perforated coffee funnel into the opening, add more freshly ground espresso, and brew on the stovetop. You should have 1¼ cups. If you have less, brew another pot of espresso (using water rather than already brewed coffee) and add enough to the double-strength brew to make 1¼ cups. If you have more than needed, measure out 1¼ cups and drink the rest.

NOTE· If you are using an electric espresso maker, brew enough strong espresso cups to make 1¼ cups total.

NOCINO

Nocino, or green walnut liqueur, is made from walnuts that are harvested while still unripe. At this stage, the outer rind is bright green and smooth and the shell and nut meat inside are transparent and partially liquid. That's what gives nocino its distinct flavor and dark color—the immature nut begins to oxidize soon after being cut open. The nuts, green rind included, are steeped in alcohol and wine, plus spices and sugar, and the brew turns dark within a few days. There are some nebulous rules around how to properly make nocino. According to various versions, the nuts must be harvested by hand on the night of June 24, the feast of St. John, by women who climb the walnut trees in bare feet. Harvesting by hand prevents damage to the soft green exterior; I'm not sure about the bare feet. Only an odd number of nuts must be used in the preparation, and they should steep in the alcohol mixture for 40 days before the filtering process. For the sake of tradition, I have adhered to a couple of the rules, but I didn't shimmy up any trees in my bare feet—I ordered my green walnuts online from California (see Sources, page 292). Nocino gets better as it ages; I know people who let it sit for at least a year before drinking. It's worth the wait; the inky brown, spiced liqueur has a pleasing, bitter finish, which makes it a good digestivo—after-dinner drink.

29 to 35 green walnuts, about 3½ pounds (1.6 kg)

Zest of 1 large lemon, in strips (no white pith)

Zest of 1 large orange, in strips (no white pith)

10 whole cloves

1 whole nutmeg, cut in half

3-inch cinnamon stick, cut in half

5 to 6 cups (1 to 1.2 kg) sugar

2 (750 ml) bottles dry white wine, such as Soave or Pecorino

1 (750 ml) bottle 151-proof grain alcohol, such as Everclear, or 100-proof vodka

EQUIPMENT

Disposable kitchen gloves (such as Playtex)

Cutting board that you don't mind staining

2 clean 3-quart glass jars with swing-top lids and rubber gaskets

Tight-weave cheesecloth

Fine-mesh sieve

Coffee filters

Narrow-neck funnel

3 clean 1-liter swing-top bottles with rubber gaskets

1 · Wash the walnuts and pat them dry with paper towels. Put on kitchen gloves to avoid staining your fingertips. Cut the walnuts into quarters with a sharp knife. They shouldn't be difficult to cut, but watch out, as they will roll around a bit. Divide the walnuts evenly between the two 3-quart jars. Add the lemon and orange zests, cloves, nutmeg, cinnamon stick, and 5 cups (1 kg) sugar, taking care to divide the ingredients evenly between the two jars. If you have a very large glass jar, you can use that instead of two; however, I find two to be more manageable. Pour 1 bottle of wine into each of the jars, and divide the alcohol between them. Clamp the lid on tightly and give the jars a few good shakes to distribute the ingredients and help dissolve the sugar.

2 · Place the jars in a sunny spot—I set them on a small table near the kitchen window, with a clean (but old) kitchen towel under them to protect the table. Let the walnuts steep for 40 to 60 days. Shake the jars once or twice a week if you think of it to redistribute the ingredients. The liquid will turn from clear to near-black. This is what you want.

3 · Set a colander lined with damp cheesecloth over a large bowl and strain the nocino to remove the walnuts and aromatics. Discard the solids. Line a fine-mesh sieve with a coffee filter and set it over a clean deep bowl. Use one with a spout if you have it. Strain the nocino through the filter to remove sediment.

4 · Line the funnel with a coffee filter and filter the nocino into the bottles. If the filter clogs with sediment, replace it with a clean one. Wipe the rims of the bottles and secure the lids. Label the bottles and place them in a cool, dark spot for several months. The flavor of the nocino will mellow and improve as it ages. Nocino will keep for several years.

COOK'S NOTE · If you would like to give nocino away as gifts, decant some of the liqueur into smaller bottles and label them.

GRAPES IN SPICED GRAPPA

I've never had anything quite like these grapes; neither has anyone I've
served them to. They are strong. A long steep in grappa leaves the fruit
pretty much saturated with alcohol and imbued with the alluring flavors
of cinnamon, star anise, and other spices. I adapted this recipe from one
in Ada Boni's classic book Il Talismano della Felicità. *Serve these chilled,*
in judicious portions—no more than one or two per person—in place of
an after-dinner drink, or as a garnish to rich cake or ice cream.

⅔ cup (133 g) sugar or vanilla sugar
 (see page 57)

1-inch piece cinnamon stick

2 whole cloves

1 whole star anise

¼ teaspoon ground coriander, or a few
 whole coriander seeds

Pinch of ground mace

2 cups (473 g) grappa

1 pound (454 g) organic large round red
 grapes, seedless or not, your choice

EQUIPMENT

2 clean 1-quart jars with tight-fitting lids

1 · Place the sugar and spices in a jar. Pour in the grappa and secure the lid tightly. Shake the jar gently but firmly several times until the sugar is completely dissolved.

2 · Snip the grapes from their stems, leaving just a small piece of stem attached to each grape. Wash and dry them thoroughly. Pack the grapes into the second jar. Pour the grappa and spice mixture over the grapes, fasten the lid, and place the jar in a cool, dark spot for 1 month. After that, store the grapes in the refrigerator, where they will keep for 6 months or longer.

COOK'S NOTE · Serve the grapes chilled: Use them to garnish your favorite cocktails, such as a Manhattan, a martini, or a Negroni. Or serve one or two alongside a bittersweet chocolate torte as an elegant dinner party dessert. When the grapes are gone, strain the spiced grappa and enjoy chilled as a digestivo.

PEACHES IN GRAPPA-SPIKED SYRUP

· · · MAKES 3 QUARTS · · ·

Think of this as the Italian version of bourbon peaches, only prettier because grappa is clear and won't muddy the blush and golden color of the fruit. Be sure to use ripe—but not mushy—freestone peaches; otherwise you'll have a hard time peeling and prying them open. Serve these peaches, along with a good drizzle of their boozy syrup, over vanilla ice cream.

2 cups (200 g) vanilla sugar (see page 57)

3 cups (710 g) water

2-inch piece vanilla bean

Freshly squeezed juice of 1 lemon

6 pounds (2.7 kg) ripe but firm yellow freestone peaches

1½ cups (355 g) grappa

EQUIPMENT

3 sterilized 1-quart jars and their lids

Basic water-bath canning equipment (see page 15)

1 · Bring a large pot of water to a rolling boil.

2 · Combine the sugar and water in a heavy-bottomed saucepan and set over medium heat. Stir to dissolve the sugar. Scrape the seeds from the vanilla bean into the sugar water and toss in the pod. Bring to a boil, reduce the heat, and let simmer gently for about 5 minutes, until the syrup is slightly thickened.

3 · Fill a large bowl with ice water and stir the lemon juice into it. Cut a small "X" into the bottom of each peach. When the water is boiling, gently drop in the peaches, a few

at a time, and blanch for 60 to 90 seconds to loosen the skins. Transfer them with a slotted spoon or skimmer to the ice water to cool slightly.

4 · Peel the peaches—the skins should slip off easily—and cut them in half or quarters. Pack them into the jars, fitting them as closely and tightly as possible without squishing them. Use a bubble remover or a clean chopstick to help position them snugly against one another. Leave about 1½ inches headspace.

5 · Pour ⅓ to ½ cup of the syrup into each jar so that the jar is about two-thirds full of liquid. Use the bubble remover or chopstick to gently jostle the peaches to make sure the liquid sinks to the bottom. Top off with about ½ cup grappa, leaving ½ inch headspace. Screw the lids on tightly and process for 25 minutes in a boiling-water bath (see Water-Bath Canning, page 15). The peaches will keep, properly sealed, for 6 months; after that they begin to lose their color and texture. Once opened, store in the refrigerator for up to 1 month. If a jar fails to seal properly, refrigerate it and enjoy those peaches first.

SOUR CHERRIES IN BOOZY SYRUP

My maternal grandmother, Maria Petrosemolo Tomassoni, made this wonderful concoction of dried sour cherries preserved in a thick syrup generously spiked with alcohol and brandy, amarene sotto spirito. *It was a treat to get a spoonful of those cherries, to top vanilla gelato or to enjoy them as is. It took me numerous tries to come up with my own version, one that I am reasonably happy with. The cherries my grandmother used—tiny, dark, deeply flavored ones called amarene—are not available in the United States (at least I've never seen them), so I use Montmorency cherries, which are typical sour cherries used for pie. My grandmother also dried her cherries in the sun; I use my oven. The result is not quite the same, but pretty darn close.*

1 quart (680 g) sour cherries, with pits

1½ cups (300 g) superfine sugar

½ cup (118 g) 151-proof grain alcohol, such as Everclear, or 100-proof vodka

¼ cup (118 g) Cognac

2-inch piece cinnamon stick

EQUIPMENT

1 sterilized 1-quart swing-top glass jar with rubber gasket

1 · Preheat the oven (or a warming cupboard if your oven is equipped with one) to 175°F, if possible, but no more than 200° F. Line two baking sheets with parchment paper and set a wire rack (the kind with a grid) on top.

2 · Do not pit the cherries; the pits add flavor to the steeping liquor. Set the cherries on the cooling racks so they are not touching. Transfer the baking sheets to the oven and leave the cherries to dry for several hours— as many as 10, if necessary.

3 · Check them after the first hour, and then again every couple of hours, to make sure they are not drying out too fast or cooking, which could make them tough. Turn them over once or twice for even drying and to keep them from sticking to the rack. After a few

(recipe continues)

hours, you will see a change in their color and appearance; they'll begin to deflate and crinkle and eventually become a couple of shades darker. Remove the cherries when they have shrunk to about one-third their original size and are no longer plump. They should still be pliable, even a little soft, but with only a little juice left. Let cool completely. You should end up with about 2 cups or a little more.

4 · Place the cherries in the jar and cover with 1 cup of the sugar. Clamp the lid shut and vigorously shake the jar to mix the sugar and cherries together. Set the jar in a sunny spot and let the cherries macerate for 2 to 3 days, until the sugar is dissolved. Shake the jar now and again to help the process along. When the sugar has dissolved and turned into syrup, they are ready for the next step.

5 · If the syrup is thin—this will depend on how much juice was left in the cherries—pour some of it out (you can save it to mix with soda water for a cherry soda). Add the alcohol, Cognac, and cinnamon stick, along with the remaining ½ cup sugar. Let the cherries steep for at least 2 weeks in a cool, dark spot. Taste and add more alcohol, Cognac, or sugar, as desired. Stored in a cool, dark place, the cherries will keep for 1 year or longer.

COOK'S NOTE · Serve the cherries any number of ways: Spoon them, along with some of their syrup, onto Almond Gelato (page 289) or vanilla ice cream. Chill the cherries and syrup in the refrigerator and serve in small glasses as an after-dinner treat. Or use the syrup in a Champagne cocktail, garnished with a few cherries in the bottom of the glass.

TROPICÁL

The evening passeggiata, *or promenade, is a ritual in Italy. Clusters of friends, arms linked; parents with toddlers in strollers; groups of signori (spry older men and women) all take to the piazzas and streets to walk and talk. Sometimes the* passeggiata *happens before dinner; sometimes afterward (sometimes both). It's a wonderful habit that helps to keep the population fit. And, depending on the time of day, it usually includes a small cone of gelato or a beverage—coffee or an aperitivo. On evenings when I accompanied my parents on the promenade in our beach town (before I was old enough to go out with friends), we would sometimes end up at the bar of a local hotel, where I would order this children's drink. Almond syrup sweetened the rich milk, and a glug of mint syrup turned it a pretty shade of green. The tropicál at the bar, made with commercial syrup, was good, but the drink is even better when the syrup is homemade. Homemade mint syrup lacks that bright green color, though; you can add a couple of drops of green food color to the milk if you like. I do, for old times' sake.*

1½ cups (360 g) cold whole milk

3 tablespoons Orzata (page 240)

3 tablespoons Mint Syrup (page 239)

A few drops green food coloring (optional)

Take a nice walk. When you get home, combine the ingredients in a large glass and stir well. Enjoy.

MOSTACCIOLI

··· MAKES ABOUT 30 COOKIES ···

*Abruzzo, Campania, and Puglia all claim this spiced Christmas cookie as their
own. They are all right; versions of mostaccioli can be found across Italy's south.
The addition of* mosto cotto—grape must syrup—*to the dough gives these cookies
their tender, cake-like crumb and rich, almost raisin-like flavor. After baking, the
cookies are thickly glazed with bittersweet chocolate. Tempering the chocolate is an
extra step, but it will ensure that your glazed mostaccioli keep their beautiful sheen.*

½ cup (70 g) raw skin-on almonds

3 cups (375 g) unbleached all-purpose flour,
plus more for dusting the work surface

1 cup (200 g) sugar

2 tablespoons unsweetened cocoa powder

1 teaspoon baking powder

1 teaspoon ground cinnamon

¼ teaspoon ground cloves

¾ cup (300 g) Mosto Cotto (page 244 or
store-bought; see Sources, page 292)

2 large eggs, lightly beaten

1 pound (454 g) bittersweet chocolate,
for glazing

EQUIPMENT
Instant-read thermometer

1 · Preheat the oven to 350°F and line two
baking sheets with parchment paper.

2 · Spread the nuts on a rimmed baking sheet
and bake until fragrant, 7 to 8 minutes. Let
cool completely. (Leave the oven on.) Grind
the nuts in a food processor until finely
chopped.

3 · Combine the flour, sugar, cocoa powder,
baking powder, cinnamon, and cloves in the
bowl of a stand mixer fitted with the paddle
attachment. Add the nuts and mix on low
speed to combine. With the mixer on low,
pour in the *mosto cotto* and the eggs. Mix until
a soft ball of dough forms.

4 · Turn the dough out onto a lightly floured
work surface and roll it out into a rectangle
about ½ inch thick. With a cookie cutter or
sharp knife, cut the dough into diamond
shapes about 2 inches wide. Gather up any
odd-shaped pieces and re-roll to make more
mostaccioli. You should end up with about 30.

5 · Place the mostaccioli ½ inch apart on the baking sheets. Bake until the cookies are set and lightly crackled on the surface, about 15 minutes. Let cool for 10 minutes, then transfer to racks to cool completely.

6 · **To temper the chocolate for glazing:** Coarsely chop 12 ounces (340 g) of the chocolate and leave the rest in large pieces. Put the chopped pieces in a heatproof bowl. Set the bowl over a pan of barely simmering water (the bottom of the bowl should not touch the water). Start stirring when the chocolate begins to melt and keep stirring until it is nearly melted. Remove the bowl from the pan and continue to stir until all the chocolate is melted. Use a digital thermometer to test the temperature of the chocolate. If it is above 100°F, keep stirring until it drops to 100°F. Add the remaining pieces of chocolate to the bowl and stir constantly until the temperature drops to 90°F. The goal is not to melt all the chocolate; in fact, if it does all melt, chances are the chocolate has not been properly tempered. Simply add another piece and keep stirring until the temperature registers 90°F.

7 · Have ready two baking sheets lined with parchment paper (I use the same parchment on which I baked the cookies). With a pastry brush, brush a thick layer of chocolate on the tops and sides of the mostaccioli and set them on the parchment. Let the chocolate set completely, for about 1 hour, before serving. Store the mostaccioli at room temperature in an airtight container. Stack the cookies in layers, with sheets of waxed paper between them to prevent scuffing. The mostaccioli will keep for 1 week.

GINO'S MINT CHOCOLATE CHIP CAKE

· · · MAKES ONE 9- BY 13-INCH CAKE · · ·

La Locanda di Gino is a gem of a restaurant in the heart of Sulmona. It opened in 1962 and has been expertly run by the Allega family ever since. The late Gino's sons, Giacomo and Marco, always impeccably dressed in colorful pressed shirts and ties, keep the front of the house running smoothly. In the back, their mother, Lucia, and wives, Titina and Marcella, dressed alike in white aprons and caps, make culinary magic, turning out fresh chitarra *noodles, tender roast lamb, vegetable terrines, and other* piatti tipici Abruzzesi.

One afternoon, while lunching there with friends, we were served this simple-looking cake, cut up into small squares, for dessert. I must have ooohed and aaahed a lot, because when I went into the kitchen to thank the chefs, they handed me a slip of paper with the recipe written by hand on it.

2 cups (255 g) unbleached all-purpose flour, plus more for dusting the pan

2 teaspoons baking powder

¼ teaspoon fine sea salt

7 tablespoons (100 g) unsalted butter, at cool room temperature, plus more for greasing the pan

1 cup plus 2 tablespoons (125 g) sugar or vanilla sugar (see page 57)

3 large eggs, at room temperature

9 ounces (255 g) fresh ricotta cheese

½ cup (85 g) bittersweet chocolate chips (see Cook's Note)

¾ cup (227 g) Mint Syrup (page 239)

Confectioners' sugar, for dusting

1 · Preheat the oven to 375°F. Butter and flour a 9- by 13-inch baking pan.

2 · Combine the flour, baking powder, and salt in a bowl and stir well. In a stand mixer fitted with the whisk attachment, beat together the butter and sugar until fluffy. Add the eggs, one at a time, until well incorporated. Beat in the flour mixture on low speed just until incorporated. Raise the speed to medium-high and beat in the ricotta and chocolate chips. With the mixer running on low speed, gradually pour in ½ cup of the mint syrup and mix until fully incorporated.

3 · Scrape the batter into the prepared pan and bake until browned on top and a cake tester inserted in the middle of the cake comes out clean, about 30 minutes.

4 · Set the pan on a cooling rack. While the cake is still hot, use a pastry brush to brush the top with the remaining ¼ cup mint syrup. Let the cake cool to room temperature. To serve, cut into squares and dust with confectioners' sugar.

COOK'S NOTE · I use small bittersweet chocolate baking chips from France that I buy at La Cuisine, a kitchenware store in Alexandria, Virginia (See Sources, page 292). The brand is Michel Cluizel. The chips are smaller than regular chocolate chips (more like tiny disks) and sort of melt into the batter as the cake bakes. They provide the necessary hit of bittersweet chocolate flavor without the hard texture of regular chips. Mini chocolate chips may be substituted.

SICILIAN LEMON GRANITA

· · · MAKES 1½ QUARTS · · ·

Sicily is famous for many sweets, including icy, refreshing granita. Flavors abound, from almond and pistachio to coffee and chocolate. Fruit granita is also popular— peach, strawberry, mandarin, and, of course, lemon. This recipe makes use of all the lemons left over from making limoncello (page 247), a win-win in my book.

2 cups (473 g) freshly squeezed lemon juice, from 10 to 12 lemons

Zest of 2 lemons, coarsely chopped (no white pith)

3 cups (710 g) water

2 to 3 cups (400 to 600 g) vanilla sugar (see page 57)

1 · Press the lemon juice through a fine-mesh sieve into a jar or lidded container and refrigerate.

2 · Combine the lemon zest, water, and 2 cups (400 g) sugar in a heavy-bottomed saucepan. Bring to a simmer over medium heat, stirring often, to make sure the sugar is completely dissolved. Taste and add the remaining sugar if you want sweeter granita. Stir until completely dissolved. Remove from the heat and let cool to room temperature. Strain through a fine-mesh sieve into a container with a lid. Refrigerate until well chilled.

3 · Combine the chilled syrup and lemon juice in a bowl. Pour into the frozen canister of an ice cream machine and freeze according to the manufacturer's instructions until solid. The granita will have a texture and appearance similar to wet snow. Scoop it into a container with a tight-fitting lid and freeze. Enjoy within 2 weeks.

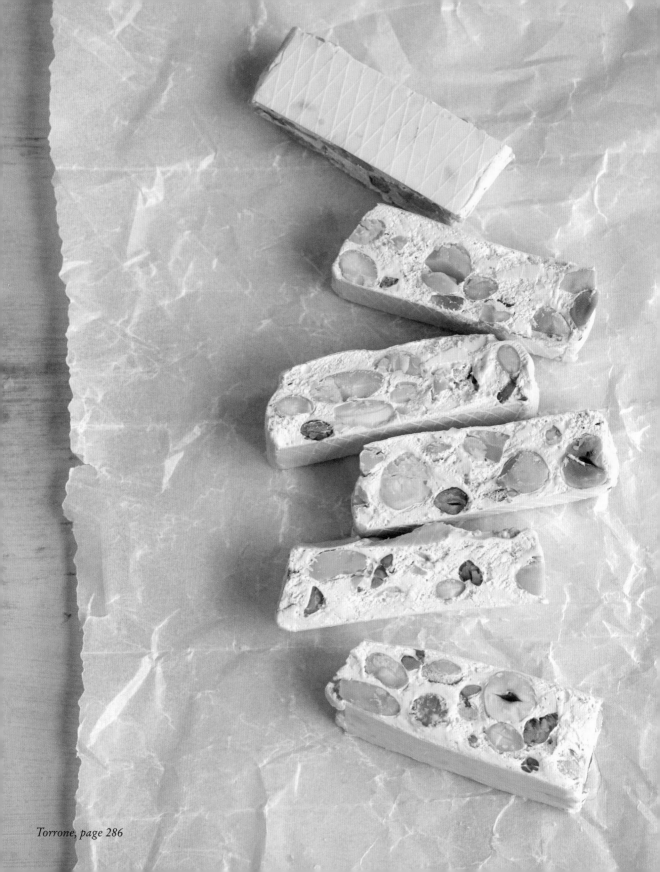

Torrone, page 286

CONFECTIONS

You might not think of confections—candies, chocolates, nougats, and other sweets—as a form of preserves, but step inside Pietro Romanengo fu Stefano, on Via Roma in Genoa, and you will soon change your mind.

The place itself is something of a well-preserved confection. Originally founded as a spice shop in 1780, Romanengo has been at its current location since 1930. Being inside the shop is like being inside a jewel box trying to choose a favorite bauble. It gleams and sparkles with polished wood and glass display cases, large mirrors on the walls, painted ceilings hung with crystal chandeliers, and marble underfoot. Inside the display cases is a spectacular array of sugar-preserved fruits, almond-paste sweets, chocolates, and more.

Confectioners still make everything by hand following a seasonal schedule: chocolates, candied orange peel, and torrone (nougat) in winter; Easter sweets, rose-infused preserves and syrups, sugared violets, and herb and spice pastilles in spring; chocolate-dipped candied figs and other fruit in summer; and candied chestnuts and fruit pastes in fall.

Shops like Romanengo can still be found in cities and towns throughout Italy, each with its own history and specialties; they truly are gems and I recommend you search them out if you are planning a trip.

And now, a (confection) confession: I am not a professional candy maker. While I adore all those gorgeous glazed fruits and delicate sugared sweets—edible works of art, really—produced at confectionary shops, I don't really want to devote all my time to mastering what really is a specialized profession. On the other hand, I am a curious and ambitious cook—you probably are, too—and I enjoy stretching my abilities and learning new techniques.

So what I offer in this chapter is a taste of traditional Italian confections—a few of my favorites—that may veer toward ambitious but are not intimidating. Well, maybe one is a little intimidating; it's torrone, the nut-studded nougat that is found all over Italy (and here in the United States) at Christmastime. Torrone calls for making both meringue and a hot sugar syrup and then combining the two to yield a billowy, sticky mess that must then be quickly wrestled into shape. I know! But when you make it you will see that it is worth it. It's impressive, and so much better than the slightly stale stuff you find in most shops during the holidays.

Far easier to make (but just as impressive) is homemade *panforte di Siena*, a dense cake of dried and candied fruit, nuts, and lots of spices that dates to the thirteenth century. The hardest part is waiting the month or so that it takes for the panforte to properly cure.

SWEET ALMOND PASTE

··· MAKES ABOUT 1 POUND (454 G) ···

Almond paste, pasta di mandorle, *is often confused with marzipan, a sweet, smooth paste that is used to make* frutta martorana—*Sicily's famed marzipan confections, which are molded into fruit shapes and painted with colorful vegetable dyes. Almond paste, by contrast, is coarser, less "finished." It is the central ingredient in many Italian sweets; often added to cake batters, baked into cookies, and used as a filling for sweet cornetti and other pastries. It makes an excellent base for Almond Gelato (page 289).*

1⅓ cups (200 g) raw, skin-on almonds
1 cup (200 g) vanilla sugar (see page 57)
2 to 3 tablespoons water
1 teaspoon pure almond extract

1 · Place the almonds in the bowl of a food processor. Sprinkle in 3 tablespoons of the sugar and process until the nuts are powdery—they will first look like coarse sand and then like fine cornmeal. Add the rest of the sugar and pulse until combined.

2 · With the motor running, add 2 tablespoons water and the almond extract through the feed tube and continue to process until the mixture forms a ball of sticky dough. Add 1 or 2 teaspoons more water if necessary to bring the paste together.

3 · Turn the paste out onto a clean work surface and divide it in half. Knead each piece into a rough log about 6 inches long. Place each log on a separate sheet of plastic wrap. Wrap the plastic around each log and roll and press the logs, one at a time, to make them smooth and even. Tie the logs at both ends with kitchen string.

4 · If not using immediately, store in the refrigerator for up to 1 month. For longer storage, place the logs in a zipper-lock freezer bag and store them in the freezer, where they will keep for up to 1 year. Let the paste thaw until pliable before using.

SWEET HAZELNUT PASTE

··· MAKES ABOUT 1¾ CUPS (400 G) ···

Hazelnuts are an important crop in Piedmont, where they are cultivated primarily for use by commercial and artisanal producers of candies, chocolates, creams, and spreads. Yes, Piedmont is the birthplace of Nutella, the iconic chocolate-hazelnut spread. This paste, though, is pure hazelnut, with a little sugar mixed in. The sugar is optional; I like the touch of sweetness it adds to the robust, toasty flavor of the nuts. In this book, hazelnut paste is the base for the Hazelnut Cream Crostata on page 290. You can also substitute it for the almond paste in Almond Gelato (page 289) to make hazelnut gelato. And it's delicious spread on toast along with Simple Strawberry Jam (page 85) or Sour Cherry Spoon Fruit (page 87).

3 cups (400 g) hazelnuts

¼ cup (50 g) sugar

1 tablespoon hazelnut or vegetable oil (optional)

1 · Preheat the oven to 350°F. Spread the hazelnuts on a rimmed baking sheet and bake until the skins have begun to crackle, about 10 minutes. Wrap the hot hazelnuts in a clean kitchen towel and let stand for about 1 minute. Roll the nuts back and forth in the towel to loosen and rub off the skins. Not all the skins will come off; this is fine. Let the nuts cool completely.

2 · Place the hazelnuts in the bowl of a food processor. Sprinkle in the sugar and process until the nuts are powdery—they will first look like coarse sand and then like fine cornmeal. Continue to process, at intervals if necessary to avoid overheating the motor. After 3 to 4 minutes, the nuts will clump together like thick, coarse peanut butter. Turn off the motor and scrape down the bowl, then keep processing; the coarse paste will soon loosen and become smoother; when it reaches that point it is done. (If the paste is being stubborn, drizzle in the hazelnut oil to help loosen it.)

3 · Scrape the paste into a container with a tight-fitting lid. (I like to divide it between two small containers.) Store the hazelnut paste in the refrigerator for up to 1 month, or in the freezer for up to 1 year.

FIG AND WALNUT SALAMI

··· MAKES ONE 6- TO 7-INCH SALAMI ···

This whimsical dried fig concoction, spiced with cinnamon, cloves, and pepper, hovers between sweet and savory. It mimics the shape of lonza (cured pork loin) or a small salami. For full effect, roll the fig salami in confectioners' sugar before serving. It goes beautifully with all sorts of cheeses, including Gorgonzola, robiola, and extra-aged Parmigiano-Reggiano.

4 ounces (113 g) dried **Mission figs**

4 ounces (113 g) dried **Calimyrna figs**

1 whole **clove**

1 small **cinnamon stick**

Zest of 1 small **orange**, in strips (no white pith)

½ teaspoon whole **anise seeds**

2 cups (473 g) **dry red wine**, such as Sangiovese

½ teaspoon **fine sea salt**

½ teaspoon freshly ground **black pepper**

¼ to ½ cup (50 to 100 g) **sugar**

½ cup (57 g) **walnuts**, toasted and coarsely chopped (see Cook's Note)

Confectioners' sugar, for rolling the salami

EQUIPMENT

1 clean 1-quart jar with a tight-fitting lid (I use a swing-top jar with rubber gasket)

Kitchen twine

1 · Put the figs, clove, cinnamon stick, orange zest, and anise seeds in the jar and pour in the wine. Cover tightly and let the mixture steep on the countertop for 4 days. Once steeped, drain the figs in a colander set over a bowl, reserving the steeping liquid. Fish out the cinnamon stick and whole clove (if you can find it) and discard.

2 · Transfer the figs to the bowl of a food processor. Add the salt, pepper, and sugar, and process to a coarse puree. Scrape the mixture into a small heavy-bottomed saucepan and pour in ¼ cup of the reserved steeping liquid. (Don't toss the remaining liquid; see Cook's Note for instructions on how to make fig wine syrup.) Bring to a simmer over medium heat and cook, stirring constantly, until the wine is evaporated and the puree pulls away from the sides of the pan. Taste and add more sugar if you like. Stir to dissolve, then remove from the heat and fold in the walnuts.

3 · Scrape the fig puree onto a piece of parchment or waxed paper and pat it into a rough log shape about 2½ inches in diameter. Roll

(recipe continues)

the log up in the parchment, smoothing it out as you go, and tie the ends tightly with kitchen twine. Set the log in an oval dish— I use a corn-on-the-cob dish; its concave shape allows the fig salami to set without flattening the bottom. Let the salami cure in the refrigerator for at least 2 weeks before serving. It should be firm enough to slice, though not hard.

4 · When the salami is ready, unwrap it and roll in confectioners' sugar to mimic the "bloom" of real salami; tap off the excess. Cut into slices and serve with cheese as an appetizer.

COOK'S NOTE · To toast walnuts, spread them out on a baking sheet and bake at 350°F until fragrant and lightly browned, 7 to 8 minutes. Let cool completely.

SPICED FIG-WINE SYRUP
Strain the leftover wine used to steep the figs through a fine-mesh sieve lined with cheese-cloth. You should have about 1½ cups. Pour the wine into a small heavy-bottomed sauce-pan and add ½ cup (50 g) sugar. Bring to a simmer over medium heat and cook, stirring to dissolve the sugar, until slightly thickened (it will thicken more as it cools). Funnel the cooled syrup into a clean bottle and store at room temperature. The syrup is delicious drizzled over Almond Gelato (page 289) or ice cream. Add a splash to salad dressing or toss with roasted or grilled fruit.

PANFORTE DI SIENA

Like other dense, fruit- and nut-filled cakes, panforte gets better the longer it hangs around. Make it ahead of time, wrap it tightly in plastic wrap, and store it in a cool place or in the refrigerator for at least a week and up to a month (although you could also serve it immediately). Feel free to adapt this recipe to your liking, substituting your favorite dried fruits, nuts, and spices. And don't be put off by the long ingredient list. This cake really does come together easily.

Butter, for greasing the pan

¾ cup (90 g) unbleached all-purpose flour

1 tablespoon unsweetened cocoa powder

¼ teaspoon salt

1 teaspoon ground cinnamon

½ teaspoon ground ginger

½ teaspoon ground coriander

¼ teaspoon ground allspice

⅛ teaspoon ground cloves

1 cup (140 g) almonds (skins on or off), toasted and coarsely chopped (see Cook's Note)

½ cup (70 g) hazelnuts, toasted, skinned, and coarsely chopped (see Cook's Note)

½ cup (70 g) walnuts, toasted and coarsely chopped (see Cook's Note)

½ lightly packed cup (70 g) dried apricots, coarsely chopped

½ lightly packed cup (70 g) dried Mission figs, coarsely chopped

¾ cup (100 g) dried cranberries

½ cup (70 g) dark raisins

½ cup (70 g) sultanas (golden raisins)

¼ cup (35 g) chopped candied orange peel

¼ cup (35 g) chopped candied citron (optional)

¾ cup (150 g) sugar

¾ cup (226 g) honey

¼ cup (59 g) water

Confectioners' sugar, for dusting

EQUIPMENT

Instant-read or candy thermometer

Kitchen twine

1 • Position a rack in the middle of the oven and preheat the oven to 300°F. Generously butter an 8- by 2-inch springform pan and line the bottom with parchment paper. Generously butter the parchment paper.

2 • Whisk together the flour, cocoa, salt, cinnamon, ginger, coriander, allspice, and cloves in a large bowl. Add the almonds, hazelnuts, walnuts, apricots, figs, cranberries, raisins, sultanas, candied orange peel, and citron, if using. Stir well to coat everything evenly with the dry ingredients.

(recipe continues)

3 · Combine the sugar, honey, and water in a small saucepan and cook over medium heat, stirring occasionally, until the sugar and honey have dissolved. Bring to a boil, place a candy thermometer in the mixture, and continue to cook, without stirring, until the mixture reaches the soft-ball stage, 238°F, 10 to 15 minutes.

4 · Remove the cooked sugar mixture from the heat, immediately pour it over the nut and fruit mixture, and stir until the ingredients are well combined. The batter will be very sticky and thick.

5 · Scrape the batter into the prepared pan and, using a heatproof spatula or your fingers, spread it evenly in the pan, pressing firmly. (If you use your fingers, you might want to wet them with cold water to prevent them from sticking.) Wrap the pan with a parchment-paper collar that rises about 3 inches above the pan and secure with kitchen twine. This will prevent the fruit and nuts on the surface of the cake from browning and hardening too much.

6 · Set the pan on a baking sheet and bake the panforte until it is puffed and dark golden brown, 1 hour to 1 hour 10 minutes. Let the panforte cool completely in the pan on a wire rack. When it has cooled, carefully remove the sides of the springform pan and slide the panforte off the bottom of the pan (or invert the panforte and gently pry off the bottom of the pan).

7 · If serving immediately, dust the panforte with confectioners' sugar and cut it into thin wedges. Alternatively, omit the dusting of sugar, keep the panforte whole, and wrap it tightly in plastic. Store it in a cool area or in the refrigerator for at least 1 week and up to 1 month. Dust with confectioners' sugar before serving.

COOK'S NOTE · To toast the almonds and walnuts, spread them out on a baking sheet and bake at 350°F until fragrant, 7 to 10 minutes. To toast and skin the hazelnuts, spread them out on a baking sheet and bake at 350°F until the skins have begun to crackle, about 10 minutes. Wrap the hot hazelnuts in a clean kitchen towel and let stand for about 1 minute. Roll the nuts back and forth in the towel to loosen and rub off the skins. Not all the skins will come off; this is fine. Let all the nuts cool completely before using.

TORRONE

*What a sticky mess this nut-studded nougat is to make! I tell you
this so that you can be ready to embrace the process, for it is worth it.
Egg whites are whipped into clouds, then beaten with hot sugar into
taffy-like candy. The air is perfumed with nuts and citrus. If you are
looking to conjure magic over the holidays, this is the project.*

Edible wafer paper (optional; see Sources, page 292)

2 tablespoons (28 g) butter, for the pan

1½ cups (227 g) almonds, blanched, skinned, and toasted (see Cook's Note)

1 cup hazelnuts (140 g), toasted and skinned (see Cook's Note)

½ cup pistachios (70 g), shelled, blanched, skinned, and toasted (see Cook's Note)

2 large egg whites, at room temperature

Pinch of fine sea salt

2 cups (400 g) plus 1 tablespoon sugar

⅔ cup (227 g) mild honey

1 teaspoon pure vanilla extract

2 tablespoons candied orange peel, cut into small dice

EQUIPMENT

Instant-read or candy thermometer

1 · If using edible wafer paper, line the bottom of an 8-inch square baking pan with it, cutting the paper if necessary to fit. Generously butter the sides of the pan. Cut out another piece of wafer the same size and set it aside for topping the nougat. If not using the wafer paper, line

the pan with parchment paper so that there is an overhang on two sides. Generously butter the parchment.

2 · Combine the nuts in a bowl and toss to mix. Set aside.

3 · Place the egg whites in the stainless steel bowl of a stand mixer fitted with the whisk attachment and add the pinch of salt. Set aside.

4 · Combine 2 cups of the sugar and the honey in a medium heavy-bottomed saucepan with high sides. Set the pot over medium heat and stir just to incorporate the sugar into the honey. Cook, stirring once or twice, until the sugar is completely dissolved and the mixture begins to bubble and foam, about 10 minutes. Continue to cook the mixture until it reaches a temperature of 315°F on a candy thermometer, about 10 minutes more. Remove the pot from the heat and stir to cool slightly.

5 · Meanwhile, once the honey-sugar mixture begins to foam, start beating the egg whites with the salt. When the whites are foamy, add the remaining 1 tablespoon sugar. Beat on high speed until the whites are glossy and form stiff peaks.

6 · With the mixer on high speed, dribble in the hot honey-sugar mixture down the side of the bowl, a little at a time. The whites will turn a couple of shades darker because of the honey and grow in volume. Then add the vanilla and candied orange peel. The mixer will slow as the nougat thickens and the mixing bowl will be hot to the touch. Continue to beat at high speed for about 5 minutes—until you can put your hand against the bowl and leave it there.

7 · Add the nuts. Either fold them in with a sturdy wooden spoon or silicone spatula, or switch to the paddle attachment of the mixer to incorporate them. Make sure you scrape the sticky nougat off the whisk and return it to the bowl.

8 · Scoop out the torrone and spread it into the prepared pan. Very lightly moisten your hands with water and press the nougat into the corners of the pan, evening out the top. If using wafer paper, press the second sheet on top. Let the torrone cool completely.

9 · Remove the torrone from the pan and, if necessary, peel off the layer of parchment (do not peel off the edible wafer paper). With a sharp knife, slice the torrone into four 2- by 8-inch bars or eight 2- by 4-inch bars. Wrap the bars in waxed paper or parchment paper and store them in an airtight container at room temperature for up to 2 weeks. To serve, cut the bars crosswise into ¾-inch-thick slices or bite-size pieces.

VARIATION · Traditional torrone does not call for dried fruit, such as cherries or cranberries. But they add a pretty holiday touch to the candy when you cut into it, so I sometimes add ¼ to ½ cup (35 to 70 g) along with the nuts.

COOK'S NOTES

To prep the almonds, preheat the oven to 350°F. Place the raw almonds in a heat-proof bowl and pour boiling water over them. Let sit for 1 to 2 minutes to loosen the skins. Drain and rinse, then pop the almonds out of their skins. Spread them on a baking sheet and let dry for 30 minutes. Bake until lightly golden and fragrant, about 7 minutes. Let cool to room temperature.

To prep the hazelnuts, preheat the oven to 350°F. Spread the nuts on a rimmed baking sheet and bake until the skins have begun to crackle, about 10 minutes. Wrap the hot hazelnuts in a clean kitchen towel and let stand for 1 minute. Roll the nuts back and forth in the towel to rub off the skins. Not all the skins will come off; this is fine. Let cool to room temperature.

To prep the pistachios, place the nuts in a heatproof bowl and pour boiling water over them. Let sit for 2 minutes, and then drain. You can either slip the skins off with your fingers or roll them in a clean kitchen towel, as you would with hazelnuts. I find the towel method to be less successful with stubborn pistachio skins, so I use my fingers. Let cool completely.

CROCCANTE (NUT BRITTLE)

When I was a teenager, our beach town on the Adriatic coast was run by the local Communist party. Every August they put on the Festa dell'Unità in the central piazza. Entertainers performed on a makeshift stage, and politicians gave speeches. Purveyors set up a row of stalls along the street and sold popcorn, roasted sugared nuts, cotton candy, and croccante—nut brittle. You could practically smell the butter and caramelized sugar from the other end of town. Looking back, it was a pretty clever way to attract people to the piazza.

Vegetable oil (if not using a silicone baking mat)

1½ cups (350 g) sugar or vanilla sugar (see page 57)

½ cup (118 g) water

1 tablespoon freshly squeezed lemon juice

2¼ cups (300 g) toasted, skinned hazelnuts or blanched, toasted almonds (see Cook's Note, page 287)

1 · Line a rimmed baking sheet with a silicone baking mat, or coat the baking sheet with vegetable oil. Set it near the stove.

2 · Pour the sugar into a shallow, heavy-bottomed saucepan and add the water. I pour the water in around the perimeter of the pan so that the sugar is surrounded by a moat of water; this helps to prevent crystallization. Add the lemon juice. Set the pan over medium-low heat and cover.

3 · Cook, without stirring, until the sugar is completely dissolved and begins to boil. This will take about 20 minutes. Uncover every few minutes to check on the sugar's progress and to make sure no crystals are forming. Do not stir; instead, swirl the mixture gently to help distribute the sugar and for even cooking. Be sure to return the lid to the pot after checking. The lid will also help prevent crystallization.

4 · While the sugar is cooking, coarsely chop half the nuts. Leave the rest whole. After about 20 minutes, the boiling liquid sugar will begin to change color, going from pale gold to caramel brown. Watch carefully, as you don't want it to burn. When it is golden, pour in the nuts all at once. Use a silicone spatula to stir and coat them with the foaming caramel. Continue cooking until the caramel is a toasty golden brown, a minute or two longer.

5 · Pour the mixture onto the prepared baking sheet and spread it out in an even layer. Let the brittle cool completely, then break or cut it into pieces. The brittle will keep for up to 1 month, or even longer, if stored properly. Wrap it in plastic or waxed paper and place in a container with a tight-fitting lid. Set the container in a cool, dry, dark spot. Do not store the brittle in the refrigerator, where the humidity will soften it.

ALMOND GELATO

This is a really simple recipe, especially if you already have a log of almond paste stored in the freezer. Honey adds body and a silky quality to the gelato. Serve it as is, or top with a little Mosto Cotto (page 244) or Spiced Fig Wine Syrup (page 282), or a spoonful of Sour Cherries in Boozy Syrup (page 267).

1½ cups (360 g) heavy cream

1½ cups (360 g) whole milk

7 ounces (200 g) Sweet Almond Paste (page 279), or store-bought, cut into small dice

4 large egg yolks

½ cup (100 g) sugar

⅛ teaspoon fine sea salt

¼ cup (85 g) honey

½ teaspoon pure almond extract

EQUIPMENT

Instant-read thermometer

Ice cream maker

1 · Combine the cream, milk, and almond paste in a heavy-bottomed saucepan and bring just to a boil over medium-high heat, stirring to dissolve the paste. Remove from the heat.

2 · Beat the yolks with the sugar and salt until thick and pale yellow. Dribble a small amount of the hot cream mixture into the eggs, whisking all the while to keep the eggs from curdling. Continue to gradually add more of the cream mixture until you have

added about one-third of it. Gently whisk this mixture back into the pot with the remaining hot cream mixture. Place over medium-low heat and cook, stirring constantly, until a thin custard forms that lightly coats the back of a wooden spoon, or until the mixture reaches 180°F. Do not let it boil. Remove from the heat and gently but thoroughly stir in the honey and almond extract.

3 · Strain the hot custard through a fine-mesh sieve into a heatproof bowl. Place a sheet of plastic wrap directly on the surface of the custard to prevent a skin from forming. Refrigerate until thoroughly chilled, at least 4 hours and up to overnight.

4 · Freeze the custard in an ice cream machine according to the manufacturer's instructions. Spoon the gelato into a container with a tight-fitting lid and freeze until firm, about 4 hours or up to overnight.

5 · To serve, remove the container from the freezer and let sit for 10 to 15 minutes to soften slightly.

HAZELNUT CREAM CROSTATA

*Hazelnut desserts are a specialty of Piedmont, where bushy trees bearing the
spherical nuts are cultivated in the provinces of Cuneo, Asti, and Alessandria.
This dessert is my own invention inspired by the flavors of that area. You might
be tempted to eat the hazelnut pastry cream by itself with a big spoon. That's fine,
except that you'll be depriving yourself of this sumptuous tart. A layer of jam or
Nutella on the bottom—your choice—makes it a standout dessert for a dinner party.*

FOR THE CRUST

3 cups (380 g) unbleached all-purpose flour,
plus more for dusting the work surface

1 cup (200 g) confectioners' sugar, plus more
for dusting the crostata

¼ teaspoon fine sea salt

Finely grated zest of 1 orange

8 ounces (2 sticks/227 g) cold unsalted
butter, cut into ½-inch pieces

1 large egg

2 large egg yolks (reserve the whites for
another use, such as Torrone, page 286)

½ teaspoon pure vanilla extract

FOR THE HAZELNUT PASTRY CREAM

2 cups (480 g) whole milk

1 vanilla bean

6 large egg yolks

⅔ cup (133 g) sugar

¼ cup (30 g) unbleached all-purpose flour

1 cup (227 g) Sweet Hazelnut Paste
(page 280)

½ cup Simple Strawberry Jam (page 85),
raspberry jam, or Nutella

Confectioners' sugar, for dusting

1 · **Make the crust:** Combine the flour, confectioners' sugar, salt, and zest in the bowl of a food processor. Process briefly to combine. Distribute the butter around the bowl and process until the mixture is crumbly. Add the egg, egg yolks, and vanilla extract, and process just until the dough begins to come together. Turn the dough out onto a lightly floured surface and pat it into a disk. Wrap it tightly in plastic wrap and refrigerate until well chilled, at least 1 hour. (The pastry may be made a day ahead. Remove from the refrigerator and let sit at room temperature for about 45 minutes before rolling out.)

2 · **Make the hazelnut pastry cream:** Pour the milk into a medium heavy-bottomed saucepan. Split the vanilla bean lengthwise with a paring knife and scrape the seeds into the milk. Discard the pod or use it to make vanilla sugar (see page 57). Bring just to a boil over medium-high heat, then remove from the heat.

3 · Whisk together the egg yolks and sugar until thick and pale yellow. Whisk in the flour. Dribble a little of the hot milk into the egg mixture, whisking vigorously all the while to prevent the eggs from curdling. Continue gradually adding milk to the egg mixture until you have added about one-third of it. Slowly whisk this mixture into the saucepan with the remaining hot milk. Cook, stirring constantly, over medium-low heat until thickened. Do not let it boil. Reduce the heat to low and cook, stirring, for 3 to 4 more minutes. Remove from the heat and whisk in the hazelnut paste.

4 · Strain the hot pastry cream through a fine-mesh sieve into a heatproof bowl. If not using immediately, place a sheet of plastic wrap directly on the surface of the cream to prevent a skin from forming. (The hazelnut cream can be made a day ahead and refrigerated.)

5 · Preheat the oven to 350°F.

6 · Remove the dough from the refrigerator and cut it into two pieces, one slightly larger than the other. Rewrap the smaller piece and set it aside. Roll the larger piece into an 11- or 12-inch circle. Carefully wrap the dough around the rolling pin and drape it over a 9- or 10-inch fluted tart pan with a removable bottom. Gently press the dough into the bottom and up the sides of the pan. Trim the overhang to about ½ inch and fold it in, pressing it against the inside rim to reinforce the sides of the tart shell. Use the rolling pin or the flat of your hand to cut off any excess dough.

7 · Spread the jam or Nutella on the bottom of the prepared shell. Spread the hazelnut pastry cream evenly on top. Roll out the remaining piece of dough and cut it into ¾-inch-thick strips. Place the strips in a lattice pattern on top of the pastry cream. Use any remaining strips to make a border around the crostata. (Save any excess dough to roll out later; you can cut out shapes and bake cookies.)

8 · Bake the crostata until the cream is set and the top is nicely browned, about 45 minutes. Let cool on a rack to room temperature. Remove the outer ring of the pan and transfer the crostata to a serving platter. Dust lightly with confectioners' sugar and serve. Store any leftovers in the refrigerator.

SOURCES

For more information on food artisans profiled in this book:
Francesca Di Nisio, CantinArte
www.cantinarte.com

Marco Biagetti and Rosina Cariani, Da Tagliavento
Corso Amendola 15, Bevagna (PG) 39-0742-360897 (no web site)

Noemi Lora and Paolo Anselmini, I Frutti della mia Langa
www.fruttidellamialanga.it

Roberto Panizza and Pesto Genovese
www.pestogenovese.com

Sabato Abagnale, Sapore di Campania
www.saporedicampania.it

Tenuta Vannulo Buffalo Mozzarella
www.vannulo.it

For pressure canning equipment:
All American Pressure Canner
www.allamericancanner.com

National Presto Industries, Inc.
www.gopresto.com

For baking steel or pizza stone supplies:
Baking Steel
www.bakingsteel.com

Sur la Table
www.surlatable.com

Williams-Sonoma
www.williams-sonoma.com

For a traditional *chitarra*, gnocchi board, plus a large inventory of preserving and cooking supplies:
Fante's Kitchen Shop, Philadelphia, PA
www.fantes.com

For Tropea onion and other Italian heirloom vegetable seeds:
Seeds from Italy, Lawrence, KS
www.growitalian.com

For Sabato Abagnale's canned tomatoes, Italian honey, and other imported Italian food products:
Gustiamo, Bronx, NY
www.gustiamo.com

For CantinArte olive oil and other imported Italian olive oil, artisan dried pasta, and commercial mostarda:
Olio2Go, Fairfax, VA
www.olio2go.com

For unbleached, tight-weave cheesecloth; high-quality chocolate; high-protein pizza dough flour; and other specialty kitchen supplies:
La Cuisine: The Cook's Resource, Alexandria, VA
www.lacuisineus.com

For Punch Abruzzo liqueur:
A Cork Above, Clearwater, FL
acorkabove.com

For raw green and ripe olives:
Chaffin Family Orchards, Oroville, CA
www.chaffinfamilyorchards.com

For commercial *mosto cotto*:
Ritrovo Italian Regional Foods, Seattle, WA
www.ritrovo.com

For green (unripe) walnuts to make nocino:
Haag Family Farm, Esparto, CA
www.walnuts.us

For fennel pollen and other seasonings:
Pollen Ranch, Lemoncove, CA
www.pollenranch.com

For cheese-making supplies, including basket molds and rennet:
New England Cheesemaking Supply Co., South Deerfield, MA
www.cheesemaking.com

For sausage- and *salumi*-making equipment, including hog casings and pink salt:
Butcher & Packer, Madison Heights, MI
www.butcher-packer.com

The Sausage Maker, Inc., Horseheads, NY and Buffalo, NY
www.sausagemaker.com

TOP: *Stacked jars in the shop of Paolo Anselmino and Noemi Lora, Piedmont*
BOTTOM: *Picking peppers at the farmers' market in Sulmona, Abruzzo*

BIBLIOGRAPHY

Barrow, Cathy. *Mrs. Wheelbarrow's Practical Pantry: Recipes and Techniques for Year-Round Preserving*. W. W. Norton & Company, New York, 2014.

Bertolli, Paul. *Cooking By Hand*. Clarkson Potter, New York, 2003.

Bone, Eugenia. *Well-Preserved: Recipes and Techniques for Putting Up Small Batches of Seasonal Foods*. Clarkson Potter, New York, 2009.

Boni, Ada. *Il Talismano Della Felicita, Serie d'Oro*. Editore Colombo, Rome (undated).

Capalbo, Carla. *The Food and Wine Guide to Naples and Campania*. Pallas Athene, Ltd., London, 2005.

Chiarello, Michael. *Michael Chiarello's Casual Cooking: Wine Country Recipes for Family and Friends*. Chronicle Books, San Francisco, 2002.

McClellan, Marissa. *Food In Jars: Preserving in Small Batches Year-Round*. Running Press, Philadelphia, 2012.

Ruhlman, Michael and Brian Polcyn. *Charcuterie: The Craft of Salting, Smoking, and Curing*. W. W. Norton & Company, New York, 2005.

For information on preserving:

National Center for Home Food Preservation at the University of Georgia, www.nchfp.uga.edu, provides comprehensive information on preserving techniques and safety.

Food Safety, www.foodsafety.gov, contains food safety information provided by government agencies such as the USDA, FDA, and CDC.

Ball Canning, www.freshpreserving.com, provides information on canning techniques, supplies, and recipes.

Food In Jars, www.foodinjars.com, is author Marisa McClellan's popular blog about preserving.

Hunter Angler Gardener Cook, www.honest-food.net, is cookbook author, forager, and wild game expert Hank Shaw's web site.

Mrs. Wheelbarrow's Kitchen, www.mrswheelbarrow.com, is cookbook author and preserving expert Cathy Barrow's web site.

Punk Domestics, www.punkdomestics.com, is an online DIY community of home preserving aficionados.

ACKNOWLEDGMENTS

Four or five years ago I had a short conversation about Italian food and cookbooks with Celia Sack, owner of Omnivore Books on Food, in San Francisco. She was lamenting the lack of written information on Italian preserves. "You should write a book," she said, or words to that effect. It was a passing comment, but it stayed with me.

In fact, unbeknownst to Celia, I was already working on a recipe to recreate my grandmother's *amarene sotto spirito* (sour cherries preserved in alcohol). I had begun to make my own liqueurs, and my pantry and fridge were gradually filling up with other experiments, some new, some based on centuries-old traditions—pickled garlic scapes, chestnut cream, peaches in grappa. Mainly I was making these foods for my own enjoyment and that of my family. Putting up preserves in the Italian tradition also made me feel connected to Italy when I wasn't there. I was skeptical that there might be broader interest in this somewhat retro, somewhat esoteric subject. But Celia's words spurred me on—after all, who could argue with the owner of such a beautifully curated cookbook store? Thank you, Celia.

In the same breath I would also like to express my gratitude to two other people: my agent, Jenni Ferrari-Adler of Union Literary, who embraced this project from the get-go, whipped my ambitious proposal into shape, and promptly found a home for the book at Houghton Mifflin Harcourt; and my editor,

Stephanie Fletcher, whose quiet demeanor, calm professionalism, and feather-light touch belie the enormous amount of work she put into organizing its many components. My deepest thanks to both of you.

I owe much gratitude to the excellent team at HMH: art director Tai Blanche, designer Jan Derevjanik, managing editor Marina Padakis, production editor Helen Seachrist, production coordinator Kevin Watt, copy editor Valerie Cimino, and indexer Marilyn Flaig. My thanks also to publicity associate Brittany Edwards and director of culinary marketing Brad Parsons.

To photographer Lauren Volo and her superb team—food stylist Molly Shuster, prop stylist Rich Vassilatos, and assistant Drew Salvatore: Somehow, you managed to conjure the splendor of Italy in a Brooklyn studio. You are amazing. Thank you for letting me watch you make magic on the set.

Over the years I have drawn inspiration from countless Italian cooks, food artisans, and friends in the kitchen. I am indebted to them all. Special thanks to Sabato Abagnale, Paolo Anselmino and Noemi Lora, Marco Biagetti and Rosina Cariani, Francesca Di Nisio, the Palmieri family at Tenuta Vannulo, and Roberto Panizza for taking time to meet with me and share your stories. Special thanks also to those who generously shared their recipes: Rosetta Costantino, Anna and Vincenzo Gasbarri, Fabrizio and Anna Maria Lucci, Ben Pflaumer, Linda Maiello Prospero,

Giulia Scappaticchio, and the Allega family at La Locandi di Gino. Your contributions have enriched this book immeasurably.

To Nancy Jane and Michael Morizio, my culinary tour partners at Abruzzo Presto, who introduced me to a number of people and places mentioned in this book, thank you for sharing your deep knowledge of and boundless love for Abruzzo. It is a delight and a privilege to work with you.

I would like to raise a glass to Michael Heny, winemaker at Horton Cellars, who kept me supplied with wine grapes and fresh must so that I could faithfully reproduce the recipes for *mosto cotto* and *scrucchjata* (with a touch of Virginia mixed in).

To my dear friend Carolyn Van Damme, thank you for turning your kitchen into a mini *macelleria* so that we could test sausage recipes together.

To Cathy Barrow, for encouraging me to become a more intrepid canner, for answering sporadic email questions, and for being such a great lunch date, thank you.

To Beatrice Ughi of Gustiamo, irrepressible spirit and champion of Italian food artisans, thank you for your support, insight, recommendations, and your uncompromising eye and impeccable taste.

To my great friends and neighbors (and ace taste testers) Anne and John Burling, thank you for keeping me supplied with that all-important ingredient: jumbo-sized bottles of Everclear.

I have never met Carla Capalbo but I would like to thank her for writing her exhaustively researched book *The Food and Wine Guide to Naples and Campania*, which led me to Tenuta Vannulo and the best buffalo mozzarella I've ever had.

Good food is meant to be shared, as the Italian people well know. I am grateful to friends in Italy who have shared not only their food but also their wine, tables, kitchens, knowledge, and expertise. Among them: Marcello De Antoniis, Marta Carrozza, Lina Colafella and Abramo Morizio, Miriam Deluca and Emanuele and Nicola Altieri, Antonella and Mariadora Santacroce, Alice Pietrantonj, the Pavone family at Agriturismo Tholos, and Emanuela Raggio and Anna Merulla of Beautiful Liguria.

Stateside, I am blessed to be surrounded by a wonderful group of food-loving friends and colleagues who have supported my work and cheered me on over the years. Special thanks to Nancy Purves-Pollard, Helen Free, Michelle DiBendetto Capobianco, Diane Morgan, and Cheryl Sternman Rule, and Adri Barr Crocetti. To my kindred spirits at Le Virtù and Brigantessa, Francis Cratil and Cathy Lee, and Joe Cicala and Angela Ranalli, *grazie di cuore*.

Thanks, as always, to my supportive family: my parents, Gabriella and Frank; Maria, Gina, and Tony; and the "Bro-Cha-Chos" Darren, John, and Xander.

Most especially, thank you to Scott, Nick, and Adriana, for putting up with all my putting up, and for being here to "preserve" my sanity during a sometimes crazy process these last few months. Love you always. *ping*

Rooftops of Sulmona, Abruzzo

Westfield Memorial Library
Westfield, New Jersey

INDEX

Westfield Memorial Library
Westfield, New Jersey

TOP: *The Langhe Hills of Piedmont*
BOTTOM: *A vegetable garden in San Tommaso, Abruzzo*

Westfield Memorial Library
Westfield, New Jersey